A PORTRAIT OF THE MENOPAUSE

black dog press

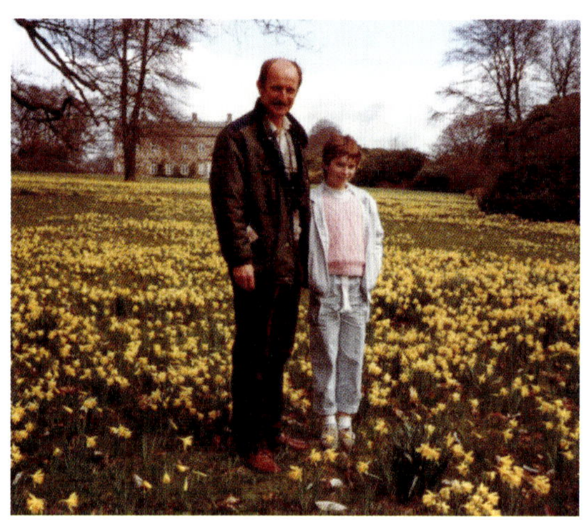

This book is dedicated to my dad
who taught me about photography,
and the power of listening.

CONTENTS

FOREWORD

As women, there are so many layers of shame attached to our physical bodies, and that also comes up during menopause. We are only recently discussing menopause, not only among ourselves but in the wider culture.

Our understanding of the menopause and the impact it has on our physical and mental health is still at the beginning. For me, the menopause was a creative and healing process and I needed a lot of quiet reflection. I would sit at my desk in my bedroom at night making little pieces of art and it felt like I was beginning again and becoming exactly who I was supposed to be. I remember saying to myself, "I was meant to be an artist." It was almost like I'd forgotten to do something.

I had two small kids and we sat at the kitchen table. I was making art with them, I was making my own art and they were making art. We had a role of lining paper and we would just paint and draw on it. "The family that draws together, stays together," I thought.

I first experienced the menopause around the age of 44. I knew what it was, even though I did not have the major hot flushes. It was this massive surge of energy and clarity to do something really positive, which I channelled into making a picture every day.

It's a great chapter and taking care of your physical and mental health becomes a priority. I built a career during the menopause; I found how empowering it was to work from home, to have a career that worked around my children, to make a living from being an artist, to sell work internationally – for example, at the New York Affordable Art Fair, which was definitely a highlight for me because it was returning to somewhere I'd lived when I was 19. I was single-minded and focused; I started painting for my mental health because I'd been diagnosed with PTSD.

There's so much more pressure on young women now to be everything. You've got to have this successful career. In our twenties you could live in a squat and still be a success. But once you can't have babies anymore, you can focus on yourself.

I met Catrin here in Ramsgate, which is a tight-knit, supportive community where people have time to stop and chat. We have friends in common.

After looking through *A Portrait of the Menopause*, I came to the conclusion that everyone's experience of the menopause is unique; nobody has an identical menopause, yet it's universal.

Catrin's book is very open, accessible and inclusive. You immediately feel a connection with each woman. I thought, "These are my people." Every woman looks at ease with herself and there's a real, shared understanding of something that's so personal.

It's a beautiful collection of stories and photographs. I love the photographs because everyone is unique, the people are relaxed and leaning in to their true selves. It's also a celebration of women and acknowledging women. I'm bringing up two boys and I want them to fully understand the beauty and complexity of what it means to be a woman.

Part of our culture is about celebrating what women actually experience – and this is just a little taster of what women go through in their lives.

Margo McDaid
Aka Margo in Margate

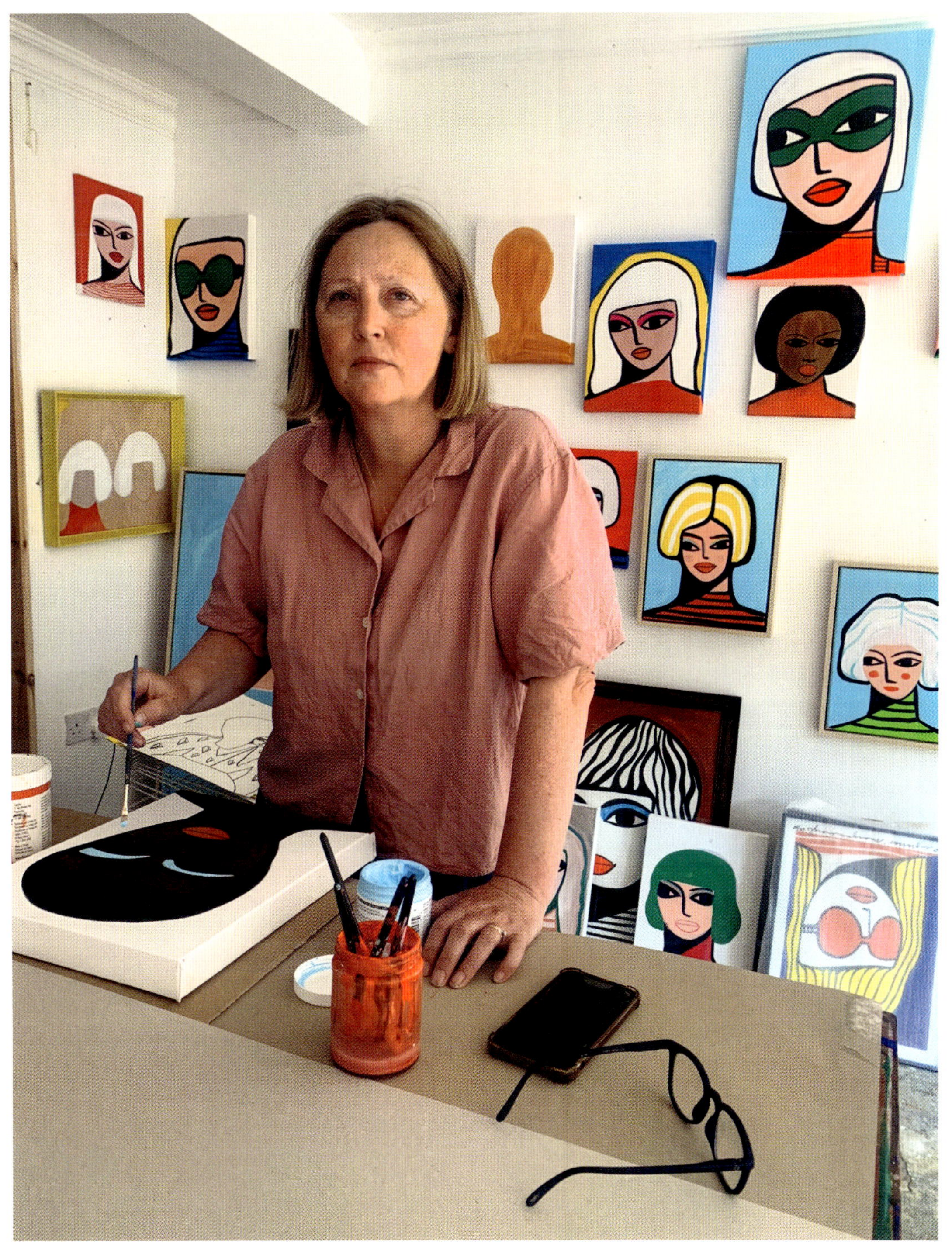

The artist Margo in Margate

INTRODUCTION

Aged 23, while completing my degree in Social Sciences, my journey as a professional artist started in the rave scene in Leeds. Then the circus came to town and I thought, "I want to do that," and went to their lessons.

After completing Circus in Performance at Greentop in Sheffield, I moved to Bristol for more training, then settled in London and worked internationally as a professional circus artist for many years. At 36, I went to Central St Martins College of Art and Design and completed a Masters in Performance: Design and Practice. It was one of the best years of my life. I remember thinking, "The things that have always got me into trouble for in my life, here I'm praised for. I've found my people." My final show was based on the book *Postcards from the Edge*. I put a fine artist from LA on the wall with gaffer tape holding her up (and a full body aerial harness). There she spouted lines from Carrie Fisher's book. There were other students performing movement on the ground to '90s classics like New Order's "Blue Monday", and a video with the protagonist Suzanne Vale repeating the mantra "Get up early every day, read more, keep a journal, talk on the phone less, do less shopping and eventually have a child with someone". I played the mother, climbing a rope to visit her daughter who was metaphorically "strung out" in rehab. The day after my MA, I was selected to become Director in Residence at The National Centre for Circus Arts, where I was mentored and given opportunities and space to develop new work.

Keen to go hide backstage and be more creative, I retired as an aerialist, aged 40, after performing in the London Olympics Opening Ceremony directed by Danny Boyle. Forming my company Osborne & What, I co-directed and toured a show based on the book *Birdy* by William Wharton, fusing circus, theatre, text, movement and music.

In 2019, aged 46, little did I know lying on my back in the dewy May grass, the early summer sun on my face, taking the selfie that I would go on to post on Twitter asking for women going through menopause to meet, interview and photograph, that more than 80 diverse women would contact me. They included ex-punks, ravers, travellers living on boats and in trucks, Roma women, a lawyer, a nurse, neurodivergent women, trans people, a furniture maker, a refugee who hadn't been allowed to work despite the fact that she'd lived in Cardiff for 16 years, a carer and even a cabaret lothario.

Little did I know that sunny May morning, having finally submitted to taking HRT gel after weeks of not sleeping, severe headaches, heat rising up my body, and giving up riding my beloved little moped around London, that ten months later the world would go into lockdown and I would lose all my work as a circus director and be forced to stay at home. This is when I first started writing the funding application to the Arts Council to tour the UK, building on an exhibition I showed in September 2019 at Bad Fruit in Hackney, curated by Serena Bobowski, Gemma Brockis and Silvia Mercuriali. And little did I know how much views on the menopause would change, with Diane Danzebrink leading a #makemenopausematter campaign and Davina McCall making a Channel 4 documentary on the subject that would teach many women more than they'd learnt from their GPs. This book aims to celebrate women whose experiences have been silenced; it turns up the colour on this stage of their lives and reminds them of their happy places (some of the women, including my collaborator, Tindara Sidoti-McNary, said they had forgotten what they were), documenting a moment in time. A moment we shared. My conclusion is people need to be seen and be heard.

Historically, women have gone through difficult experiences and had to keep them a secret. Frida Kahlo was one of the first artists who painted pictures about her miscarriage and the pain it caused her; societal norms have forced us to hide these experiences and feel shame. I went through some of these experiences – miscarriage, infertility – and I felt shame. So when I reached the age that I wasn't able to have children anymore I got excited about life, the possibilities of the other things I would do.

Little did I know that then the menopause would hit me like a ton of bricks. My mum had once said, "When menopause comes, everything dries up," which didn't sound great, I must admit; but nobody warned me about the nights of not sleeping, the anxiety I would feel, the loss of confidence, sudden ageing, the rage, the anxiety and the headaches. Symptoms are different for every woman, but the fear of taking HRT that older women I knew passed down to me at that time was resounding: "It gives you cancer", "Don't take it whatever you do".

I fought against taking it for a year and a half, and I tried all the natural alternatives; but one night I hit rock bottom and cried at the doctor's surgery the next day, begging them to prescribe me. Two days later, I was sleeping like a log and diving into the ponds on Hampstead Heath.

That's not to say HRT is for everyone or that everyone needs it. Everyone's experience is unique. For me, HRT isn't the only thing that's helped. I've evolved since menopause, made some radical life changes and moved home. I've grown as an artist and person. Put simply, in the words of David Bowie, "Ageing is an extraordinary process where you become the person you always should have been".

I hope you enjoy my journey as much as I did.

Catrin Osborne (She/They)

HOME

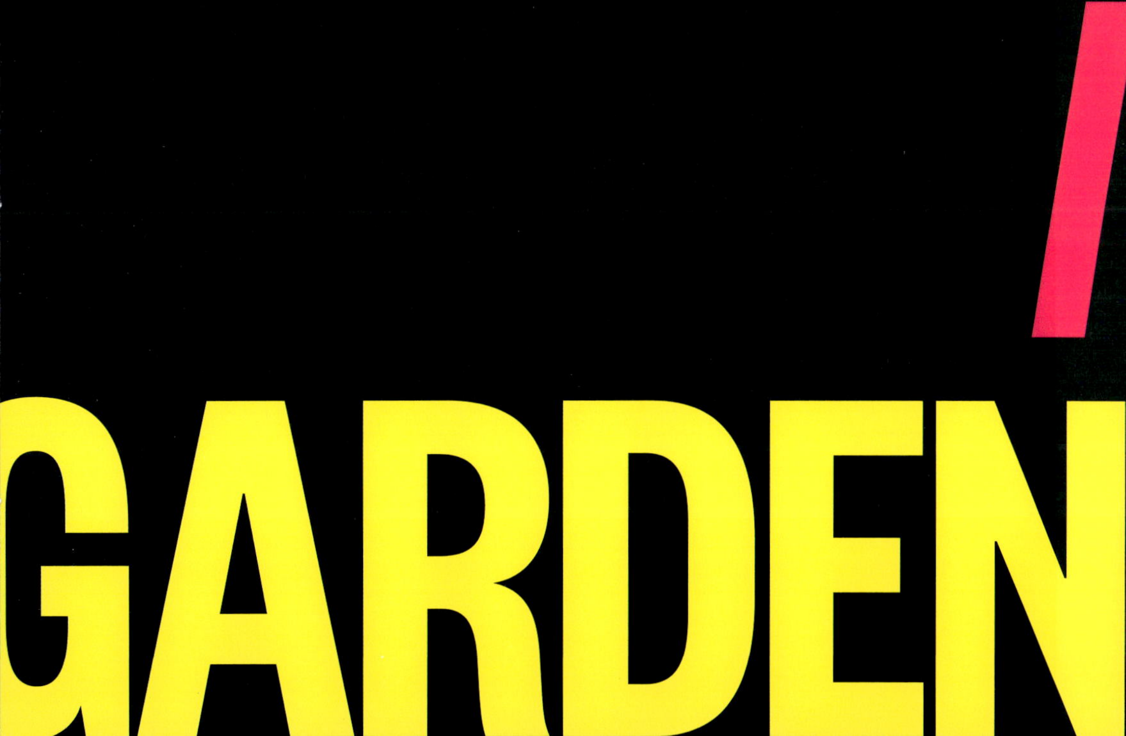
GARDEN

SHAENA

She / Her

Somerset
Age 46
Circus performer, artist, mother,
partner, producer, director, choreographer
and occupational traveller

I know myself better, am more confident and established within circus, and understand my strengths and limitations after performing physically for 28 years. It's been a journey; I had full-on headaches for ages. During lockdown I realised they were coming on around the time of my period. I was more anxious, anti-social and putting on weight, which because I'm a performer I noticed and found hard.

The doctor gave me strong migraine relief and antidepressants. I feel I was misdiagnosed and a few people said it could be perimenopause. They tested my hormones and they came back normal, so I went on a journey of self-discovery and menopause diagnosis. I found out about an app called Balance, where I could track my symptoms. I had no energy to train, despite having a little circus space at home. I would lie and feel exhausted. I tried herbal options, saw Davina's documentary, changed doctors and got a brilliant nurse who was trained in the menopause, and eventually got HRT. It feels like a postcode lottery. I've been on it nine months now. I feel so much better; I've got loads more energy and capacity, and the anxiety has gone. It's been brilliant.

Work-wise, I still want to perform aerial, but it's not all that I do now. I want there to be a creative pathway for ageing circus women. I've recently stepped into the role of aerial director in a women's circus in Ireland. I've got a Developing Your Creative Practice grant from the Arts Council for directing/choreographing. I'm researching and developing an idea for a show about "women, ageing and community", which I will write and direct – but I'm not going to produce it!

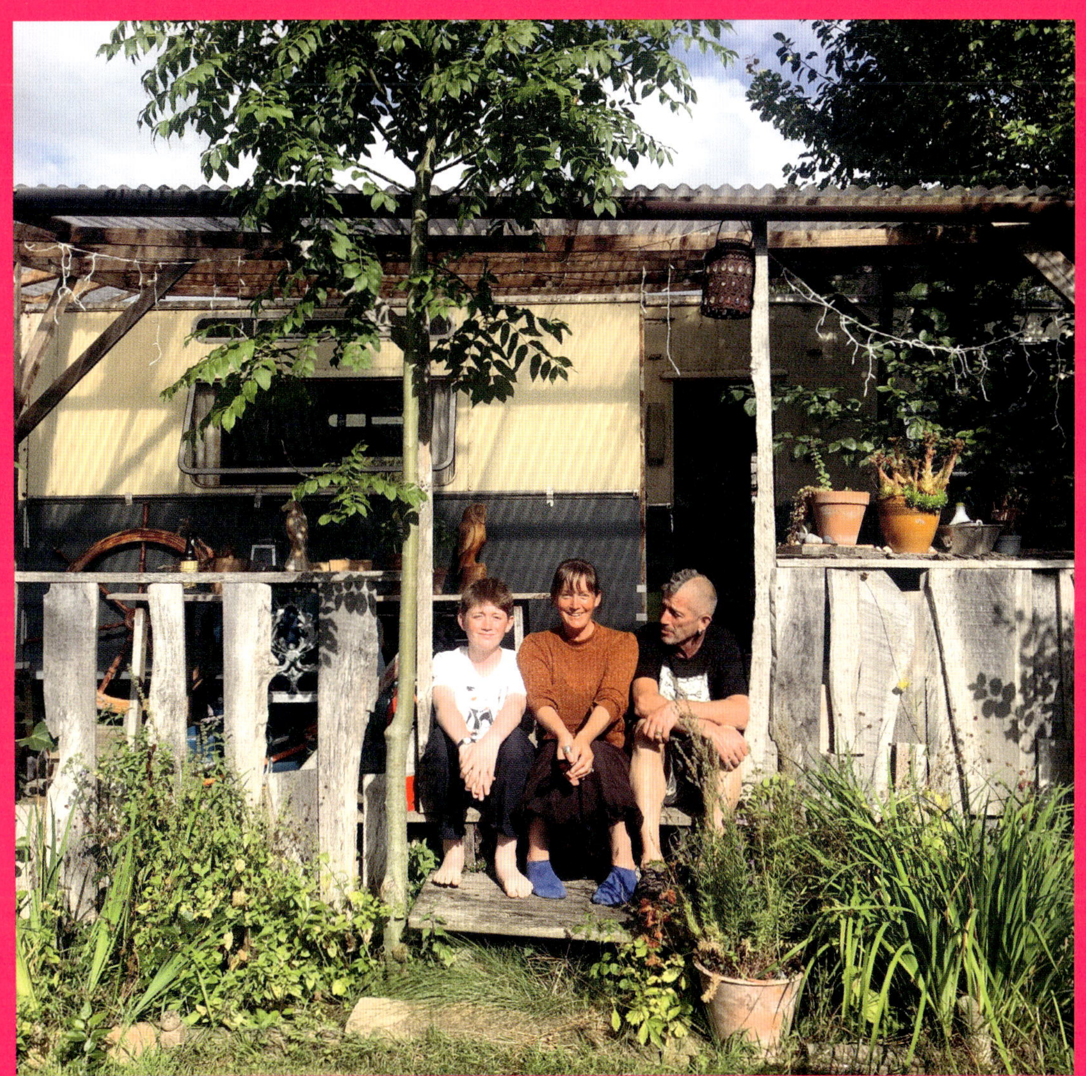

Shaena with her husband Barnz and son Taidgh outside the showman's caravan they live in

Keisha sits in her kitchen in her London flat

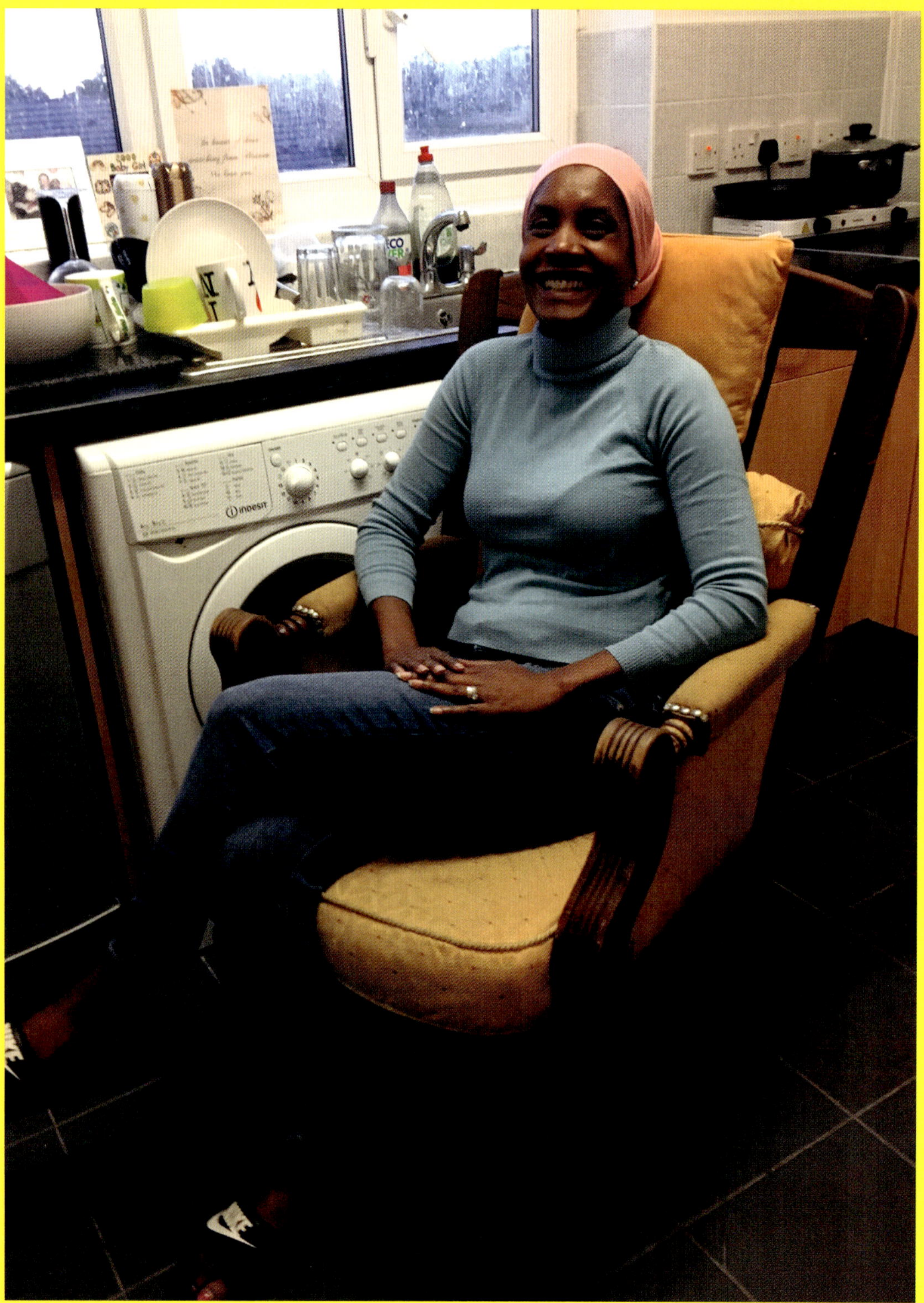

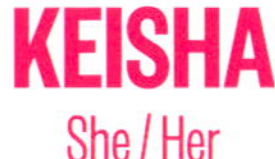

KEISHA

She / Her

Stamford Hill, London
Age 42
Support staff at
college and mum

I'll start off with the negatives. The changes that happened in my body: numbness in my fingers, pain in my lower back and hair loss, which is something that has affected me a lot because I'm wearing the headscarf all the time. I'm insecure about my hair and my hair falling out.

The positives are that I have gone on recognising what's wrong and being able to take control. Finding a way to listen to my body and understand what's going on with it has helped a lot; getting enough sleep, drinking water. When I feel a bit fatigued, I go for walks.

Understanding what's going on was the difficult transition for me; a lot of things were happening. I was on a group chat with Homerton Hospital and all the points were there. I'm like, "Oh yeah, that's that and that's that." It's nice to be able to pinpoint all the signs and know that it's okay and to be able to work with the signs.

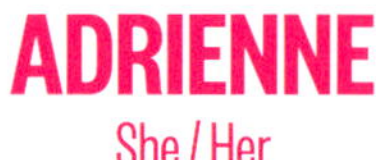

Penarth, Wales
Age 54
Actress, trainer
and educator

You've walked up a hill, gone higher and you reach a plateau so that you can look at life clearly. Lots of things happen around brain fog, but you do get a lot of clarity as well.

You get a lot of connection to other women. I'm very fortunate I've got a mother and three sisters who've lived through it. It puts to bed that whole thing in your teens, twenties, thirties, around getting attention from men. It just stops being there, which is so freeing. As a young actress and with the work that I've done over the years, you are objectified as a woman.

When you're at the top of the hill, you might have children, partners and other people you're supporting on the other side of the hill going down. You may have ageing parents and you are probably at the peak of your career (which I was) and people respect you for your work. And there you are, going through all of these things with various symptoms and trying to hold on to all the other people that you're supporting.

I'm hugely angry about the postcode lottery and the medical profession being completely inadequate with their support. Not being helpful to women going through it. Some women don't experience any symptoms. They just sail through it. I know menopause can come at different times, but once you have symptoms, some can stay for the rest of your life.

The only people I know that have managed can afford to pay privately, but for your average woman they're just offered antidepressants, which is so wrong. It's not something that you just give a tablet [for] and that's it. It changes.

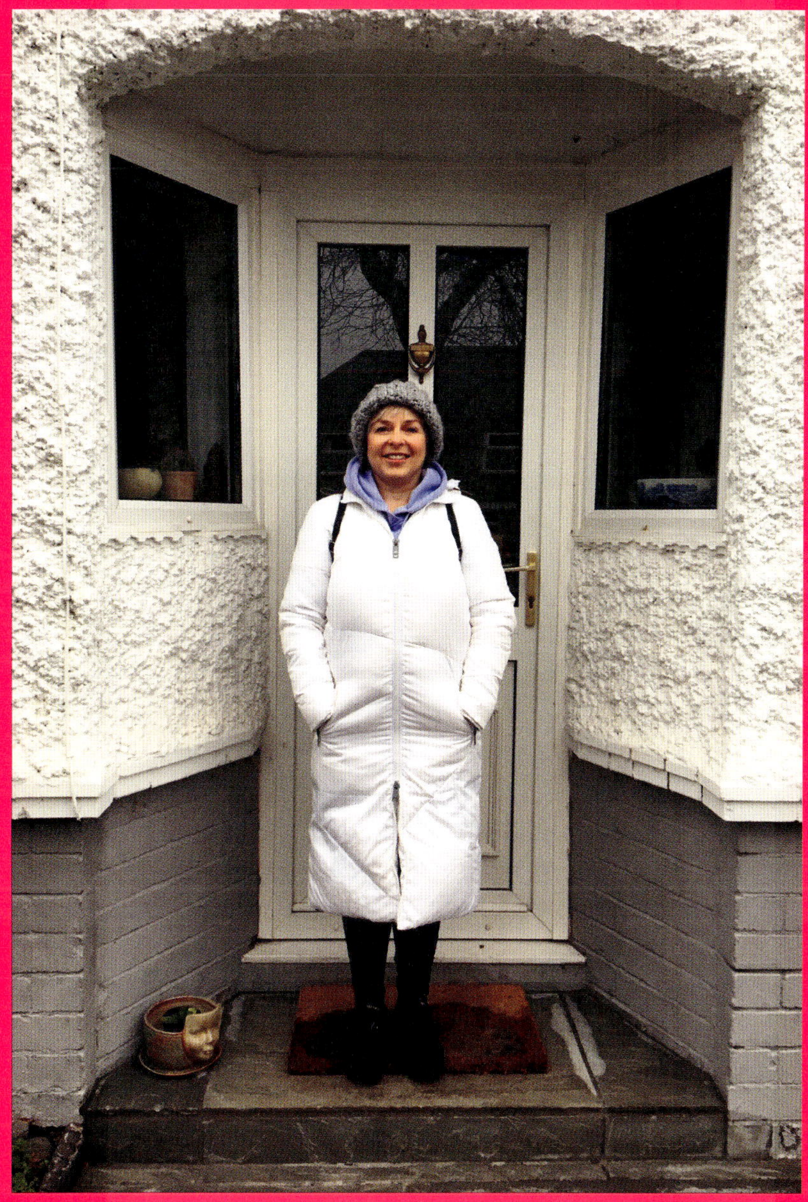

Adrienne stands in the porch of her childhood home in Newport, Wales

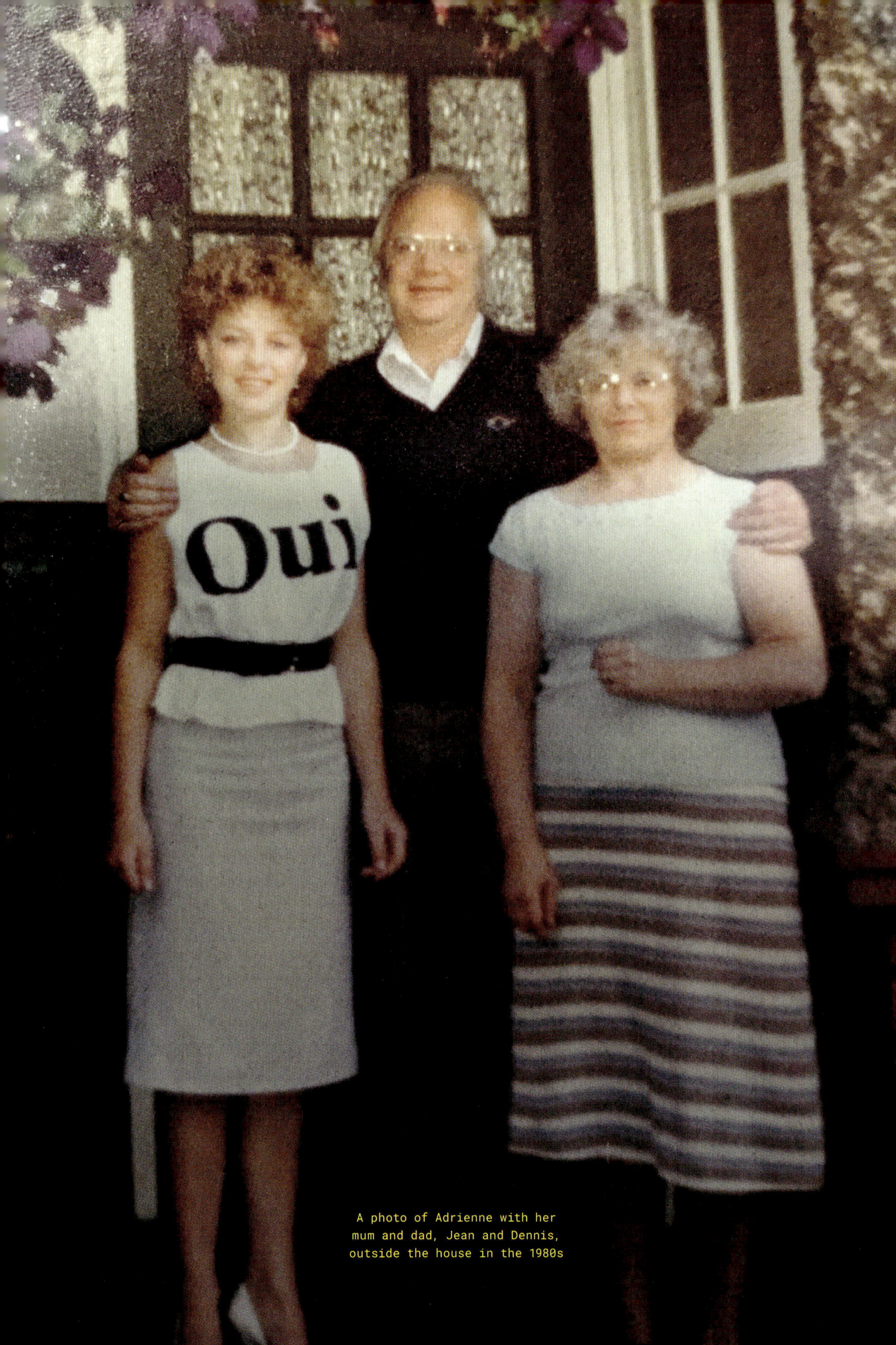

A photo of Adrienne with her mum and dad, Jean and Dennis, outside the house in the 1980s

You've walked up a hill, gone higher and you reach a plateau so that you can look at life clearly. Lots of things happen around brainfog but you do get alot of clarity aswell.

You get a lot of connection to other women. I'm very fortunate I've got a mother and three sisters who've lived through it. It puts to bed that whole thing in your teens, 20's, 30's around getting attention from men. It just stops being there, which is so freeing. As a young actress and with the work I have done over the years you are objectified as a woman.

When you're at the top of the hill you might have children, partners and other people you're supporting on the other side of the hill going down. You may have aging parents and you are probably at the peak of your career (which I was) and people respect you for your work. And there you are, going through all these things with various symptoms and trying to hold on to all the other people that you are supporting.

I'm hugely angry about the postcode lottery and the medical profession being completely inadequate with their support. Not being helpful to women going through it. Some women don't experience any symptoms. They just sail through it. I know menopause can come at different times but once you have symptoms some can stay for the rest of your life.

The only people I know that have managed can afford to pay privately but for your average woman they're just offered anti-depressants, which is so wrong. It's not something that you just give a tablet and thats it. It changes.

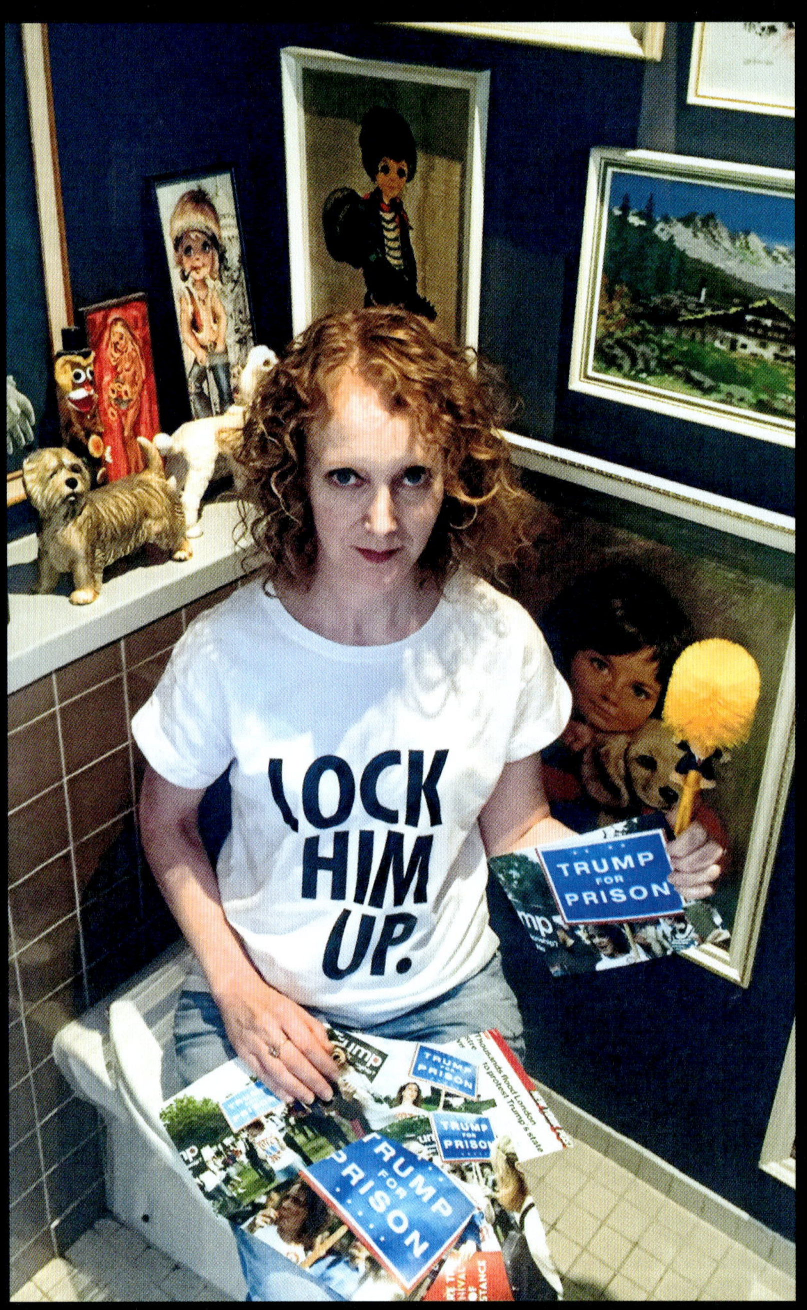

Marcia sits on her toilet holding a Trump toilet brush and the pictures she took at an anti-Trump protest that went viral

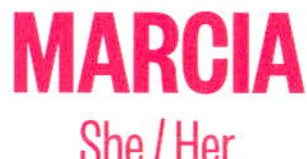

Stoke Newington, London
Age 53
Visual creative

It smacks you in the face, the reality that life is passing you by. I knew nothing about it and then it was suddenly here, and it confirmed that I was middle-aged. In the same breath, it doesn't mean that life stops in any way. I haven't changed my lifestyle at all.

Having conversations with friends who are going through the same thing and also didn't know anything about it is comforting. I think I've been extremely lucky that it hasn't affected me that badly.

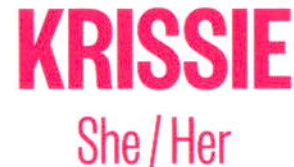

Meanwood, Leeds
Age 49
Yoga teacher, artist
and mother

I'm not getting many symptoms. My periods have changed, I've had a tiny turning up of temperature and a few headaches, which are probably hormonal, but I don't have trouble sleeping. So, it's mostly the emotional, mental changes of not being a "young" woman anymore. It's massive in our society. Trying to work out how to feel comfortable with myself, reconciling with myself. I choose to practise what I preach (yoga), acknowledging the changes and staying true to the person I am inside.

I don't feel like I have to act like an old woman, but my personal choice is not to dye my hair. My hair is grey – which comes with judgement from other women – so I'll be looked at as an older woman, but I'm on the journey towards accepting that. It's the time of life when I'm looking forward to and deciding what I want to do with the rest of my life. That includes assessing what I want to keep and what I want to let go of.

As women we're taught to give. You have to turn inwards and put yourself first. That's how I see the menopause – it's positive. I embrace change and I feel like change is always a good thing.

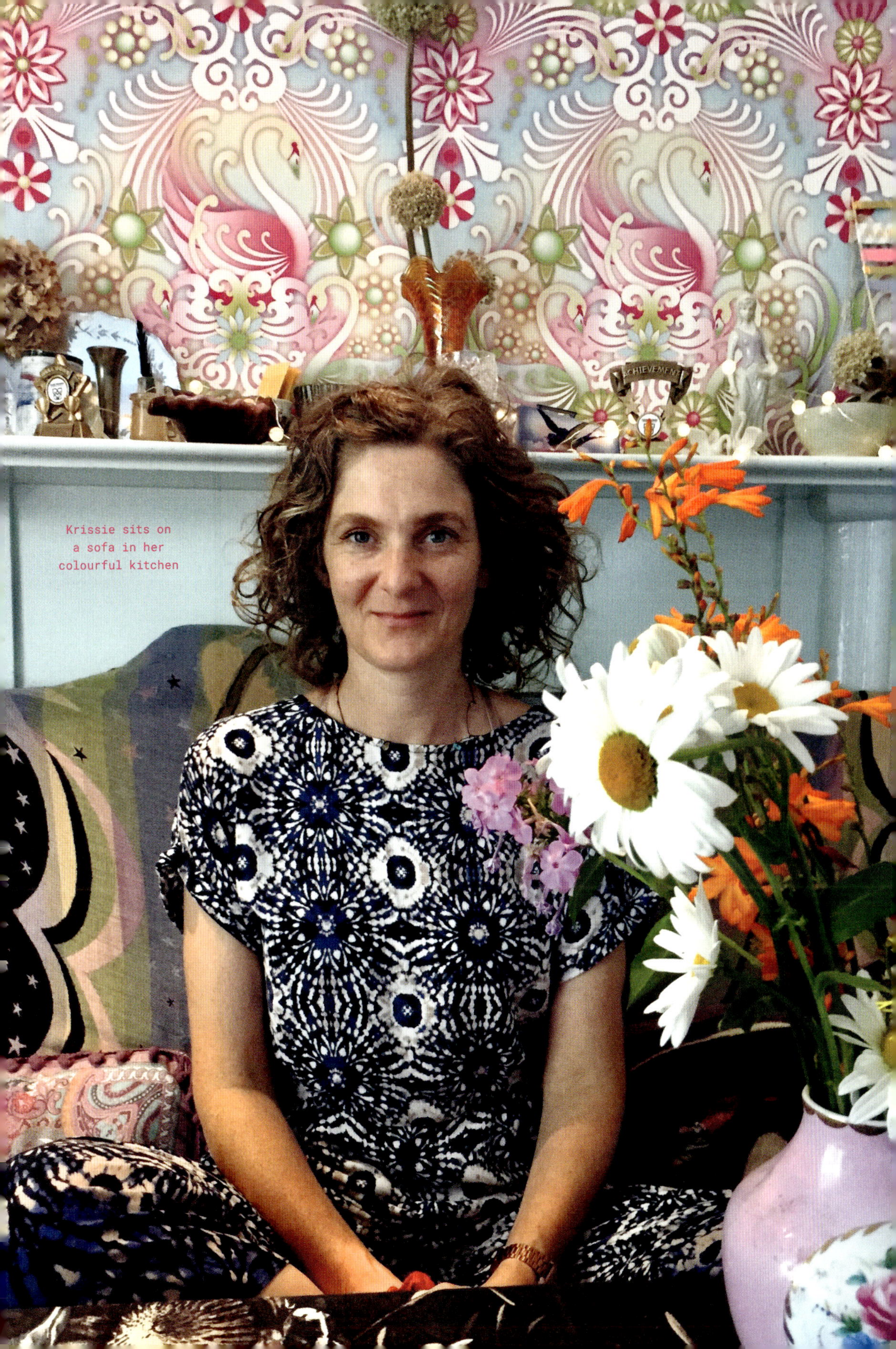

Krissie sits on
a sofa in her
colourful kitchen

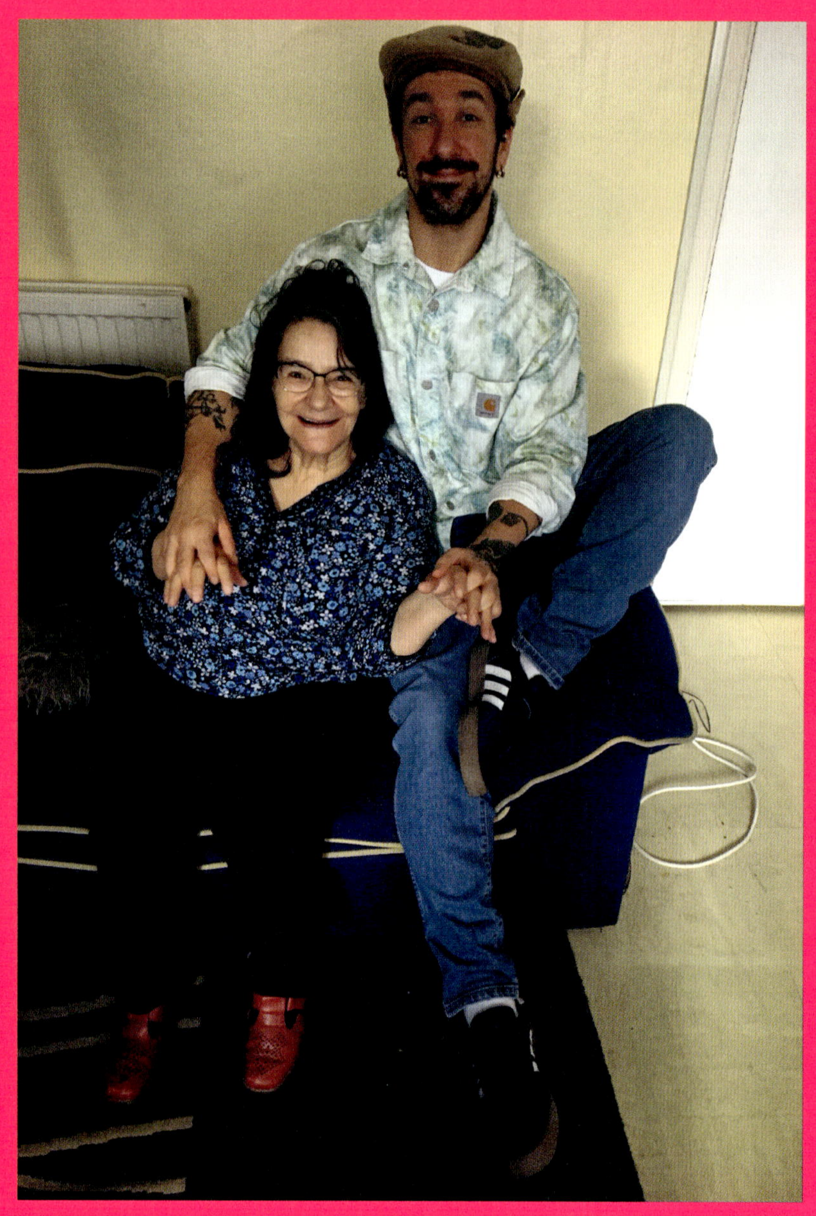

Ines with son Joseph in her living room

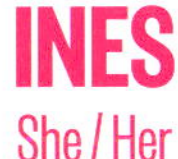

INES

She / Her

King's Cross, London
Age 72
Retired housekeeper,
mother and dog minder

I am originally from Colombia and have been based in the UK for 43 years now.

I had my menopause at about 42 or 43, and then I just thought, "It's funny I keep sweating and feeling tired and a bit nauseous." I thought I had something wrong and went to the doctor a month later and was put on HRT patches. I was given 25 milligrams of oestrogen.

It helped a lot, I felt like a new woman. Really youthful and happy. Not grumpy. Before, I was irritable and tearful and everything bothered me. I was either very happy or very, very angry. I became much more relaxed and I could do my work.

By the time I was 42, I'd already had fibromyalgia for 12 years. It took five years to get a diagnosis, so I didn't understand what was going on. It was a really bleak part of my life. Oh, I remember everything all right!

I only took the patches for six months, I'd got through it. I'm still on medication, Prozac, to keep things calm.

I worry because even now I'm sweating. I still get hot flushes. Positives are that I understand everything happens for a reason; it's no big deal, tough luck, that's it. You pace yourself and don't frustrate yourself too much. Just do what you can, when you can, slowly, you know.

Because I still have fibromyalgia, which kills me all the time, I do whatever and I pay the next day.

You know what? I'm happy! I'm not hungry or cold. I get along with my son, live on my level, and I don't want anything else.

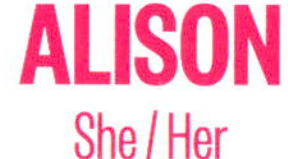

She / Her

Meanwood, Leeds
Age 54
Heating engineer

When it happened – it was early for me – I didn't know what was happening. I was confused. I didn't like the person I was, I got bitchy, paranoid; I thought I'd got over that years ago. I lost friends – I had low tolerance and looked too deep into things, analysed things too much and then found a way to be pissed off with them. Being single, fear of losing youth. Finding that the time is now.

Feel the fear and do it anyway. Not "making do" or "settling" for aspects of your life that you have done, ie previous marriage. There's a whole world out there that needs to be conquered. Taking HRT has balanced my anxieties and fear and I've found rebirth, strength; hence I'm doing my first degree, the idea of which used to scare me, as not having one had made me feel inadequate.

Also, I'm really funny now. I used to be funny, but I'm super-funny. When things go through my mind I used to feel anxious, but now I think, "Fuck it." I'm inspired to be more creative – I always have been, but now it's coming out and I'm expressing it through the mediums that I love.

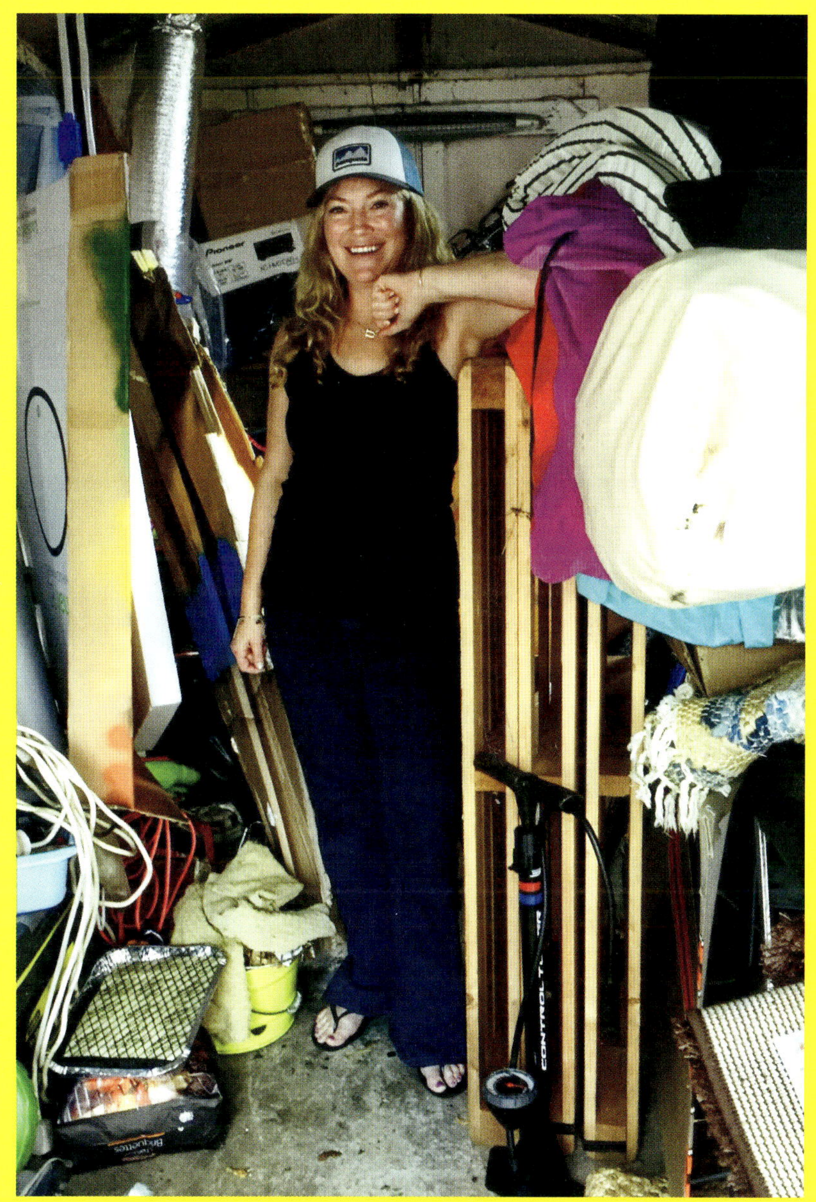

Alison in her garage: "It's not all junk! Clearing my mind and this space"

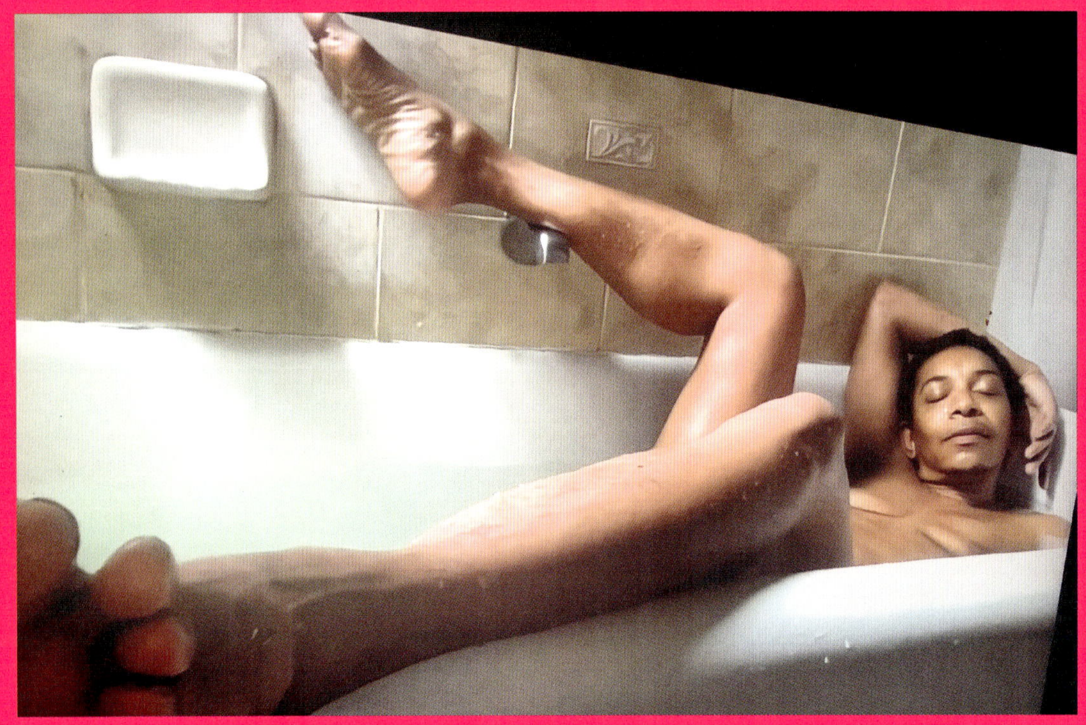

Kiebpoli photographed in the bath at home in Brooklyn

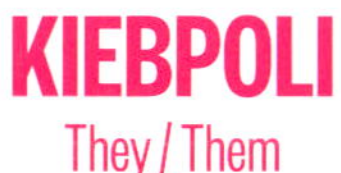

KIEBPOLI

They / Them

Brooklyn, New York
Age 52
Queer, black, trans masculine
and gender-expansive creative

I never had to talk with anybody about it. I never had to feel shame. I saw other female-bodied people have so much shame around it, and nobody talked about it and everybody was embarrassed. I was like, that's not me, that will never be me, and if that was me, it's not something that I'm going to be embarrassed about; it's just another part of life that we go through. I didn't want to get stuck in that narrative, like "I'm a crone now" – I didn't want to link my body to a child-bearing status. I didn't want to link my body to the medical industrial complex.

We live in a cis, heterosexual, white, patriarchal, capitalist society and so, of course, anything to make a woman feel "less than" is how we're socialised and taught to feel and to think. It makes me sad when women are nervous about talking about it or embarrassed or feel shame. Thank goodness we're a coven; I really wish that women could step into their power, into our witchy coven power. We're ruled by the moon, we hold life. I wish we could rise up and change some legislation or something.

HRT is important for people of all genders because at a certain age our bodies don't produce as much. And I feel it should be a different class of drugs, so it can be a helpful supplement for anyone who needs it.

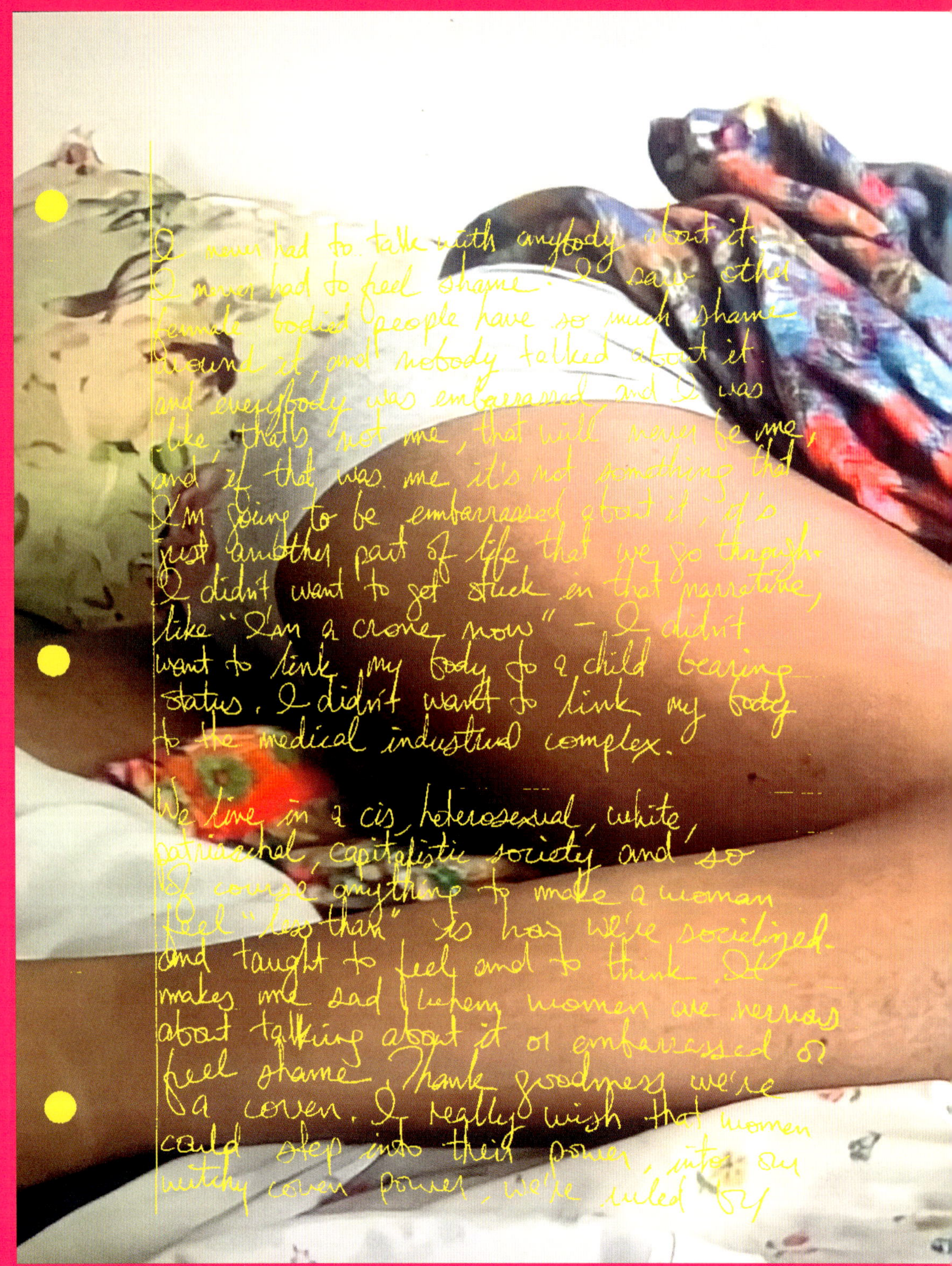
I never had to talk with anybody about it.
I never had to feel shame. I saw other
female bodied people have so much shame
around it, and nobody talked about it
and everybody was embarrassed and I was
like, that's not me, that will never be me,
and if that was me it's not something that
I'm going to be embarrassed about it, it's
just another part of life that we go through.
I didn't want to get stuck in that narrative,
like "I'm a crone now" – I didn't
want to link my body to a child bearing
status. I didn't want to link my body
to the medical industrial complex.
We live in a cis, heterosexual, white,
patriarchal, capitalistic society and so
of course anything to make a woman
feel "less than" is how we're socialized
and taught to feel and to think. It
makes me sad when women are nervous
about talking about it or embarrassed or
feel shame. Thank goodness we're
a coven. I really wish that women
could step into their power, into our
witchy coven power. We're ruled by

Kiebpoli on her bed

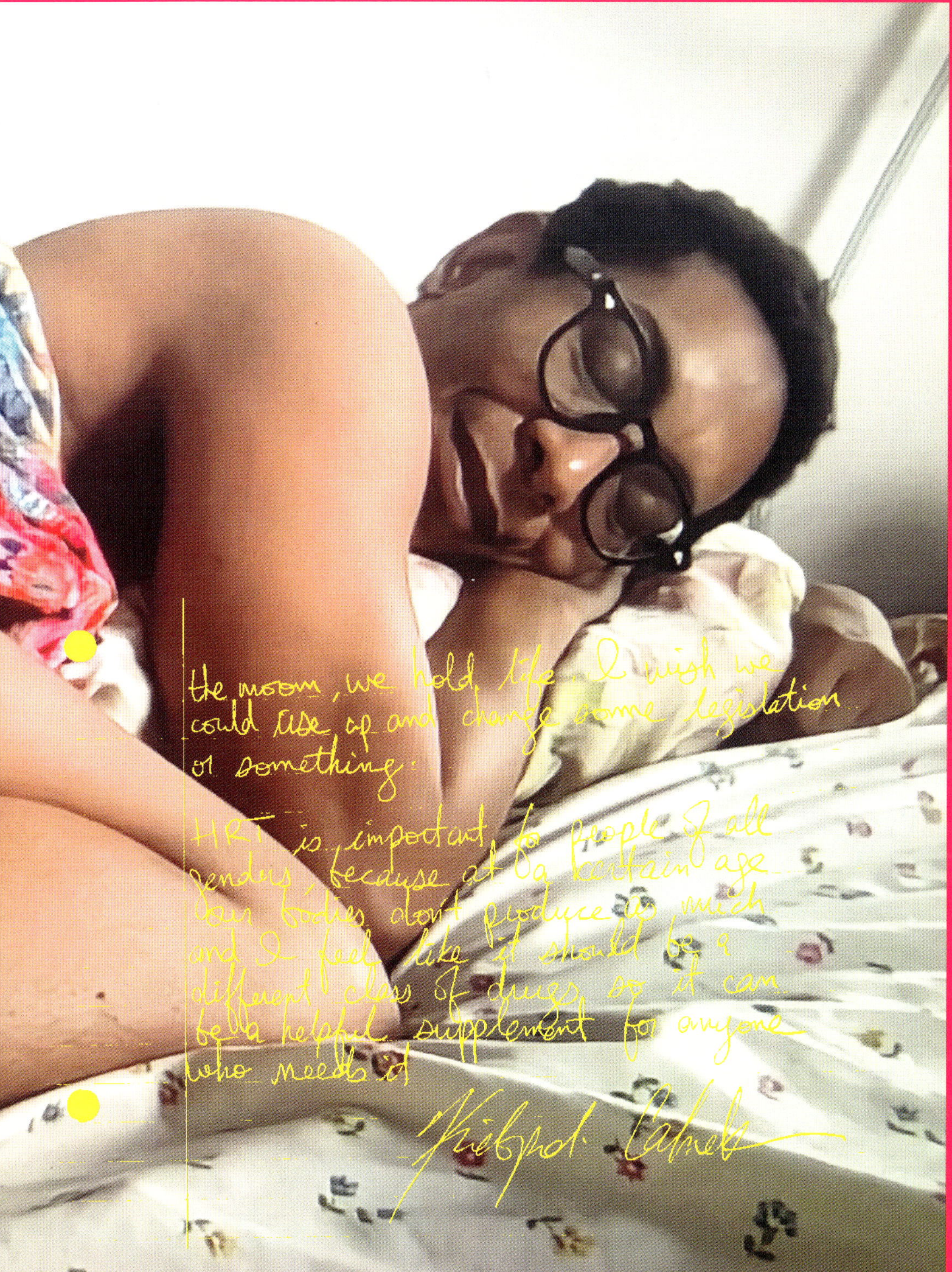

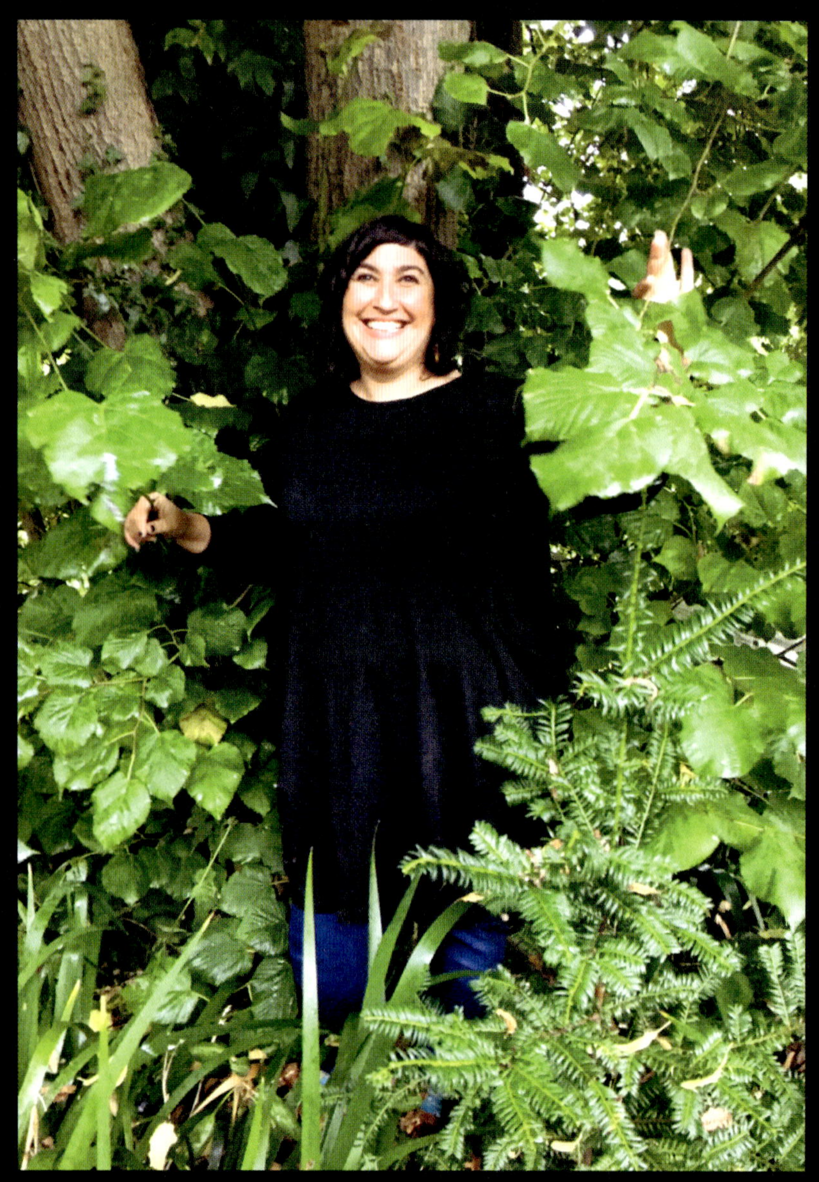

Handan stands among the foliage in her garden

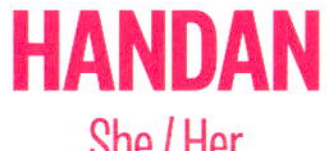

She / Her

Sheffield,
South Yorkshire
Age 45
Teacher

I worried about how my extreme moods would affect my child's formative years. When I developed insomnia and my daughter's teenage brain and hormones had kicked in, we both became teenagers in the same space. Which is not ideal if you have the intent to raise a confident and kind person. They gave me antidepressants, which I didn't take, because there weren't any reasons per se for me to be feeling down. I went on forums, found Facebook groups, a menopause café, lectures, multiple books and then went back to the doctor's, and he said, patronisingly, "You've been googling it." It was decided I was in the perimenopause.

They suggested the coil, patches, but I knew what I wanted. I took a picture in. I got the body identical gel and the tablets, I wanted the freedom to play around with the dose until I got the right one for me. I'm much calmer now. I laugh a lot with my kid again; she's in the category of miserable teenager and I find it hilarious, whereas before I would have felt insulted or disrespected. I'm like, "What was I on?" that I just became so reactive. I wasn't holding space for her, even though I tried. I've developed gluten intolerance, impatience and brain fog, but I feel empowered. I've become this "80-year-old woman" who isn't filtering her responses anymore. I call a spade a spade now. Another thing is toxic friendships, which I used to hold on to – I can just let go of them without feeling guilt, sadness or misery. I can't be bothered with drama anymore.

SOPHIE

She / Her

Peasdown St John, Somerset
Age 53
Jewellery designer and
higher education adviser

So, I'm perimenopausal, getting closer to it. I'll have a period and then stop for six months, then I think that's it, and then I'll have another.

At 45, I got chronic migraines. That's getting better. I'm really enjoying not having periods and not getting those huge mood swings within the month. It really defined me. If I had a job interview when I had PMT, I knew I wasn't going to get the job! It's plateaued now.

I'm more relaxed towards people. I can be more democratic towards everybody.

The way I've controlled my migraine and improved my whole wellbeing is that I do Wim Hof [breathing]. You do 30 breaths, lie down. Breathe all the way from your belly up, and take 30 deep breaths, then hold your breath for as long as you can. That makes you very relaxed, and then you go under a cold shower. I've been doing that for about three years; it makes me feel high in the mornings. Not many people want to have a cold shower but, for me, because of bad migraines I was desperate.

I exercise a lot and do gardening. There is no reason to change just because you are menopausal; you can just do things differently and adapt to suit you.

I've learned to be more assertive in work meetings. When I was younger I found it easier to say very little in a meeting and then regret it afterwards. Now I simply say, "I've got something to say!" and feel less self-conscious than when I was younger.

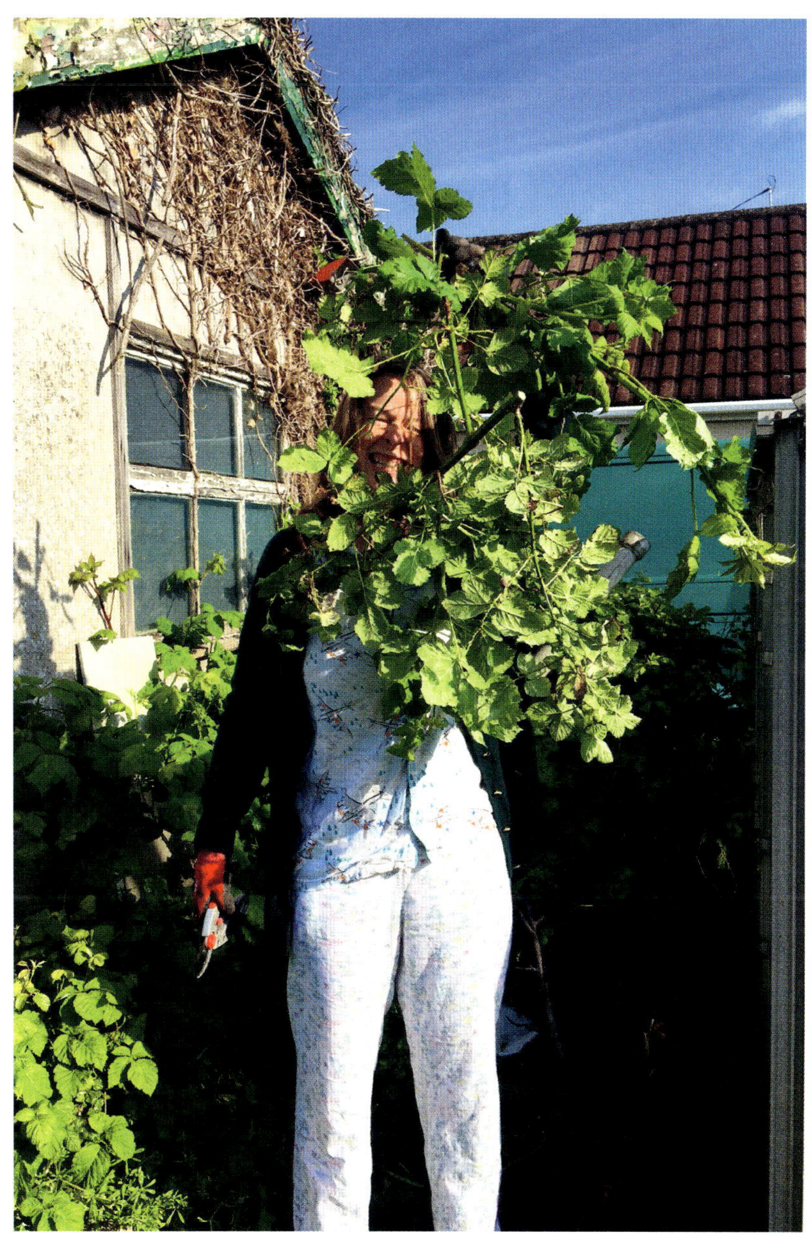

Sophie pruning her Somerset garden

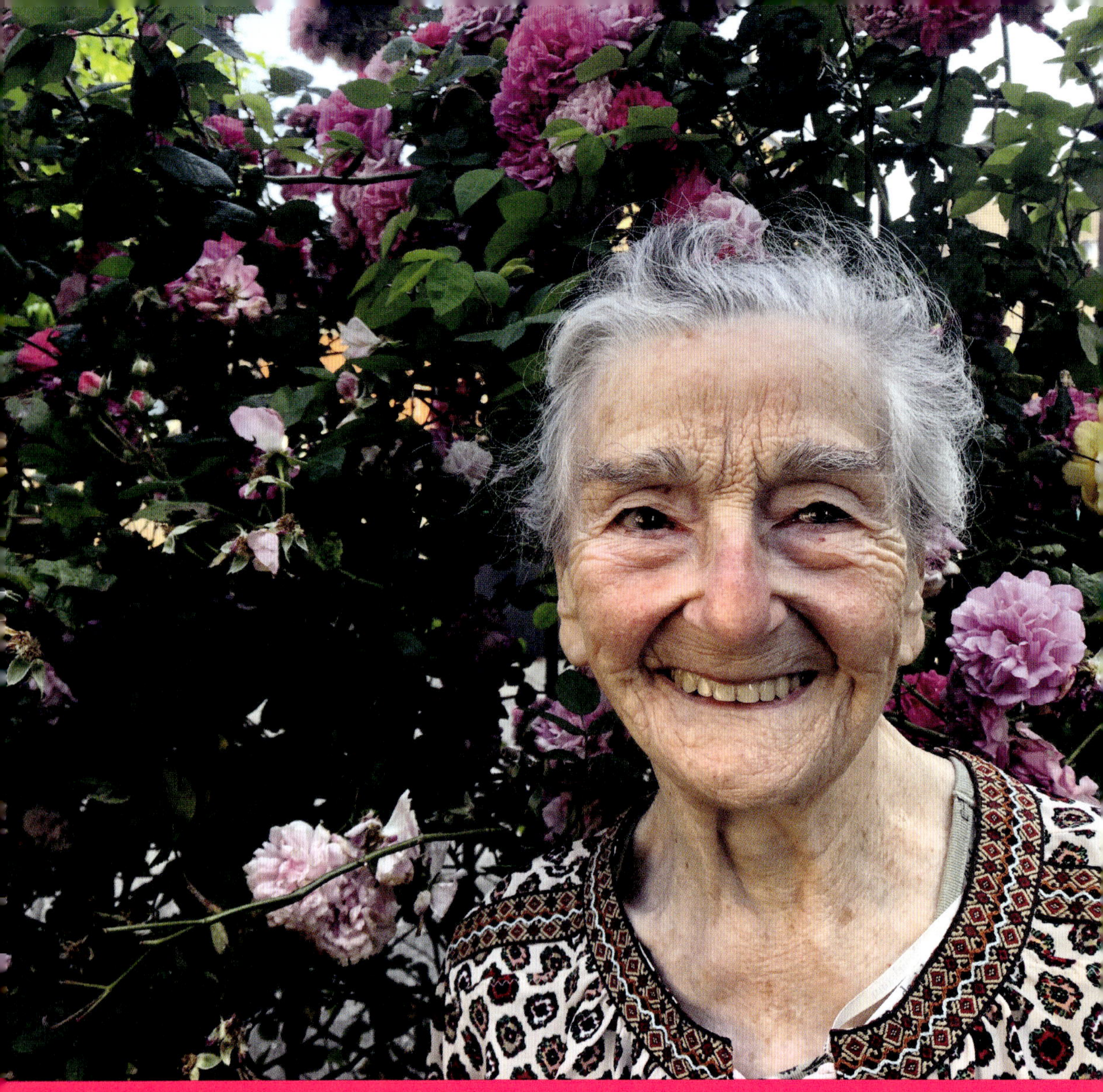

Irene pictured against the roses in the communal gardens where she lives

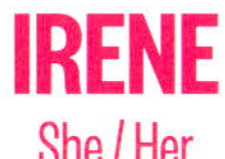

She / Her

Stamford Hill, London
Age 96
Retired, volunteer, gardener, mother, grandmother, great-grandmother and great-great-grandmother

I never went through the menopause. Mind you, I was so pleased when I didn't have a period anymore. You don't have to wait for that monthly [use of] a towel and keeping clean and everything else.

I didn't know what hot flushes were until I saw my mum going red as a beetroot. Sweat used to pour out of her; she always used to have a cloth with her. I always wondered what it was, because when you're young, you don't understand what goes on for older women.

I've got a very positive attitude, although it's only since I've got this elderly that I do panic if I miss a hospital appointment. I go tenpin bowling, I go short mat bowling, and I belong to a little men's club called the Hackney Dudes. We travel; next week we're going to Margate. We go all over London. Some of the men are slightly disabled and I'm a helper. When I'm not doing that, I'm doing the gardens.

PERSEPHONE

She / Her

Haringey, London
Age 65
Urban left-leaning lady
and trainee counsellor

There's a feeling of being more knowledgeable, wiser, and I can inhabit my unapologetic self, knowing that I've left behind the traditional, desirable woman. It is thought-provoking knowing that people, and the opposite sex, will be more interested in your character and personal qualities than the way you look.

The menopause is closely linked to the ageing process, and my body has changed. There are elements that I'm not entirely happy with – like parts of my body have become more prone to the effects of gravity. I knew in my last few years I could no longer have a child, but the finality of menopause was difficult to deal with. I've embraced postmenopause and the freedom of not having periods. During perimenopause my moods were all over the place, but now my mood is much more stable, and I'm inhabiting calmer seas.

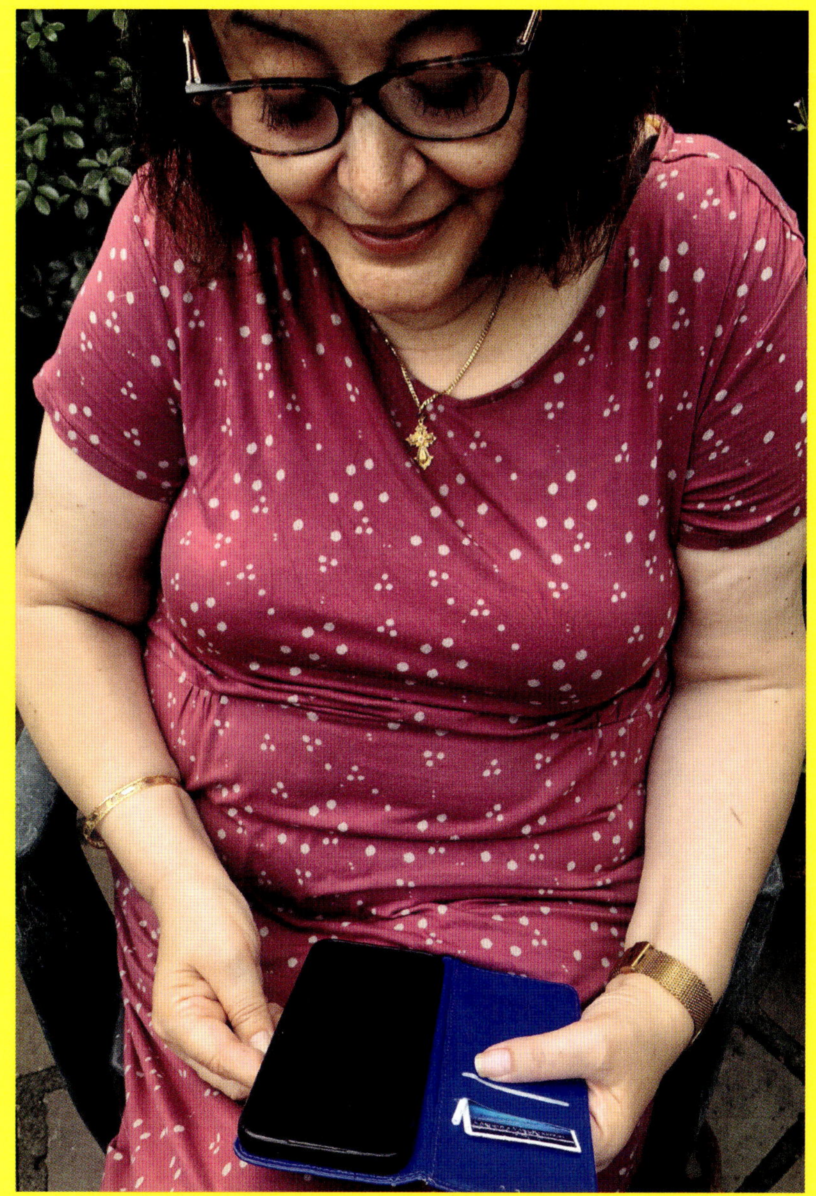

Persephone checking her phone

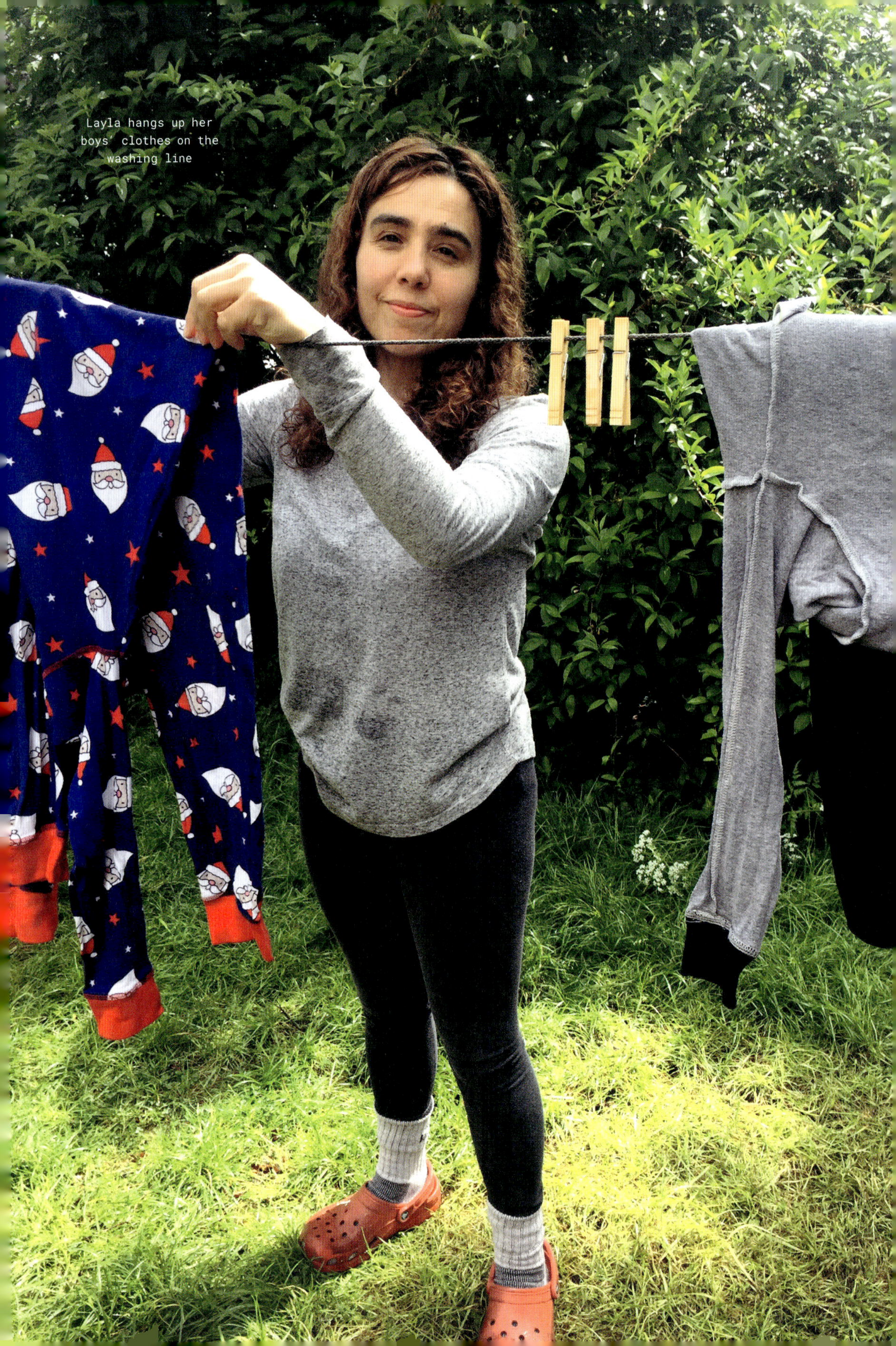

Layla hangs up her boys' clothes on the washing line

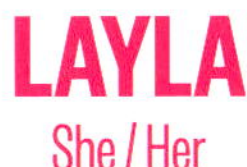

LAYLA

She / Her

Walthamstow, London
Age 47
Mother and primary carer of two boys, circus theatre teacher and maker

I live one day at a time and try to let go of things I can't cope with, recognising the change and the desire to change. There's total exhaustion and not being able to manifest the changes I feel into my work, because of trying to keep on top of raising my sons. [I have a] fear of being alone and asking for help.

FEAR
BEING
AND
FOR

OF
ALONE
ASKING
HELP

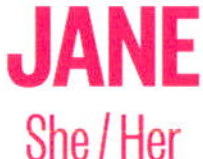

She / Her

Woodhouse, Leeds
Age 54
Homeopath, administrator
for Leeds Little
Free Libraries

For a while I thought I was going completely mad. Rage/suicidal thoughts, aches, pains, hot flushes. And when I realised what was happening, it got a bit easier. I read a book called *Passage to Power*, which made me look at it in a different way. It is the change; it's a time to reassess what I want to do with my life now. So, I left my job and put my home up for sale.

I don't tolerate too much noise, or people talking at me who don't listen anymore. Hence I spend a lot more time on my own, doing my own thing. I don't feel the need for a partner anymore. I don't feel joy like I did before. I've lost a lot of physical strength, so I've started doing yoga and Pilates and taking supplements. I feel like I'm just happy to please myself now; I don't need to please anyone else. I've stopped partying and poisoning my body, which is good, because I've started to look after myself. I really don't care what other people think now.

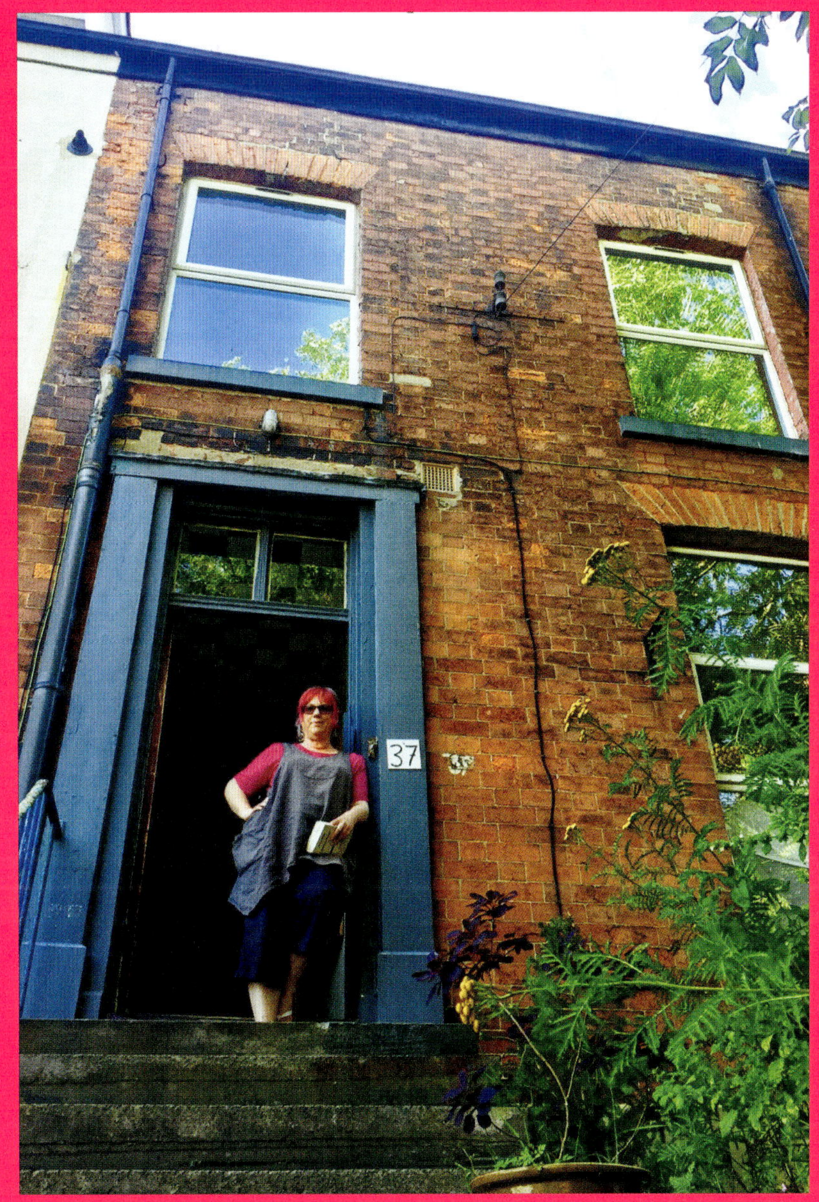

Jane in the doorway of the home she put up for sale

Emma enjoys the sunshine in her garden

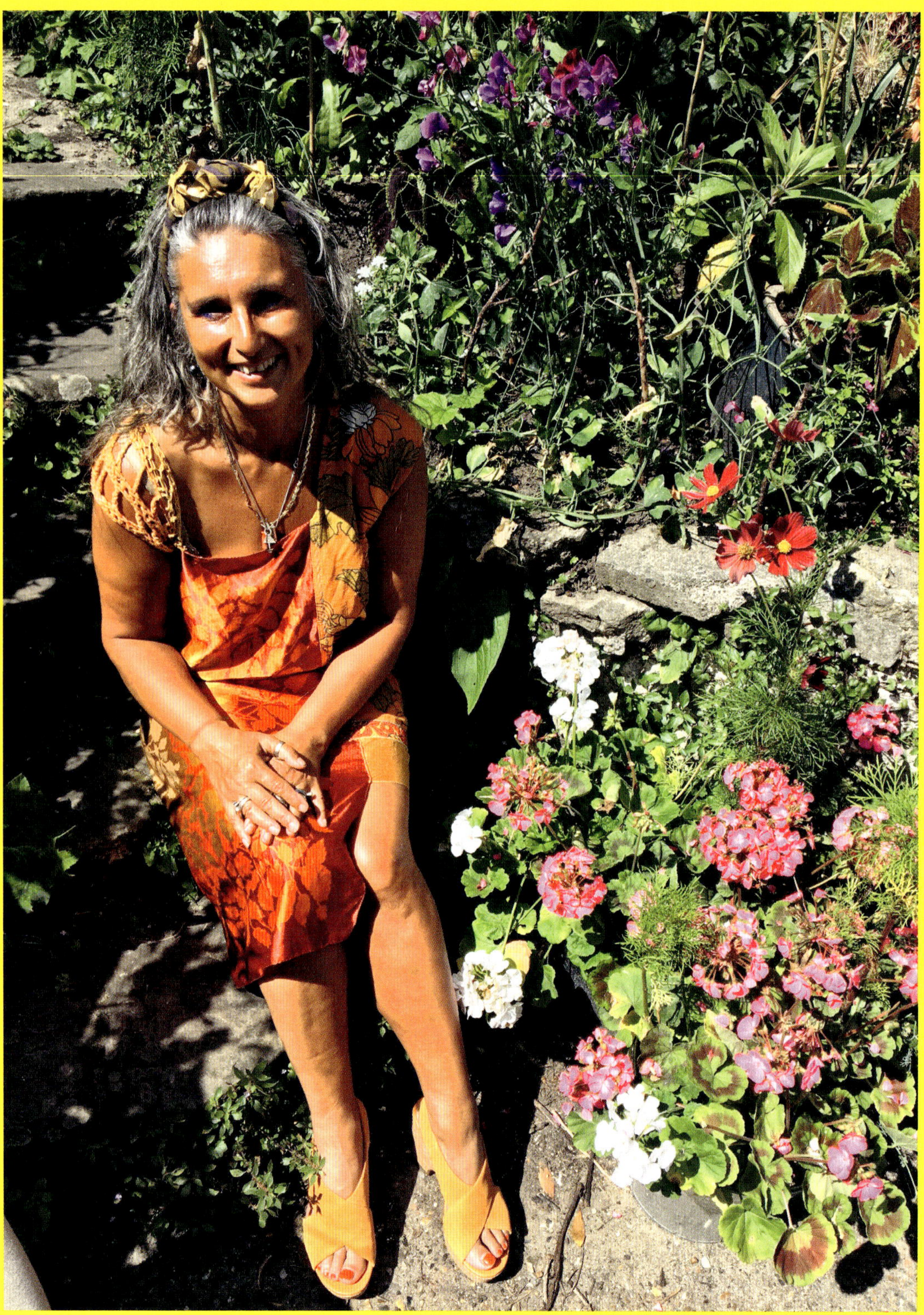

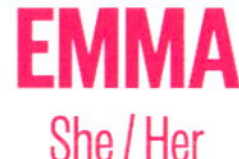

EMMA

She / Her

Ramsgate, Kent
Age 54
Educator and school
governance professional

Because my mum had womb cancer when she was around that age, she had no kind of menopausal experience to share with me, so I didn't really know what to expect. I wanted to go through it as naturally as I could, so I'm not taking HRT, even though other people have said it's amazing. I think I've soldiered through, and I think I'm OK without it, but it's a bit like having an epidural when you have a baby: I would never rule it out.

I've had to give up certain things that I really enjoyed, like caffeine; I was always saying to my mum, "What's the point of having decaffeinated coffee? I just don't understand." But when you get the anxiety attacks and the palpitations, you totally understand! I was never much of a drinker, but I drink even less now, because the time it takes to recover does not justify it. My sleep patterns continue to be very erratic. Sometimes I have an amazing night's sleep and I don't get the sweats, and other times I do. Through observation, if I do adequate exercise it sort of sweats it out. I recognise that exercise is a super-important part of it.

Not having periods, combined with the fact that my children have grown up (with no prospect of grandchildren any time soon), gives me personal freedom. I feel really comfortable with who I am and what I'm about; I don't have to prove anything to anyone, other than myself. I'm just enjoying my life. The textile exhibition I just did was the first one I've ever done in my life. I've always been a maker, but it's a really difficult field if you want to make a decent living. As long as I'm creating in some capacity, I'm happy.

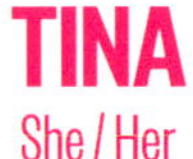

She / Her

Whitstable, Kent
Age 50
Retired aerial performer, aerial coach and researcher specialising in inclusive and accessible practice

I discovered I was menopausal when trying and failing to have children. It took doctors a long time to determine that it was the menopause, as I was in my early forties. I struggled with hot flushes (up to 22 a day!), night sweats and brain fog that impacted much of my life. This pushed me into depression, but ultimately led to me doing a PhD, as I sought something meaningful to do.

In 2018, I performed in a disability-led comedy performance about the menopause at Stratford's Olympic Park. I sang about feeling old and tired and forgetting what to do, while climbing and dangling in the air on the aerial silks. My memory was so shocking that I had someone hold up cards with prompts for me. Here's the chorus: *"My menopause brings me delights / Sweats – night and day / Sleep – then and now / What's not to like? Muscle decay? Crisis mid-life? What did you say? Mem'ry? What's that? Mem'ry? What's that?"*

When diagnosed with cancer in 2021, I was lucky to get the treatment I needed, but being on oestrogen-blocking tamoxifen has brought elements of the menopause back again. I'm grateful to be here, and the flushes – "my personal summers", as a friend used to call them – can at least be a blessing in winter!

I also performed in the "This Is What the Menopause Looks Like" exhibition opening night at The Horsebridge Arts Centre in Whitstable. This brought my menopause and cancer journeys together, as well as access, as a friend BSL [British Sign Language] signed next to me.

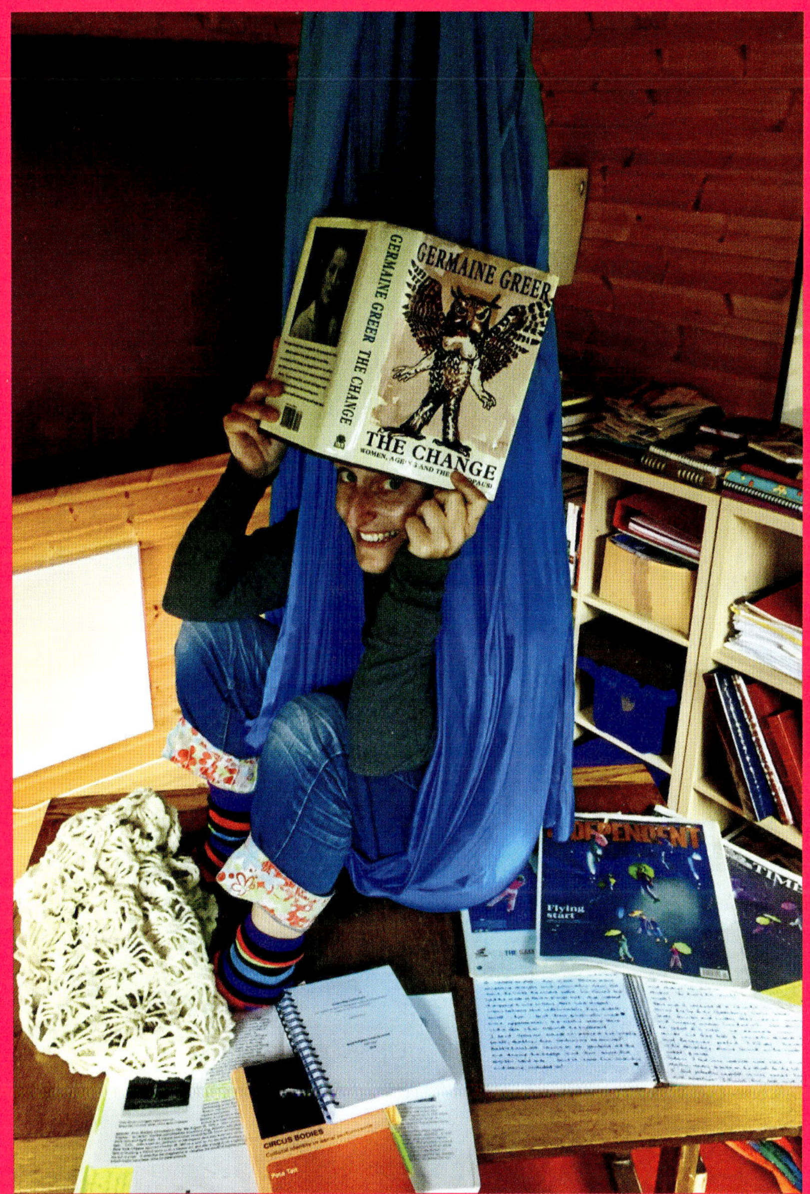

Tina sits on her aerial yoga hammock in her garden cabin and holds Germaine Greer's book on women, ageing and the menopause

PETS

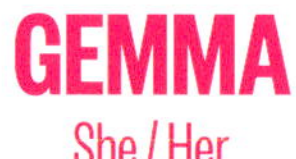

GEMMA

She / Her

Margate, Kent
Age 39
Social prescriber
for the NHS

I was in severe pain, things weren't how they were supposed to be, and I went to the GP and felt ignored. I was ringing every month about the same problem. My first appointment was in February, and by July I only ended up in A&E because I rang the hospital in London, and the nurse there said, "You need to go to A&E." Eventually, I was diagnosed and treated for Stage 3 terminal cancer.

The radiotherapy and the chemo have caused me to go into premature ovarian failure. I was told it would happen, but I wasn't told that it would happen instantly. I found that really hard – trying to recover from all the treatment and experiencing the symptoms such as hot flushes, insomnia and extreme night sweats. I panicked, thinking it was a fever, and I was sick. I didn't want to go back to the hospital. We were trying to get pregnant just before the diagnosis, and now I won't be able to have children naturally. I still thought I had plenty of time. I've been offered to discuss options, HRT, but I'm worried about the potential cancer risks. I don't want to go through that experience again.

Now I know what I'm going through, I don't have it to come later on, and the not having to worry about my period, because I don't have them anymore. When I had the tumour, periods were extremely painful. Because I'm going through it first, I'll be able to help my social group of friends when they go through it. I'm looking into alternative therapies – like diet, cold water swimming, reflexology and acupuncture.

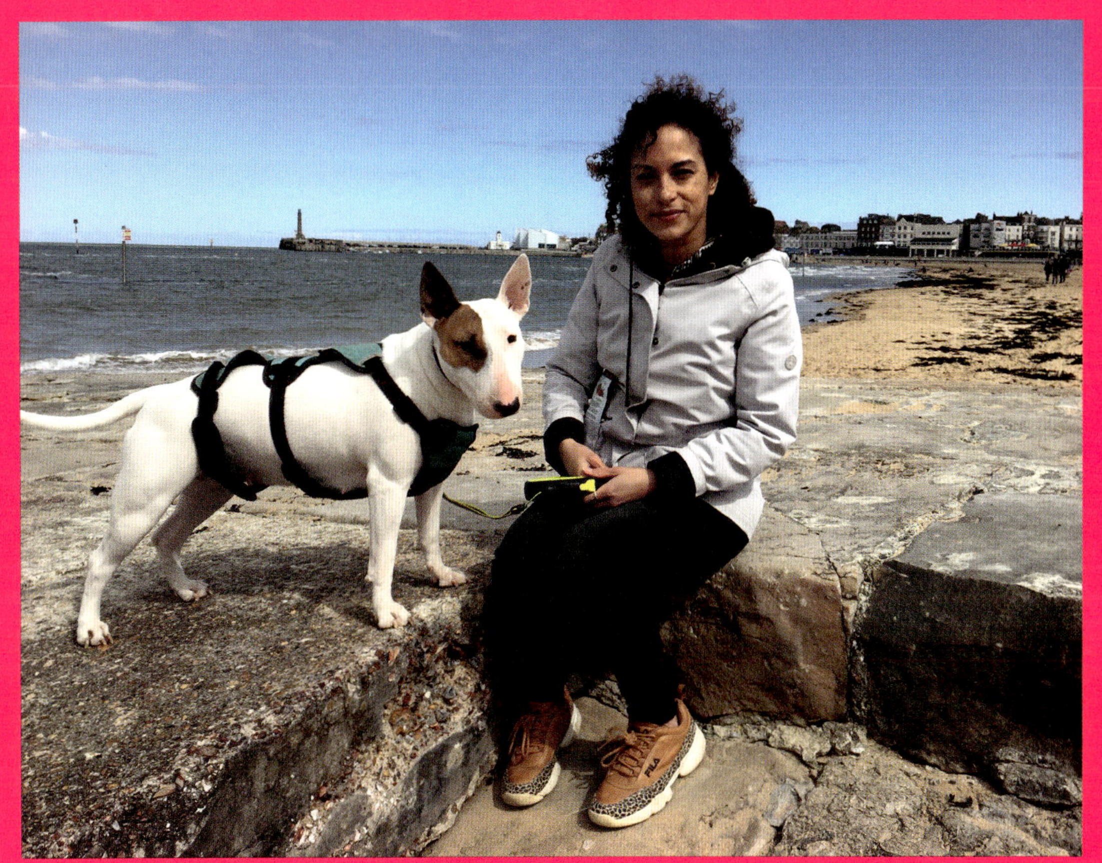

Gemma on the beach in Margate with her dog, Bow

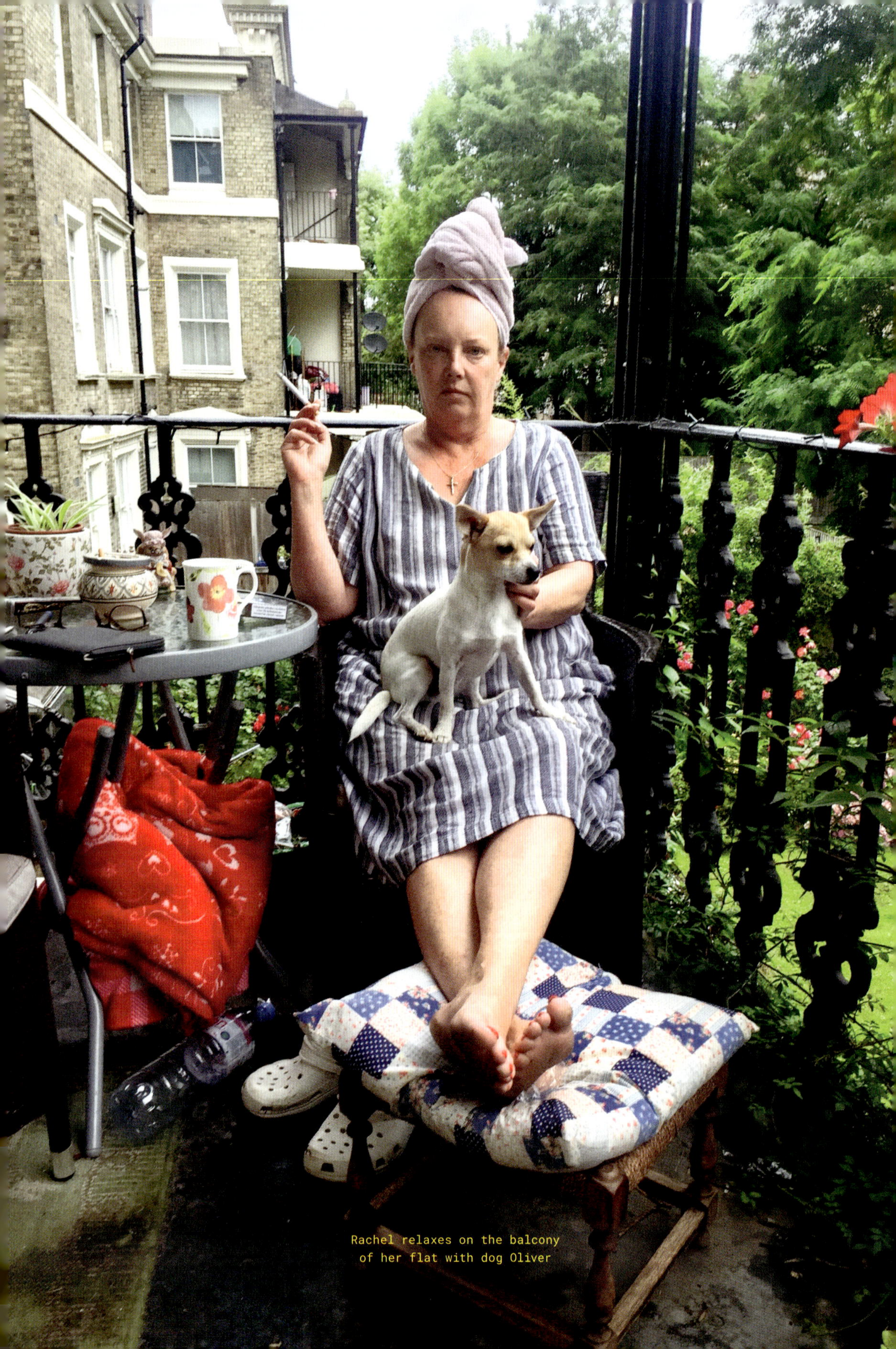

Rachel relaxes on the balcony
of her flat with dog Oliver

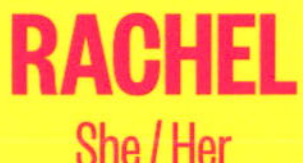

RACHEL

She / Her

Stoke Newington, London
Age 52
Receptionist and
teaching assistant

Low moods, bordering on depression. You don't know whether it's the menopause or not, because there's a lack of information out there. Less tolerant of bullshit, I can look forward to developing a different life. Not getting PMT and not having to think about carrying sanitary wear with me. The not caring what other people think. It's like my daughter's 17 and she won't leave the house without make-up. It's all about what she looks like, whereas now I don't care. I'm not that bothered what people think about me anymore. I've now got the freedom to go where I want, to do the things I want to do with the people I want to do them with, and I don't care what anyone else thinks.

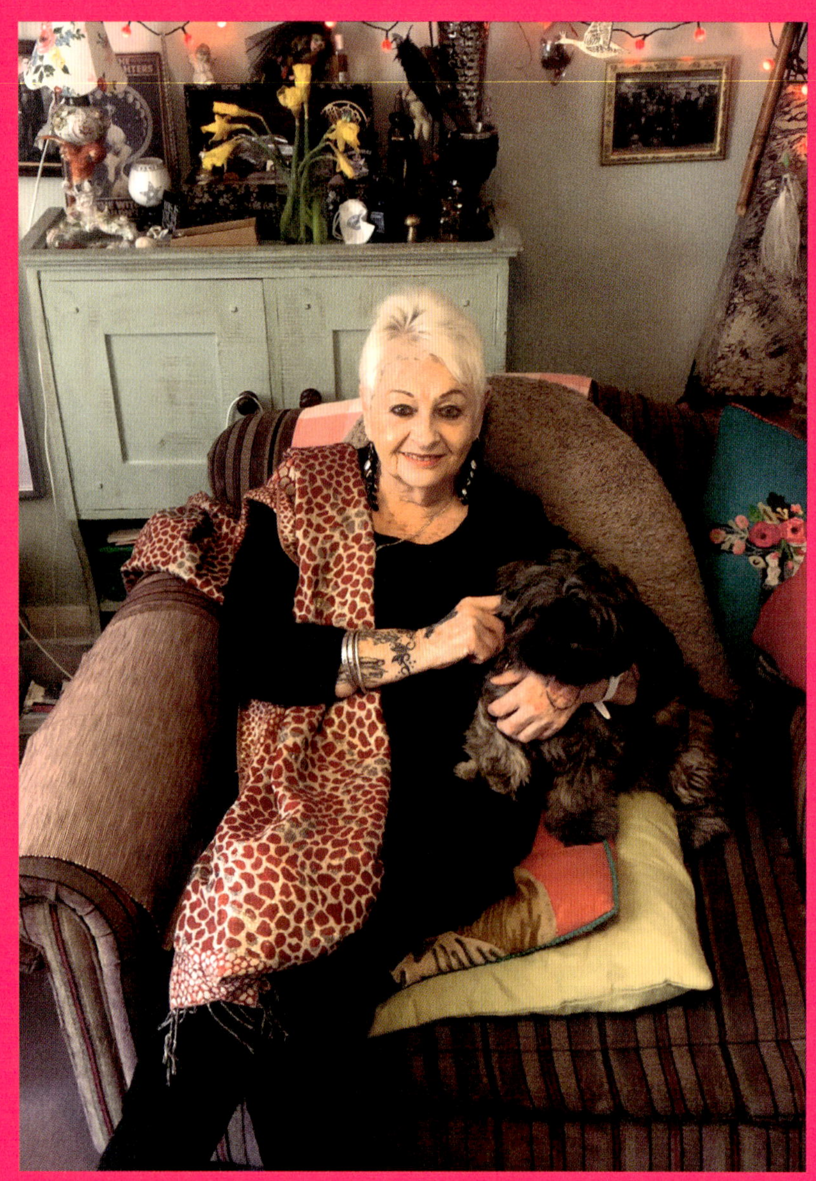

Anni at home on her sofa with Kiki

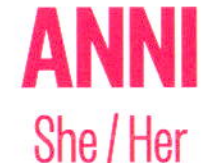

She / Her

Ramsgate, London
Age 76
Pagan mother

I had a partial hysterectomy at 36. I've had three children. I was 15 when I had Cathy. She was born in 1962 – she was given up for adoption, like all kids of that generation. I had gynaecological problems right from when I had her. Heavy bleeding, excruciating pain. I've had multiple miscarriages, in between giving live births.

People today only look at the instant, they're not looking at the past or the future. I remember marching for the contraceptive pill. The women who were in the trial for the contraceptive pill in the '60s were the young who had already given birth in the mother-and-baby homes.

In 1984, I had a hysterectomy due to fibroids. I bled constantly from when I had Luke up to the hysterectomy. They just took the uterus so I'd have a menopause. At 49, my menopause started. HRT was brand new then, and hardly anyone got put on it. I couldn't have HRT because I had a liver condition. That's when I figured out I was in the autumn of my life: I've got no period now; the pain and constant breakthrough bleeding was gone. I'm living happily at this point.

Being a pagan woman, I had my croning ceremony then. I had a gathering of 13 women – most from my coven. One of the women made a scroll and wrote out the transference from mother to crone. It's in the cycle of the moon: new moon, maiden; full moon, mother; waning moon, crone. Hence, now I'm 26 years postmenopausal, I'm happy, happy, happy. Grandmother, great-grandmother, matriarch – I carry the wisdom, and that brings happiness.

DEBORAH

She / Her

Clapton, London
Age 51
Civil servant

Hot flushes wake me up and they're dehydrating. I've started to suffer with brain fog, which is frustrating. I can identify what it is, as other women have described it to me, but nobody can prepare you for the complete blank that happens. For someone who's generally able to express themselves quite eloquently, it's quite unnerving. I'm just going into it and it's hard to know what to do because the advice that's out there is so contradictory.

I've thought about HRT, but my doctor refused to discuss it with me. She said as I'm still having periods I'm not menopausal. I'm going to have to ride it out and see how I get on. I'm thinking about trying acupuncture to try and find some "normality" because everything feels all over the place. It's hard to think of any positives, although it's been really interesting connecting and talking to other women about their experiences. And I hadn't realised that other women were so conscious and considerate about their experience. Being the age I am, I feel able to talk to other women, which is different to when I was 14 and I started my periods. I wasn't able to do that then. Not even my mother talked to me about it.

I suppose I'm very lucky to be the age that I am in the time that I live, in that society is more open about it in terms of understanding the symptoms, although we've still got a long way to go – as in, I wouldn't be able to walk into a job interview and say, "I've corpsed because of the menopause."

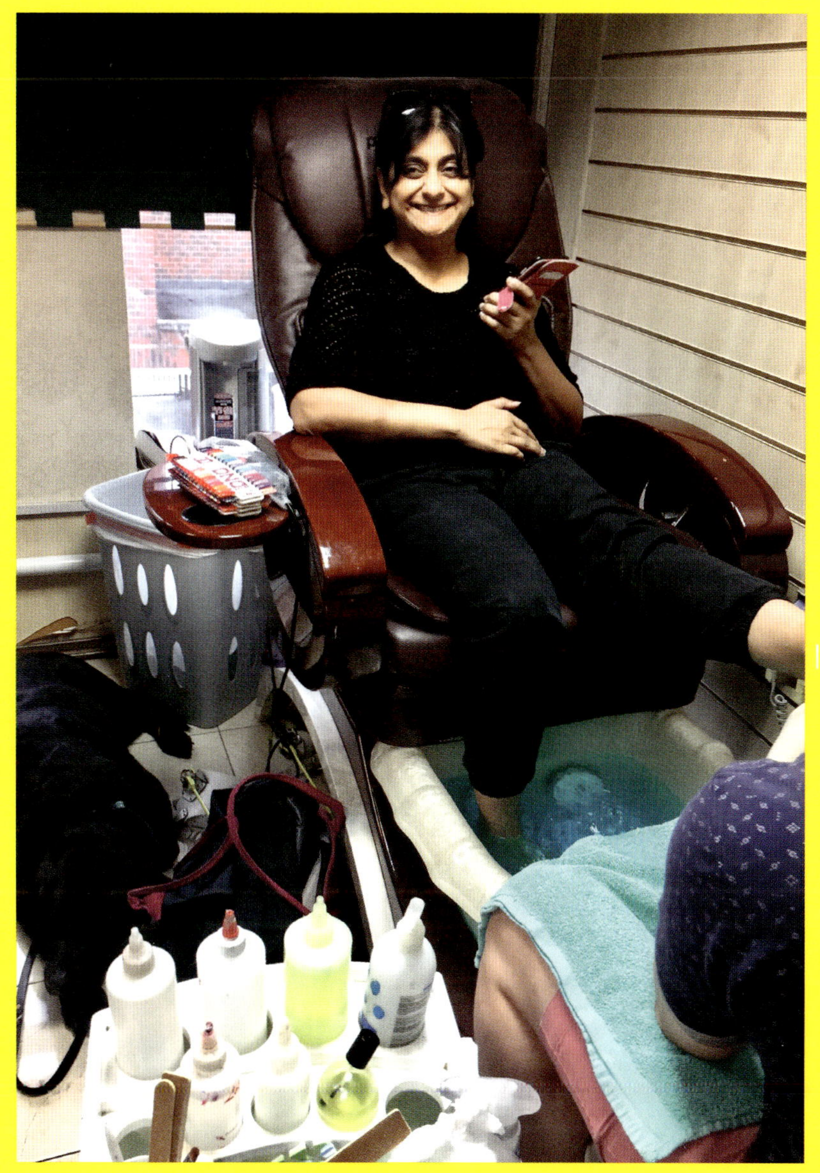

Deborah at a nail bar in Dalston with her dog, Louis

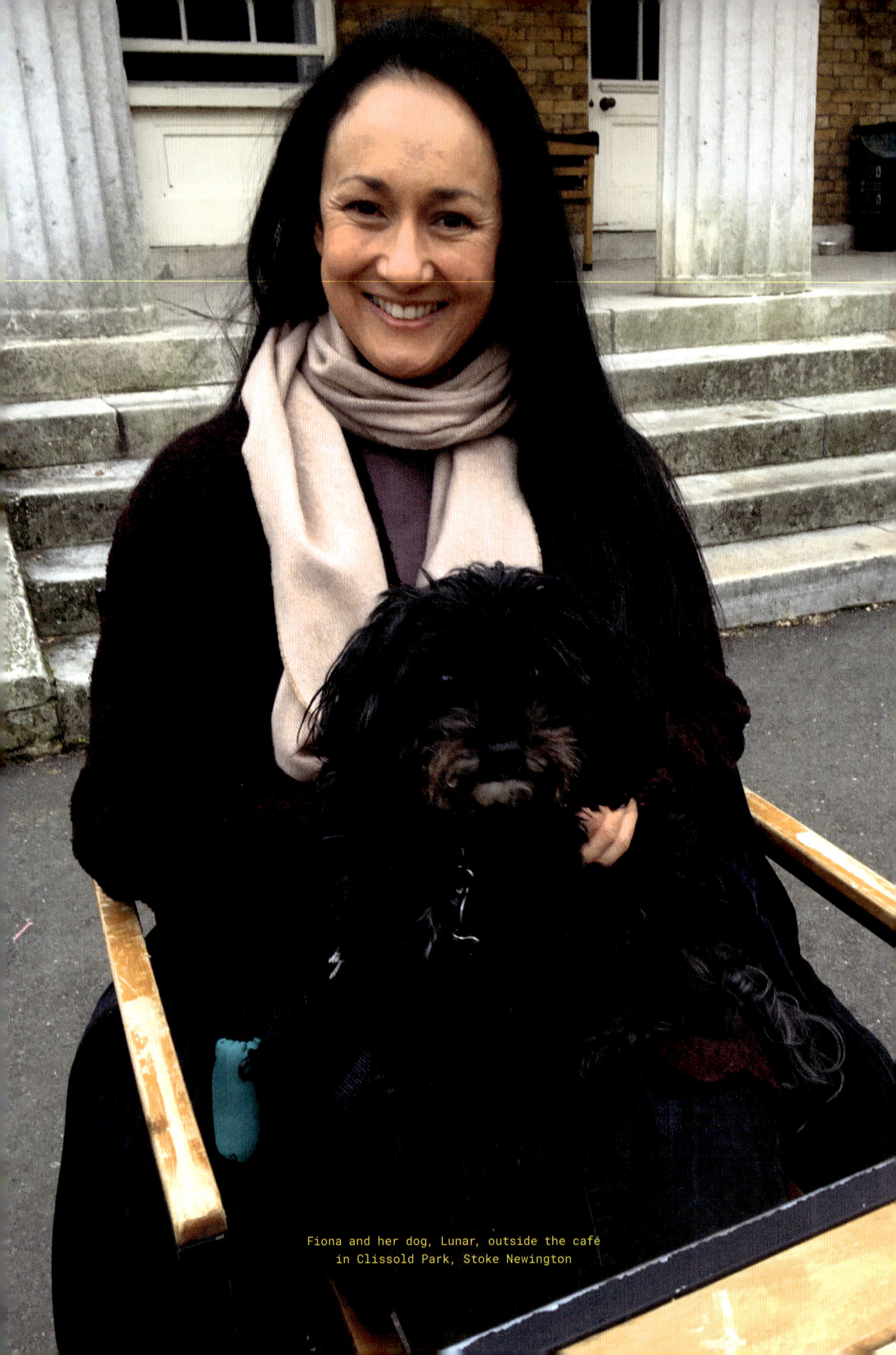

Fiona and her dog, Lunar, outside the café
in Clissold Park, Stoke Newington

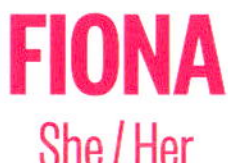

Stoke Newington, London
Age 43
Ballet mum, dog sitter, actor, aerial performer and teacher

Looking back, it was a couple of years with unexplained anxiety, hot flushes, night sweats, insomnia and waking up in a panic that I just put up with before going to my GP.

I put it all down to ageing and hadn't really considered there was any help I could get with things. I had cut out alcohol, as I just couldn't tolerate it, taken up exercising again, improved my diet, but actually starting HRT is what finally helped.

I can now sleep a bit better and the anxiety has calmed, meaning I can enjoy my life and family again. I'm still not wanting to go back to a stressful full-time job, but can manage part-time circus teaching, which I love.

My children are definitely no longer babies, so dog sitting is our new thing. The odd glass of wine is also possible on occasion, if I'm willing to put up with a couple of days' recovery time.

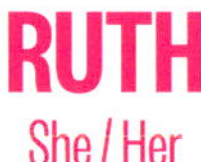

RUTH

She / Her

Burnley, Lancashire
Age 58
Recovering addict, poet
and spoken word artist

Menopause is all the rage now, isn't it? Since Davina went through it, it's trendy! I found it quite horrendous. I felt like I was losing my mind. I was working at the time in quite a stressful job. I lost that job. I believe that was because of the mental health problems that I was having at the time.

I remember being very negative about HRT. I'm a bit of an alternative person; I have massive issues with the pharmaceutical industry and just wanted to do it naturally. I thought HRT was damaging and toxic. I've now realised that was wrong. I'm going to have to rewrite one of my poems that talks about that!

On the first page of the book I bought, called *How to Get Through the Menopause Naturally*, was a list of symptoms; the list was basically everything! As so often happens, I bought the book, didn't read it and just carried on with my lifestyle, which didn't help. I was drinking a lot, still smoking and using recreational drugs. You can sort of get away with that stuff in your twenties [to] forties, but when you get to menopause you can't. Well, I couldn't!

I remember one day at work, I was on the phone to somebody and writing down his address and I forgot how to write letters; my brain had just completely frozen.

[Menopause is] just not giving a shit about what other people think and no periods. My boobs, which have always been quite pert, just sagged. My skin's really dry, it just looks like an old person's.

I've got massive incontinence issues. I saw something on the internet saying it can be caused by a lack of oestrogen and that once you get to a certain point with it, you're fucked!

Ruth photographed on her street with Nancy

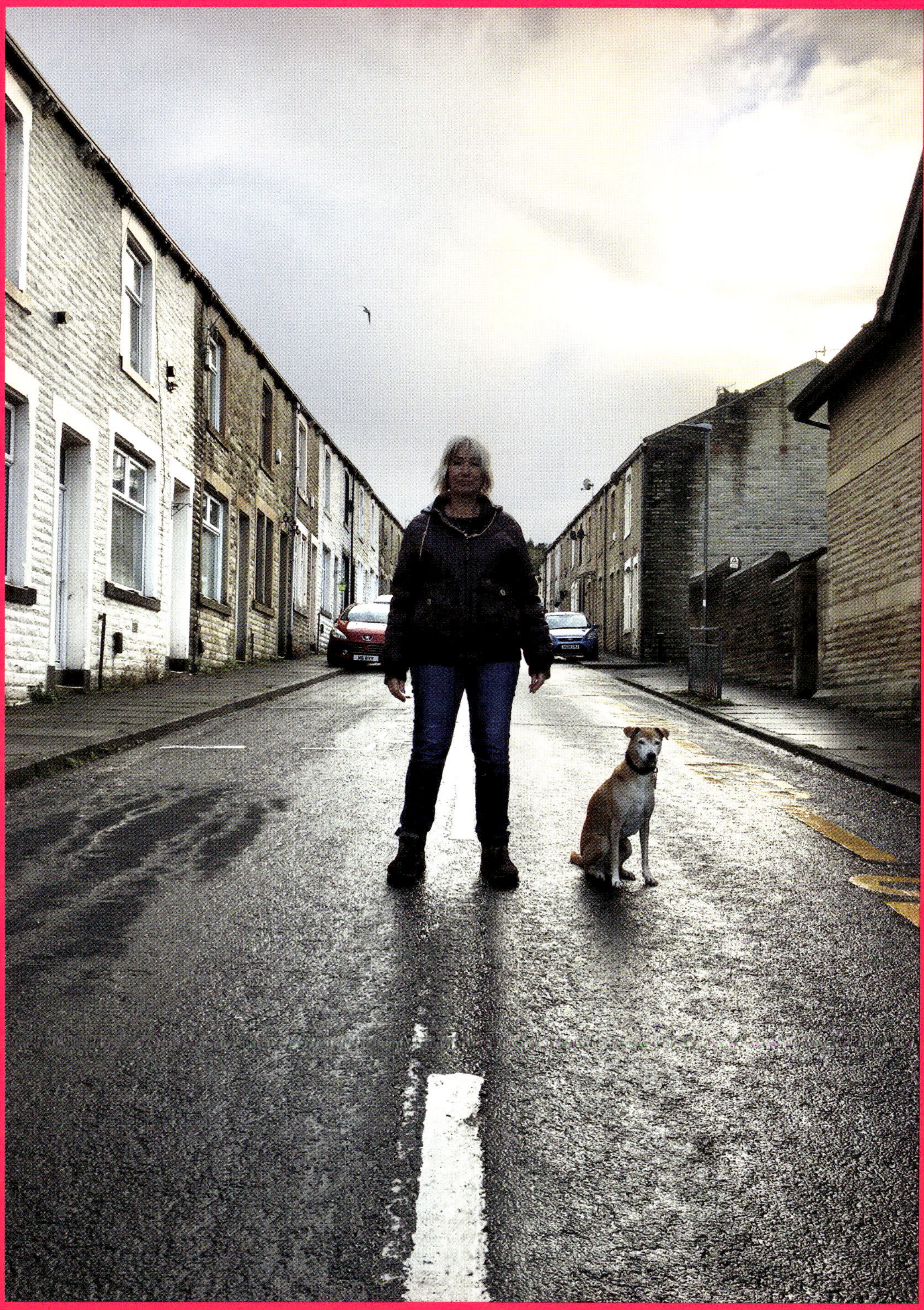

ONCE Y
TO A
POINT
YOU'RE

OU GET
CERTAIN
VITH IT,
FUCKED!

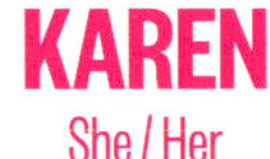

KAREN

She / Her

Ramsgate, Kent
Age 52
Artist, mother, lover, teacher and art psychotherapist

I didn't understand what was happening to me, because I'd just had my first child, aged 32. I thought my perimenopausal symptoms were symptoms of tiredness, breastfeeding and stress. It was only when I began to feel mentally ill I decided to go to the doctor's, and they told me I was going through perimenopause. I was in shock and felt sad because no support around what this really meant for me was given. Apart from the advice that if I wanted another child, I should get on with it.

I remember feeling shame, and having an irrational fear, as if somehow I was being punished for something surrounding my sexuality. By the time I was breastfeeding my second child, at 35, my periods never returned. I felt alone with this experience, as my friends and peers were not experiencing the same feeling of loss. Now, 17 years on, all my friends are talking about the menopause and I have a feeling of "job done".

I wasn't initially treated with HRT, which has resulted in me now having osteopenia, which I regularly have bone scans for. I am now taking HRT for my bones and memory, but wish more care had been taken of me from the beginning. I now read articles and books that express hope and guidance, but when I experienced the menopause, literature felt quite negative and sparse.

I feel positive about my life, I love living by the sea – close to my children and with my dogs. I love my work and my friendships and often feel inspired by opportunities and experiences that come my way. Although my journey was a challenge, I feel I'm at peace with it now.

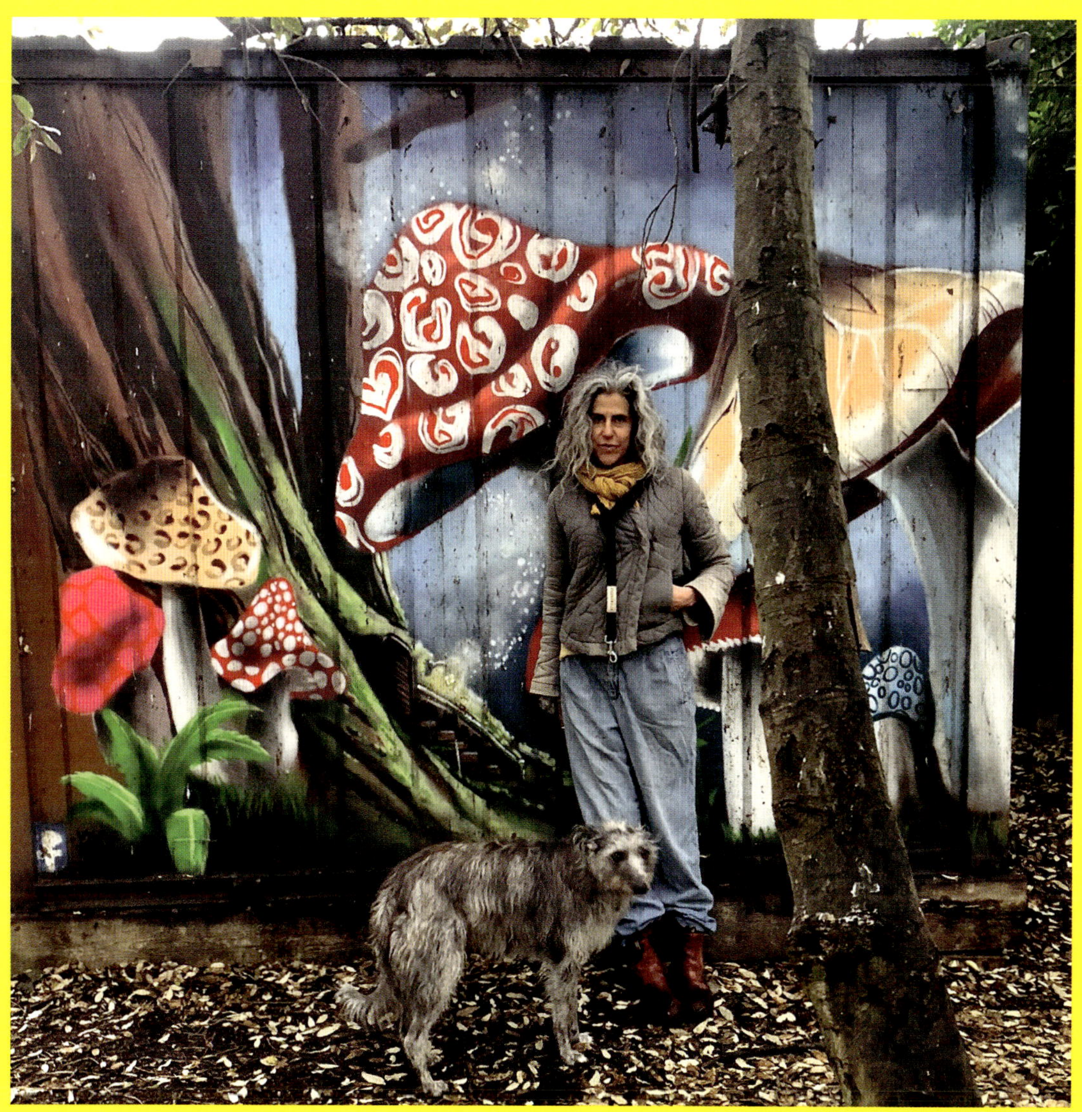

Karen and dog Bea on an early morning walk in Ramsgate

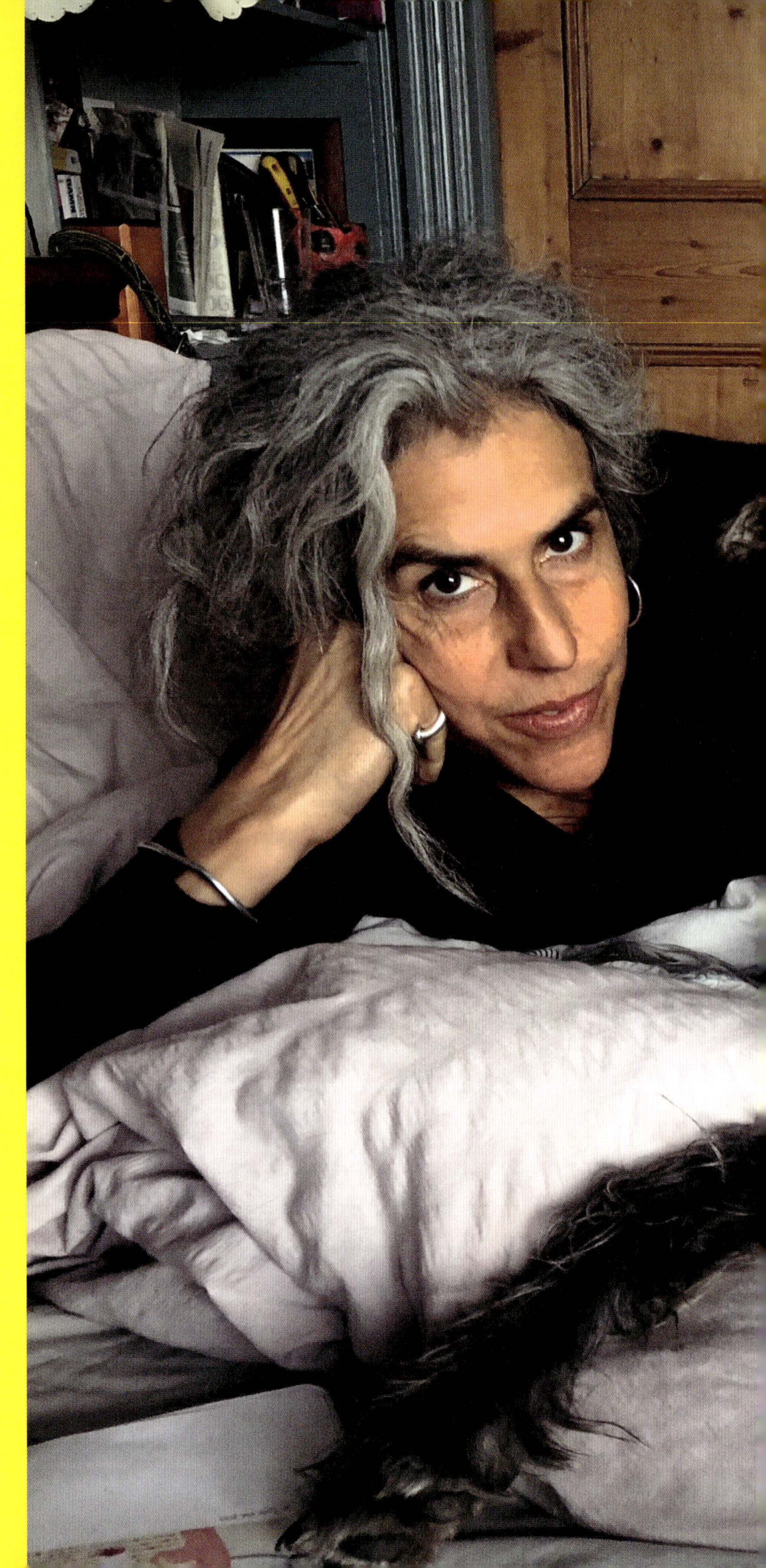

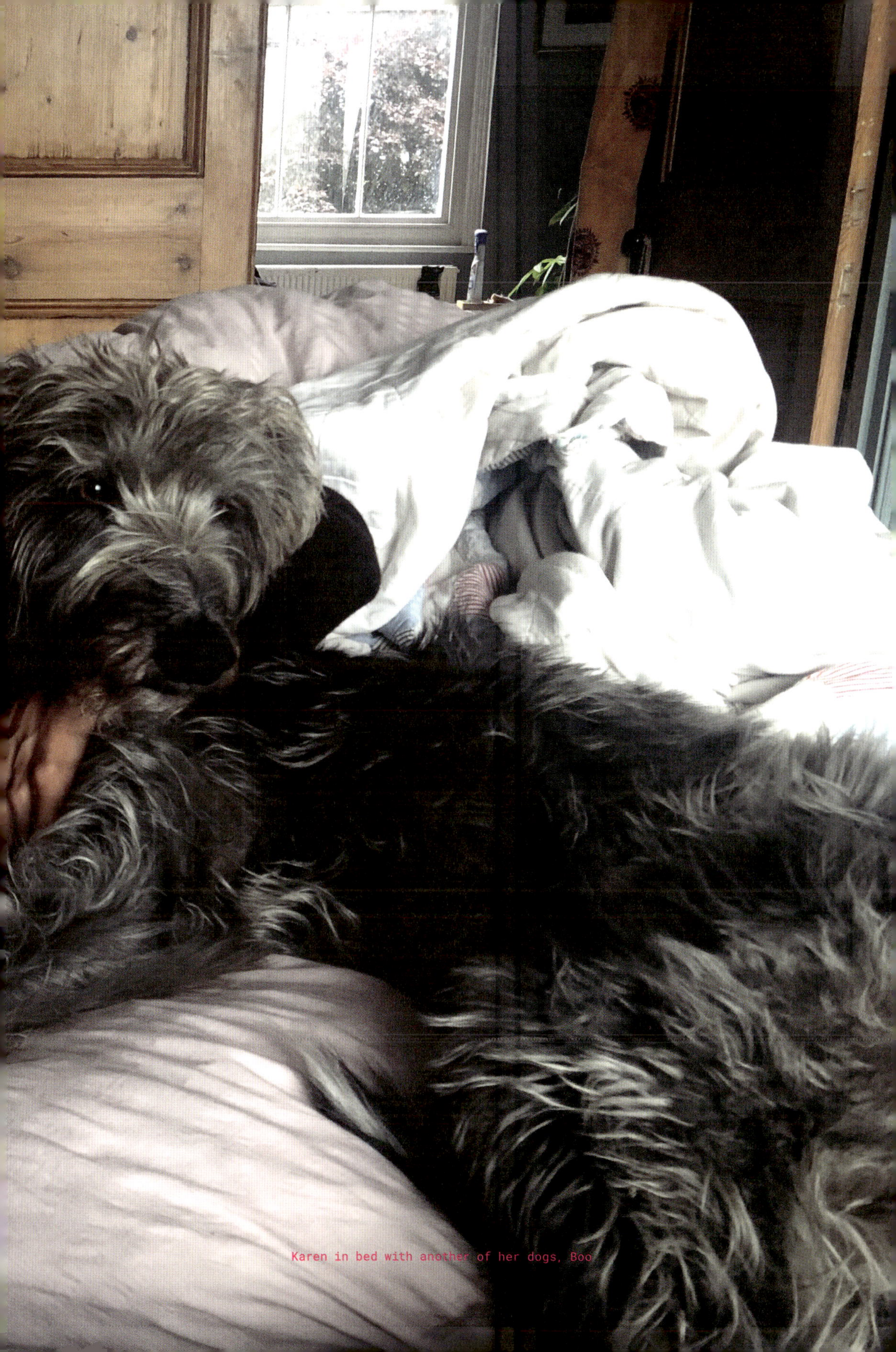

Karen in bed with another of her dogs, Boo

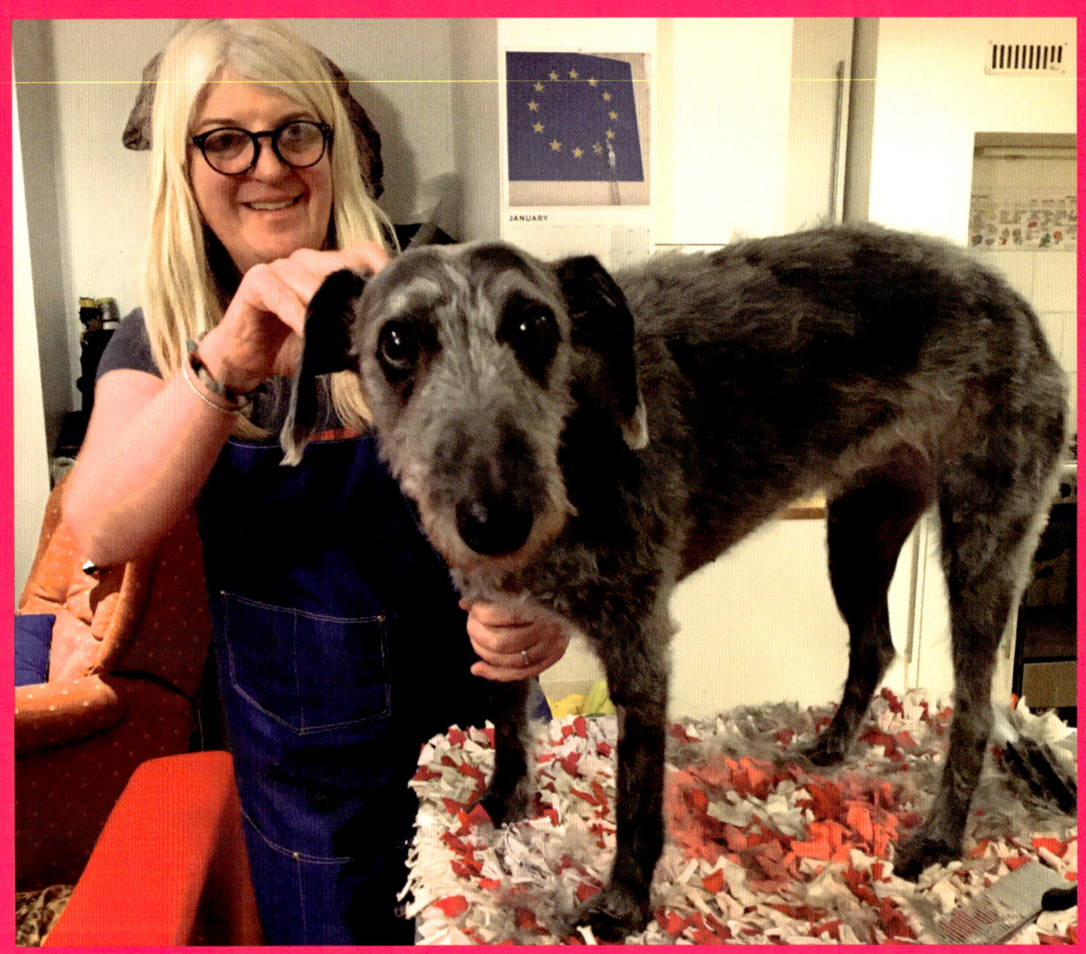

Lisa grooms Mabel, Catrin's dog, at home

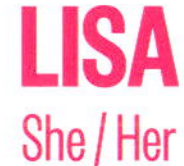

LISA

She / Her

Maidstone, Kent
Age 51
Dog groomer and mum

At 47, I was diagnosed with breast cancer, and the treatment I had forced me through an early menopause. I had tamoxifen, which caused hot flushes. I have tried cycling, running and sea swimming for three years, and that really helps.

I am hoping to go on HRT. My GP refused me HRT because of the oestrogen [receptor] positive breast cancer, but I am seeing a specialist menopause doctor in a few weeks and am hoping to go on HRT.

I have got to go private, but I don't mind. I feel quite positive, and I am hoping that once I'm on the HRT it will help with the brain fog, hot flushes and the anxiety. I wake up in the night and my heart starts pounding.

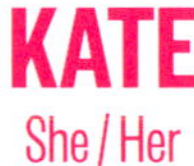

KATE

She / Her

Lives in a cabin in the woods
Age 52
Shoemaker, care home manager, biker, TV extra and sign language interpreter

I'm really dyslexic, and I'm really glad I had a Steiner education, because it gave me a different outlook. We did metalwork, woodwork and drama. We learnt life skills at the age of 14. How to build benders and saunas.

No periods, no costs, not having to spend money on Tampax. No period tax on Tampax! To be honest there aren't any positives. But not being able to have a baby has put a final stamp or closure on whether I'll ever conceive. There are so many kids out there who are unwanted or unloved, and I've got so much love. Especially living up here. Having a kid would inspire me to share the freedom to live like this outside.

I've got a goat, a horse and a dog who have given me responsibility since I left my life in the city. I always had a really high sex drive and this has enhanced it. I'm a sex pest. I feel more confident in my body, like a porn star.

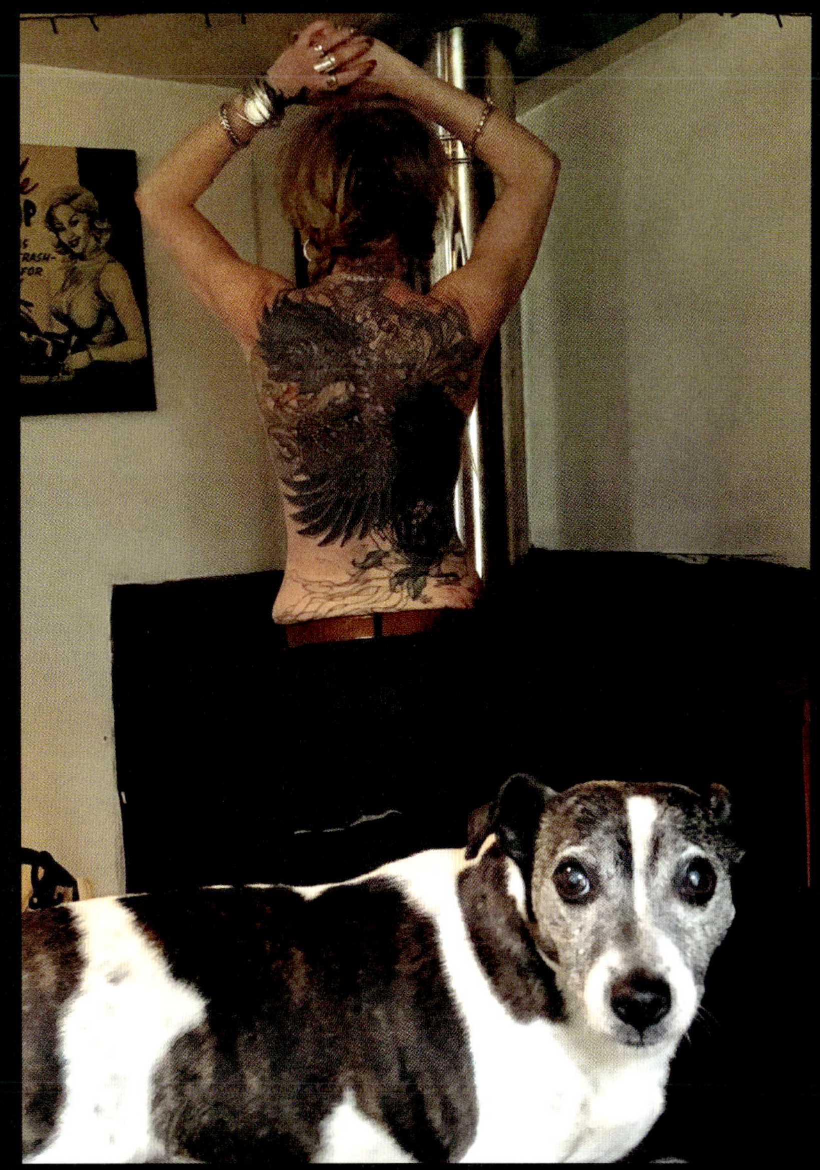

Kate in her cabin with Betsie

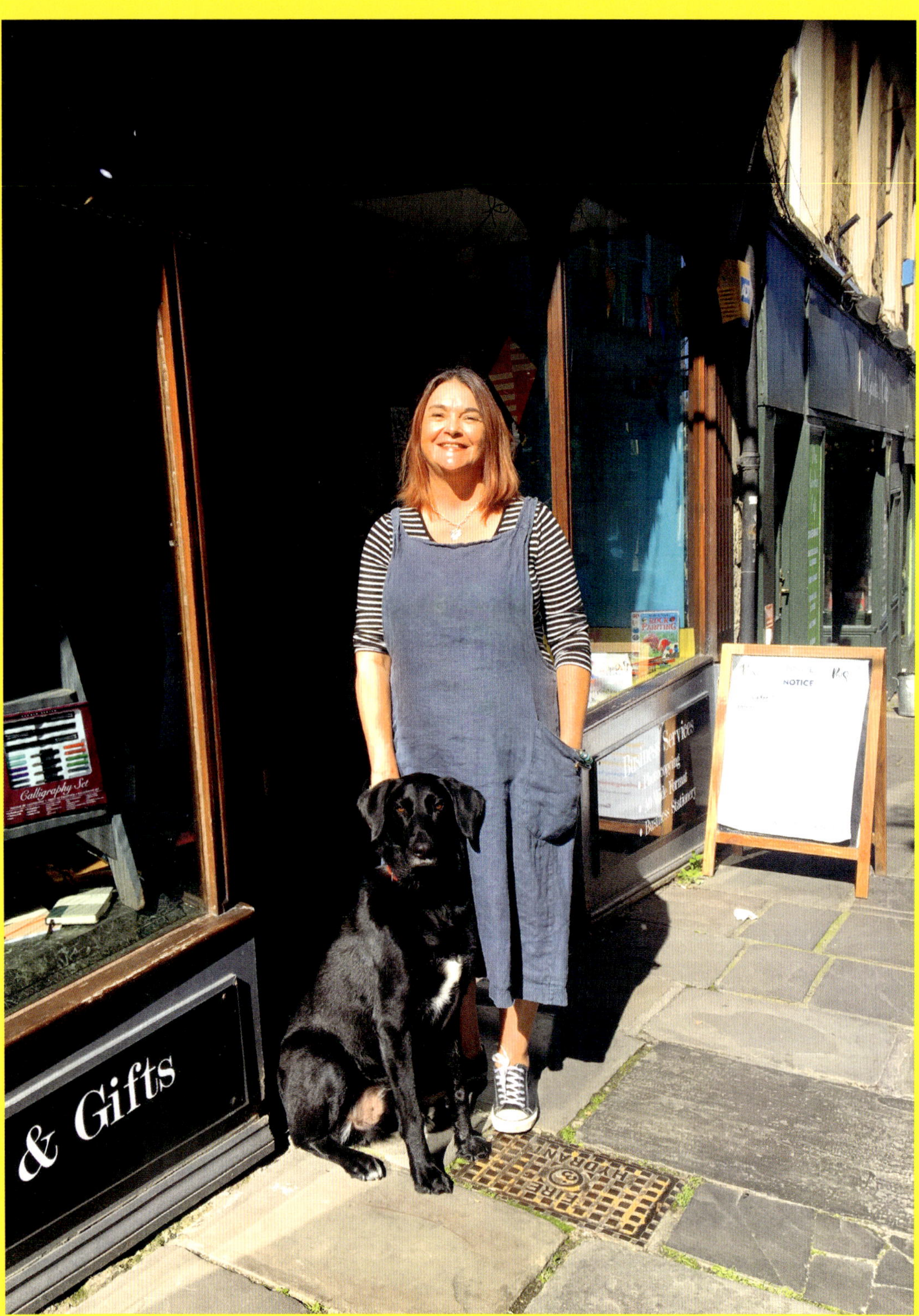

Rachel with Otis outside her stationery shop in Frome

RACHEL

She / Her

Frome, Somerset
Age 49
Stationery shop
owner and mother

I run a business and am an artist and have a large family, so have a lot to juggle! My eldest stepdaughter has just gone through pregnancy, while I've been going through the start of menopause. She's been talking about hormonal changes and lack of shape in her body. As women, we experience so much change to our bodies, through adolescence, pregnancy, menopause and general ageing – and the need to almost keep reinventing how we feel about ourselves and our ever changing bodies is very interesting.

I'm a sculptural artist working in bone china and wire; my work is influenced by the female body and movement of the form, so that whole idea of change is very much part of my work.

I have a very creative brain and don't think you can compartmentalise as much with menopause; everything is a little bit of a jumble when you've got lots of balls in the air.

Menopause has meant hot flushes, mood swings and totally overthinking, resulting in sleepless nights. I've had to start counting backwards from 100, just to get my brain to stop! Outdoor swimming has been helpful, just to be in a space of calm in nature where nobody can get to you. The body of water really helps in terms of the weightlessness: being enclosed in something that holds and supports you.

I've heard all the horror stories about HRT, and I am still fact-finding and trying to decide what menopausal path to take. It's not something that my friendship group talks about; there is sometimes still a feeling that by going on HRT you are almost a failure. It shouldn't be this hard for women, but it's an interesting journey!

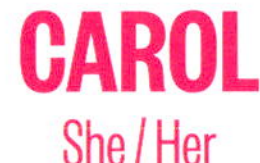

CAROL

She / Her

Ramsgate, Kent
Age 69
Retired mother,
wife and dog lover

When you first start the menopause, you really don't know what's going on. Other members of the family generally haven't experienced it. In my generation, it was a bit of a taboo subject. It's always been associated with old age. Menopause, old people.

You experience things like your hormones changing when you have periods, but then this other time in your life comes along that you're not expecting. I was in my forties; it's relatively young. I remember being at work. I was a manager, I had to be calm, interact with others, and I found I was totally doolally!

I didn't feel there were any positives at the time, and I can't even remember how I got to the doctor's. It was wonderful, she put me on HRT and I was back to more or less normal within weeks. I was on it for seven years. I didn't want to come off it, and she said, "You're probably through the menopause now." She took a blood test and I was. When I came off it, I lost a lot of weight. I still don't sleep, I get sweats, but it's not as bad as it was.

Life is more or less back to normal now. My daughter is having a horrendous time; she's gone private. The NHS doctor put her on antidepressants.

I do wonder how much harm people are doing to their bodies by not going on HRT. I see people at the doctor's with sticks and zimmers, and I hear them say their age, but they look so much older. I do wonder whether that is caused by not dealing with some of those things at an earlier time in their lives. Or not being able to, because doctors aren't trained in it.

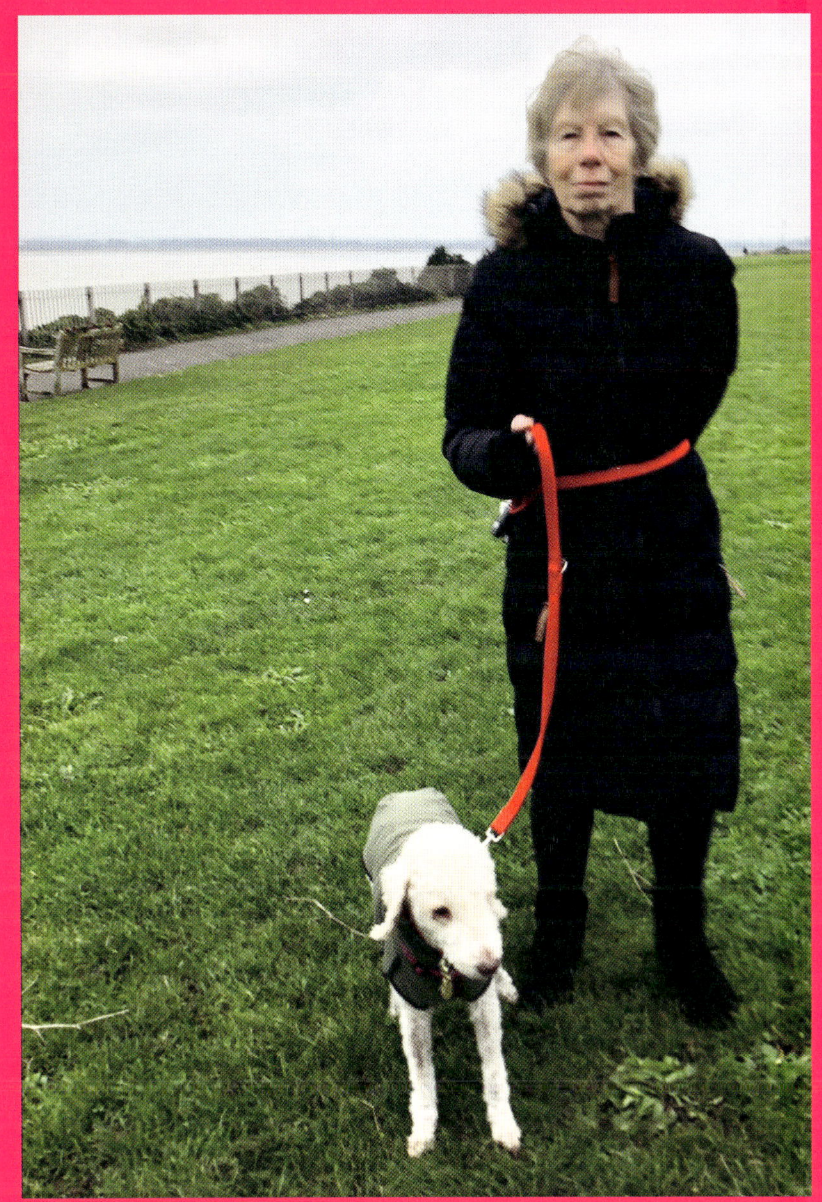

Carol walks her dog KC along the seafront in Ramsgate

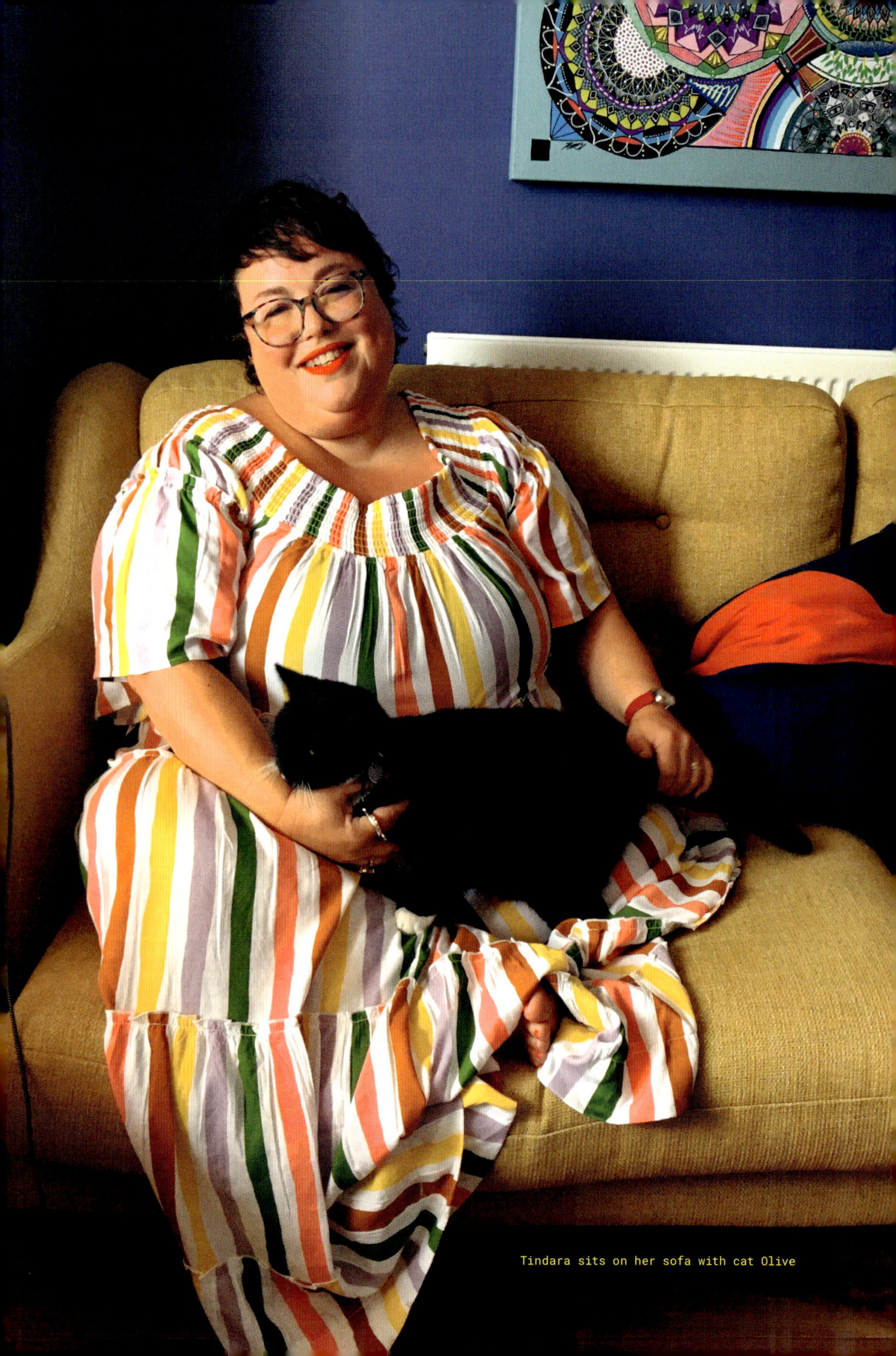

Tindara sits on her sofa with cat Olive

TINDARA

She / Her

Margate, Kent
Age 50
Artist and
art teacher

People listen to you in shops. What I say goes! In some ways you get ignored, but in other ways it's like, "Here comes trouble!" I never thought I would experience rage like that in my life (before I got on HRT, which is positive, by the way). I couldn't control the way that I was feeling. Everyone talks about the sweats. That is horrible, but this was like a real roller-coaster. And the anger about nothing. Then you realise there's something else going on here. HRT has lessened that a hell of a lot.

Me and my husband were talking about how we tried to have kids and couldn't conceive. Very shortly after that I was told I was perimenopausal. I do feel a tinge of sadness sometimes, but most of the time I feel that part of my life is over and it's "What's next?"

There are other people and children in your life that you can have amazing relationships with, and you can be maternal/paternal in other ways.

Being menopausal allows me to think about what happens next, moving on to a second or third phase. Exploring creativity, exploring how I feel about being an older woman in today's society, because it's such a tough time. But, at the same time, things are really febrile politically and with feminism. Things are changing quickly, which is a good thing, and it might feel a bit panicky, but it feels like there's something happening, something in the air... at a time when I feel like I can express myself more and don't really care what other people think, so that is positive, definitely.

People listen to you in shops. What I say goes! In some ways you get ignored, but in other ways it's like "Here comes trouble!"

I never thought I would experience rage like that in my life (before I got on HRT – which is positive by the way). I couldn't control the way I was feeling. Everyone talks about the sweats. That is horrible, but this was like a real roller coaster. And the anger about nothing. Then you realise there's something else going on here. HRT has lessened that a hell of a lot...

Me and my husband were talking about how we tried to have kids and we couldn't conceive. Very shortly after that I was told I was peri-menopausal. I do feel a tinge of sadness sometimes, but most of the time I feel like that part of my life is over and it's like, "What's next?"

There are other people and children in your life that you can have amazing relationships with and you can be maternal/paternal in other ways

Being menopausal allows me to think about what happens next, moving onto a second or third phase. Exploring creativity, exploring how I feel about being an older woman in today's society because it's such a tough time... But at the same time things are really febrile politically and with feminism. Things are changing quickly which is a good thing, and it might feel a bit panicky but it feels like there's something happening, something in the air... at a time when I feel I can express myself more and I don't really care what other people think, so that is positive definitely.

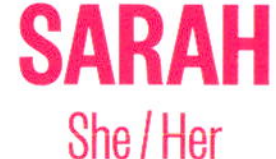

SARAH

She / Her

Cardiff, Wales
Age 57
Mother, family-centred, introverted extrovert and cat mum

I couldn't sleep and my behaviour became erratic. I was anxious, and I had a feeling of numbness and disassociation.

I felt different mentally and physically, a bit lost, and had the feeling that my motherly role was done now my two boys were young men! Of course, we are always needed, but maybe it's just historic that menopausal women should feel this way.

At the time I was watching a sci-fi series on TV where there was a parallel world called "the Upside-down" where everything was kind of the same as in the real world, but scarily unfamiliar at the same time! I remember thinking, "That's where I am. I'm in the Upside-down!"

Throughout, I've been very lucky to have had the support (and patience) of my fantastic husband, sons, sister, parents and great bunch of friends. A big positive for me has been being part of a choir, Only Menopause Aloud, which was started by my friend Bethan. Being part of this has been brilliant. Not only the singing, but spending time with a big group of women of a similar age. Having a big laugh has been invaluable, and I can't wait to get back to it.

Coming through the other side of the menopause, I'm more relaxed about who I am and what I have/or haven't achieved. When I was young, I never had big aspirations career-wise, but I always hoped I would have a family, and I feel lucky to have achieved that.

Spending time with my family and friends is my most favourite thing.

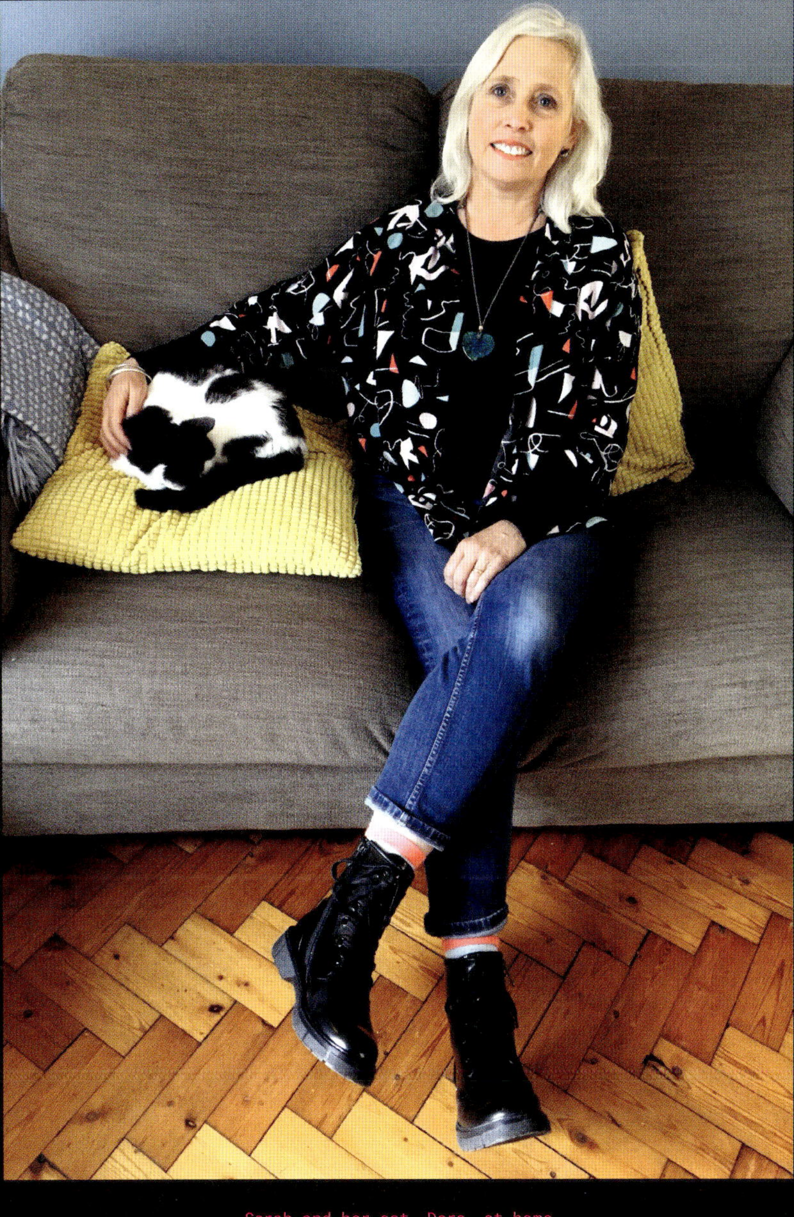

Sarah and her cat, Dora, at home

Karen on her stairs with Lucky

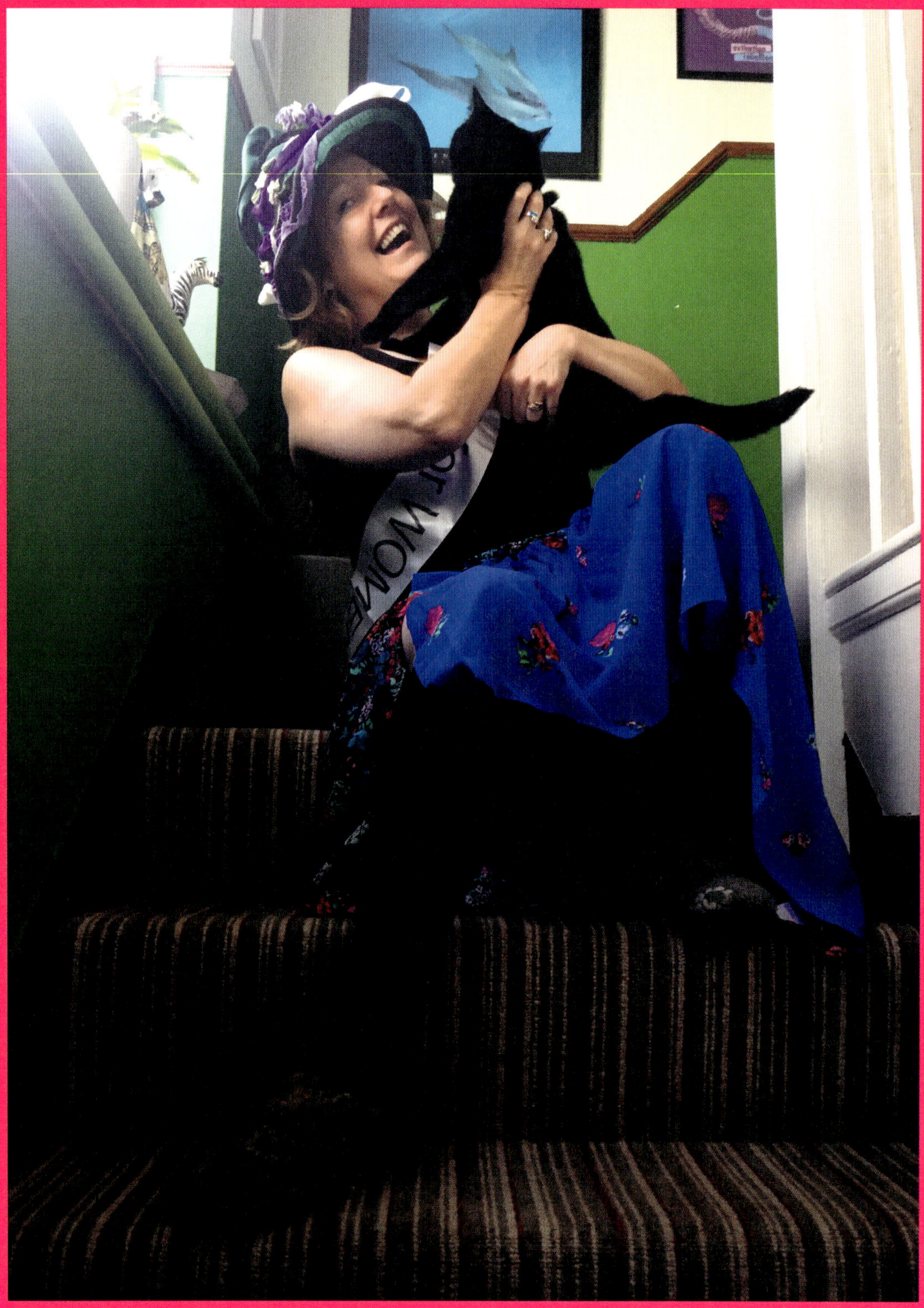

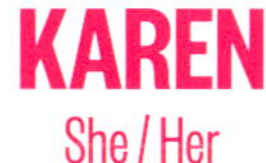

Brighton, East Sussex
Age 56
Writer, performer and
steward gallery explainer

I'm not on any particular career trajectory and have embraced the fact that I'm a failed actress. The acting gave me a great foundation for other things. I was able to write, enjoy and find time to revisit all of those wonderful artists I'd had to rush through exploring.

There's a realisation that sometimes when challenging things happen, something great comes out of it. Like the lotus flower that's on murky waters but produces this beautiful flower.

I did feel a bit invisible, and I couldn't fall back on my looks or my sexuality anymore, but I can now actually talk to anybody. That's really freeing. I really love older women, but it's important to have all different-aged people in your life. If I see a woman looking uncomfortable, I will speak up for them. It's lovely when I recognise an anxiety in someone that I've had before. I can tell them it doesn't matter.

I have to withdraw. I need to feel rested. I was always a really energetic person who could party all night and still get up the next day; now, I need to be like a cliché of an oil painting that needs to be restored in a darkened room. I like watching mind-numbing TV. I like being in the kitchen as well; it's like an artist's studio. I like finding the herbs that are in the garden. If you put sage in a tea bag, it's quite good for hot flushes, apparently. I like nettle tea and also mugwort – you can have quite lucid dreams when you've had that.

I still believe in love; it transcends everything. I've learnt to trust my spirituality now. I'm not angry about anybody else's beliefs, that's their thing. If it comes from love, there's a chance.

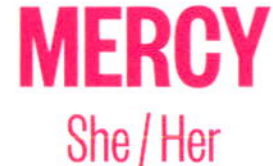

She / Her

Herne Bay, Kent
Age 55
Sells houseplants

I think I'm about three years postmenopausal now. What I thought initially was negative, and is now positive, is being invisible. While I am invisible to the rest of the world, like a lot of women in their fifties, it's quite nice because I'm not quite so paranoid about what I look like now.

[Menopause is] having my brain sucked out through my ears. My memory doesn't work; I live with brain fog. I get overwhelmed really easily. As I understand it, that's because of the drop in oestrogen, which has led to me being diagnosed with ADHD.

It was almost all mental with my menopause, which was really unexpected. I don't think the rest of the world prepares younger women for that. I had to leave a job because of the mental changes; I just couldn't understand how to do it. And this is quite often the time of life where women are at the top of their jobs. So, if you were a high-functioning executive in your mid-forties, having your brain just suddenly stop working in the way you are used to is quite a dramatic thing to happen.

A big positive is that I found cold water swimming. My friend Sarah persuaded me to go once, when I was very depressed. That really makes a difference; it lifts my brain fog. It's a massive positive, and being friends with lots of other bonkers menopausal women!

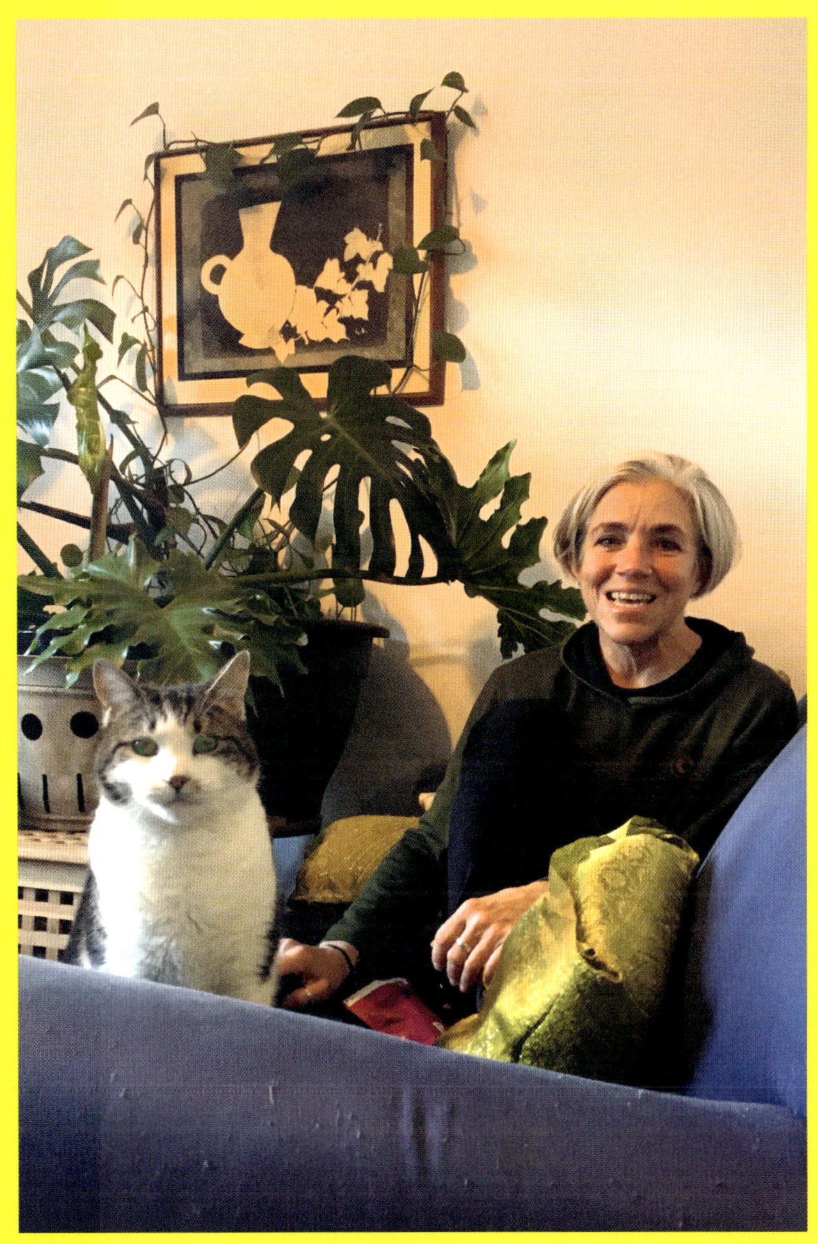

Cat Tiberius on the sofa with Mercy

PERFOR
ART
BACKST

MANCE /

AGE

Lara on stage at Screaming Alley, the Red Arrow Sports and Social Club, Ramsgate

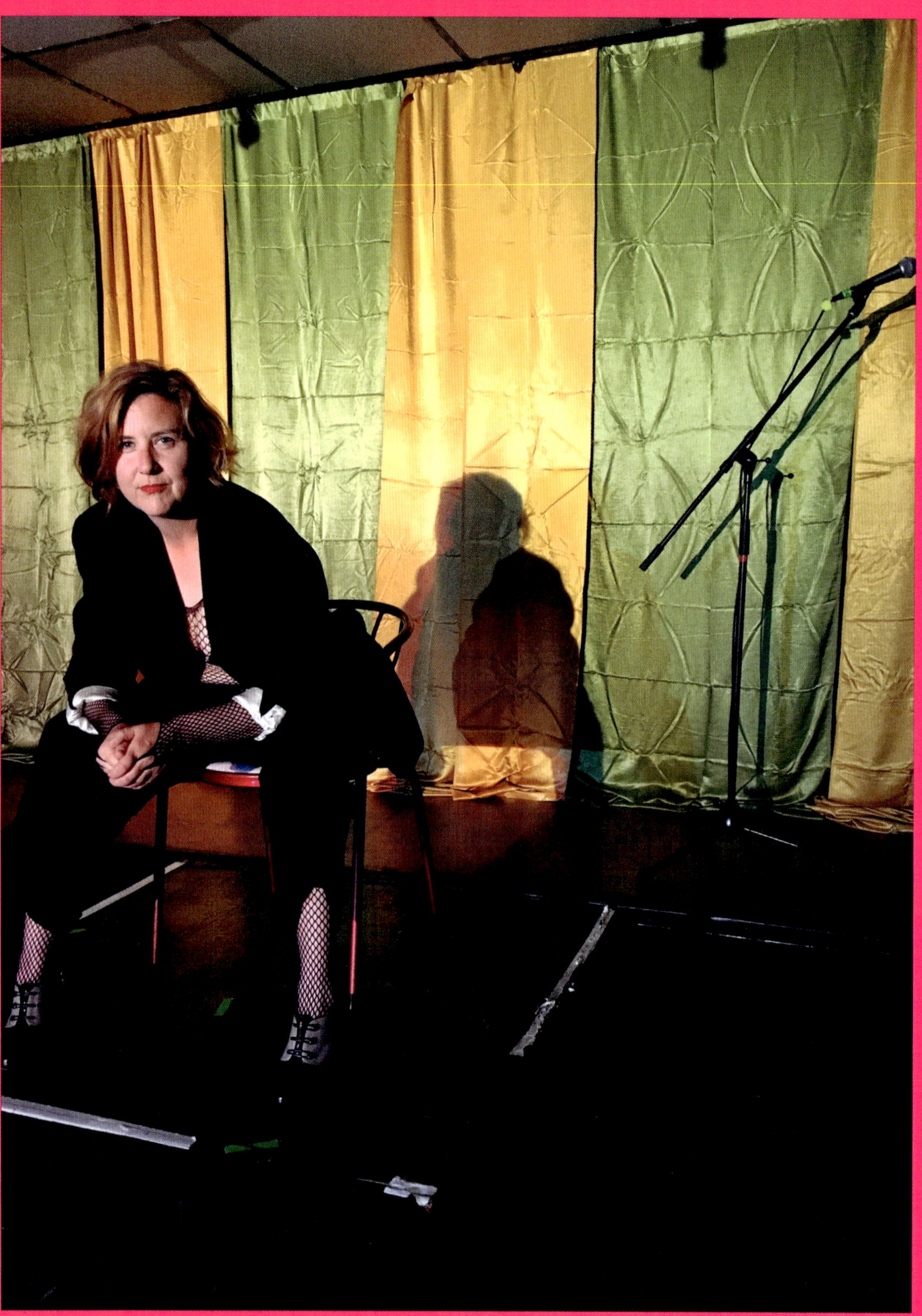

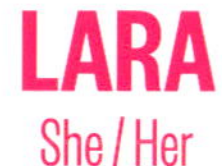

She / Her

Ramsgate, Kent
Age 50
Independently producing sex-positive/feminist/queer performance and cabaret, since 2003

I never wanted children and I now can't have them, so people don't pressure me or ask me when I'm going to, which is great. I haven't had to lie about my age on OkCupid, because people presume that if you're in your forties you're there to have a kid, so they don't want to go on a date with you.

There's this teenage energy. I had troublesome mood swings with periods; I have suppressed them through most of my life with the pill and coils. I think with the menopause those hormones that I suppressed for years are back. [There's] a kind of vibrancy, being very emotional, very present, more linked to my physical self, which feeds into creativity.

I still have a coil in, giving me some progesterone. I was advised by a mate to keep it in. My friend said to me that after the menopause you become this better version of yourself that isn't governed by hormones – just straightforwardly you. I'm feeling that coming on, in between feeling more hormonal than ever before. I'm feeling a new kind of calmness and confidence.

The menopause has affected my dyspraxia and made it worse. I've looked for connections between neurodiversity and the menopause and have found nothing online, but I feel that my condition became pretty severe during this time.

There's been a reinventing [of] one's self that I've enjoyed. I've got a new boyfriend just as I was coming into menopause, so I've been enjoying feeling sexy. Enjoying the sensual things has been part of this transition, I think.

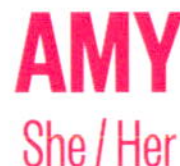

AMY

She / Her

Brighton, East Sussex
Age 47
Psychiatric nurse
and mum

It really feels like you're definitely entering a different phase of womanhood and life. That is really quite difficult at times. I mean, I'm 47, I wouldn't want to have a baby anymore, but it's the fact I wouldn't be able to.

My opinions of my friends going through perimenopause haven't changed, but I guess there are so many negative connotations about the menopause that you can't help but take them on board. I'm really trying to challenge them outwardly and in my own head.

Positives are finding out more about the menopause, experiencing it and being able to talk to younger women about it. I didn't have anyone to talk to, because my mum didn't talk about anything she really didn't like. She's not around anymore, either, so even if I wanted to talk to her about the menopause, I wouldn't be able to. I have a really open relationship with my daughter. I hope that as she goes through her life as a woman it'll be a different experience for her.

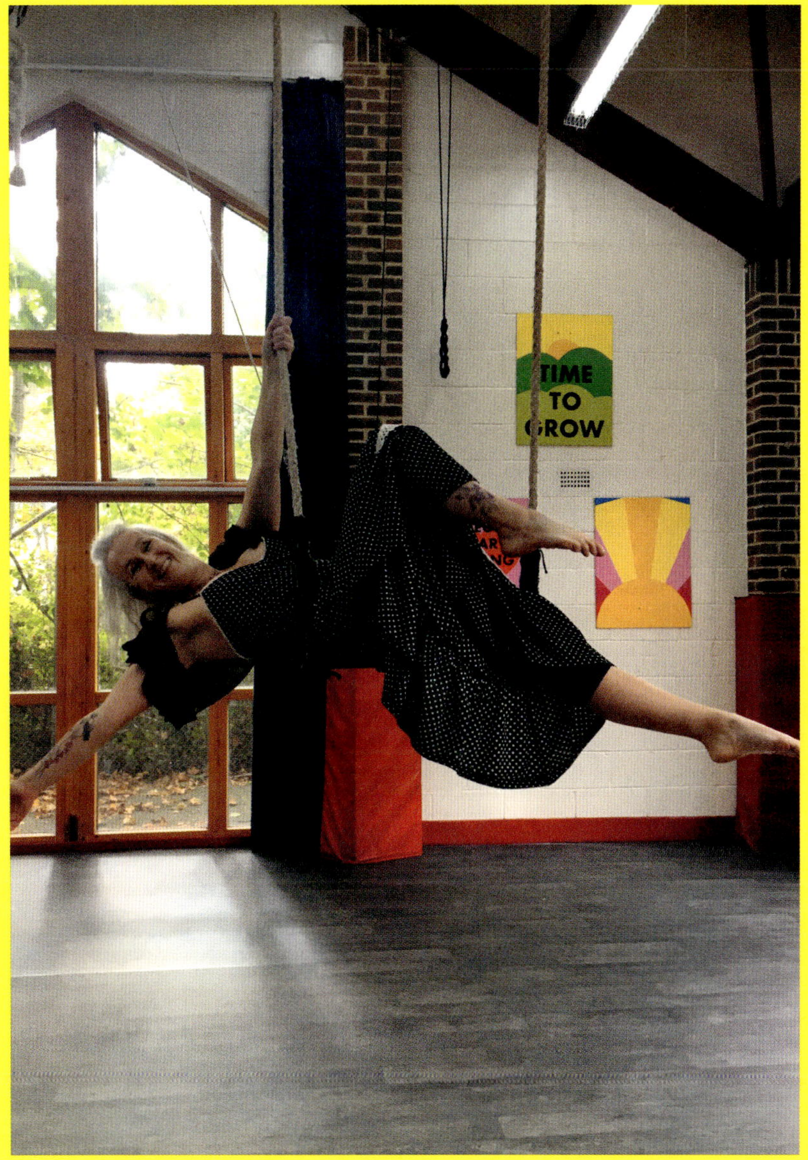

Amy on the trapeze at The Circus Project in Brighton

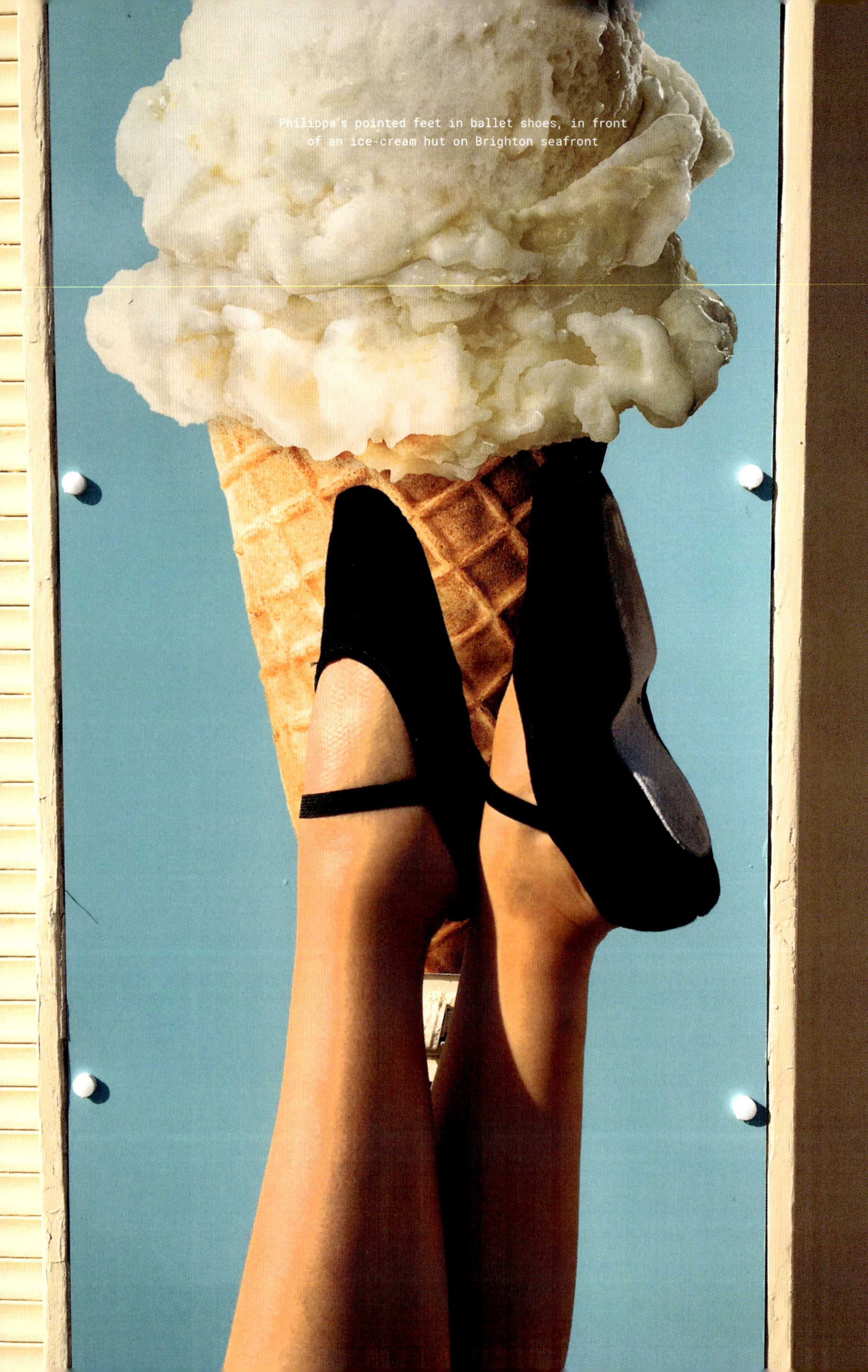

Philippa's pointed feet in ballet shoes, in front of an ice-cream hut on Brighton seafront

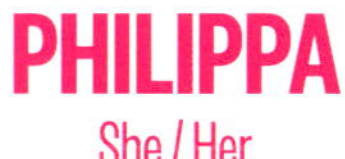

PHILIPPA

She / Her

Brighton, East Sussex
Age 56
Psychotherapist, yoga teacher,
mother and partner

I didn't really notice it hugely. My periods stopped seven years ago. I don't think I was particularly grumpy or difficult, but my husband might disagree!

Coincidentally, I started retraining as a psychotherapist, so there was another sort of transition and a change of life in a different way. It really changed how I perceived myself and how I was perceived by other people. There was a lot of introspection through the course. I had six years of therapy around this time that supported me through a whole load of things, and probably it was at perimenopause that I really did have a crisis in my marriage (which did survive) and life.

I remember a massive physical hormonal surge and sexual surge as well, like a last hurrah of masses of sexual energy, and that being very confusing and throwing up questions around my marriage. You shift into a completely different gear with the menopause and issues around sex, because you've got to be lubricated. If you do have those dialogues it's amazing, but if you find it difficult to discuss it, it must be really hard to say that intimacy doesn't work in the same way. That was difficult, but then it was negotiated and is good now.

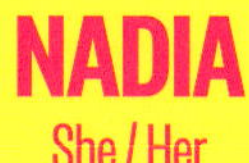

NADIA

She / Her

Dalston, London
Age 59
Special needs primary school
teacher, musician and painter

Hot sweats, being dripping wet and getting really hot; it saved me on heating in the winter – I just wrapped a blanket around myself when it got cold. My periods stopped and I thought, "I don't have to buy sanitary products anymore," and then my daughter's periods started. Freedom from periods – the bane of my life! At the same time I was going through this time, my daughter was leaving home, so I had to rediscover myself after devoting myself to my children for years. Like food, for example, I'd forgotten what I liked.

Sometimes my daughter would look at me and what I was wearing and I learnt to say, "No, I want to wear this." I learnt about self-love in this period, and through loving myself I could really appreciate others. I watched a German video and it explained that there's a male menopause called "andropause", which I'm interested in. I've been interested in what affect hormones have on you for years. Mine had more affect on me in my fertile years – they were really strong. The fact that you can't control them, and I allowed them to control my behaviour.

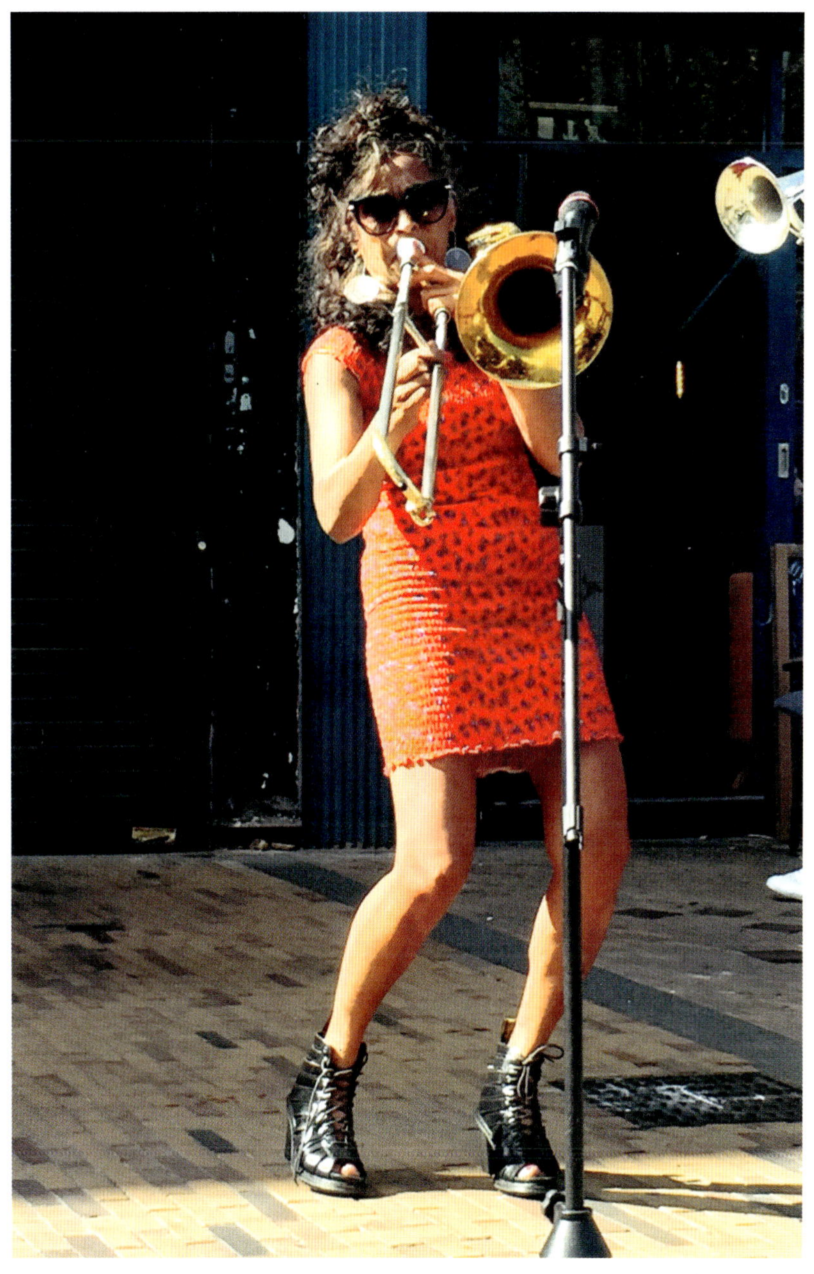

Nadia plays the trombone with The Stamford Hill Billies at Hackney Carnival

hot sweats, being dripping wet and getting really hot, it saved me money on heating in the winter – i just wrapped a blanket around myself when i felt cold.
my period stopped and i thought 'i don't have to buy sanitary products anymore'... then my daughter's period started. freedom from periods – the bane of my life!
the same time i was going through this my daughter was leaving home, so i had to rediscover myself after devoting myself to my children for years, like food for example. i'd forgotton what i liked.

sometimes my daughter would look at me and what i chose to wear and i learnt to say 'no, i want to wear this.' i learned about self-love in this period, and through learning to love myself i could really appreciate others.

i watched a german video and it explained that there's a male menopause 'andropause' which is interesting. i've been interested in the effects hormones have on us for years i feel i was very affected by hormones in my fertile years- - really strong effects, i felt i could not control my behaviour due to hormones.

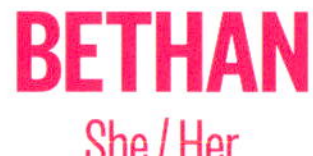

BETHAN

She / Her

Cardiff, Wales
Age 62
Musician, mother
and grandmother

Now, when I look at young women I think, "Oh God, they might be having a period, how dreadful." At one point, I was a teacher in London and I can remember the awful business of trying to get time to go to the loo in between lessons, and the horrible flooding that I'd sometimes get. It must happen to so many people, and it's this huge thing to deal with.

For me, the negative side is that I got osteoporosis, and that's had a huge influence on my life. At the moment, I'm wearing a sling because I've got two fractures in my upper arm, and that's been quite difficult; obviously I can't play the violin, so that has a massive impact.

When I was first diagnosed, at about 54, I did my left wrist – I broke it three times. At that time, I was working full time as violinist and I had to stop completely. That was hugely concerning for my friends and my sister; and some close friends said, "We're going to come round and sing," and I said, "I ain't singing, I'm not going to sing," but they said, "Come on, it'll make you think about music and we can sing in your front room."

There were so many people who wanted to come that we started to hire the Mackintosh centre, and 56 people joined. There are physical benefits to singing: when you sing with other people, you breathe at the same time and your heart rate becomes the same – in the same way that women menstruate together when they live together. I think women are good at blending and collaborating.

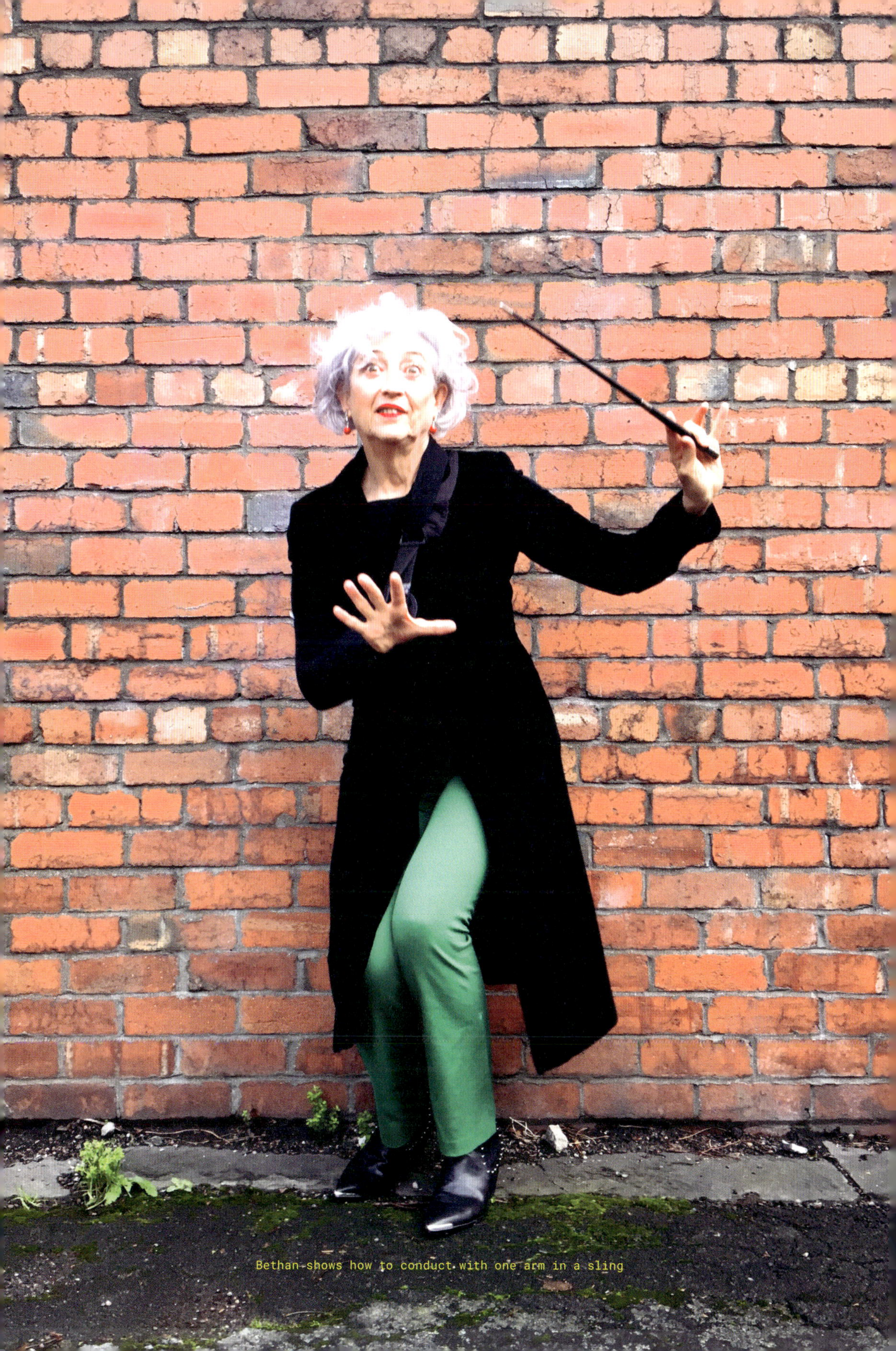

Bethan shows how to conduct with one arm in a sling

Karen DJing on the main stage at the Beat-Herder Festival in Lancashire

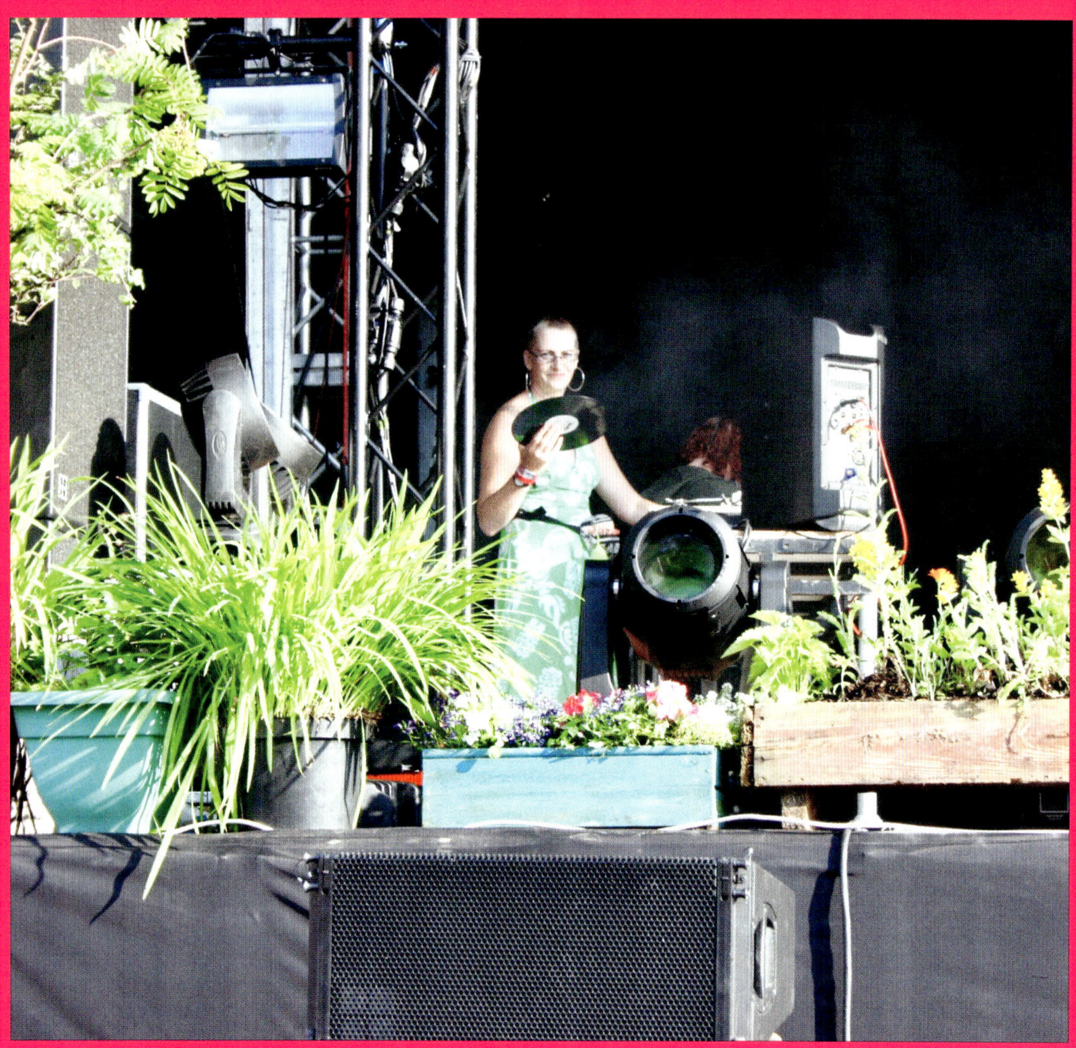

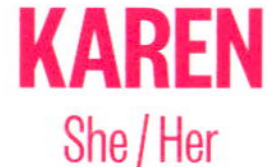

KAREN

She / Her

Newcastle upon Tyne
Age 50
Social worker, DJ

You're halfway through your life, so a bit more self-aware and wise. I had the horrific night sweats and not sleeping, and then it calmed down and disappeared. I couldn't talk about it, I felt silenced. I haven't got kids, but I see my nephews as the next best thing. I know me mama had a really bad time – she suffered night sweats and had to shower through the night. The only reason I knew about it was because of that, because it's not talked about in society; it's just brushed under the carpet.

I'm in this team at work and everybody in the team is menopausal. We've got the fans on and we laugh about it, but it's an age thing. We call it "Club 50, 60", and we can at least talk about it with each other.

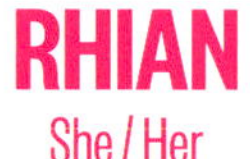

She / Her

Cardiff, Wales
Age 49
Circus tutor, teaching assistant and mum

I'm more confident now, and in my forties I now know what I want, and what I like, and I'm definitely more conscious of walking away from things that I don't want or need.

[I'm] feeling past the peak of many things: my fitness, the physicality of my body. My hair went grey at an early age, and although I dyed it for a while I really enjoy the freedom of not dying it anymore. I still want to feel attractive, and I still want people to find me attractive because I find this exciting, but there's no longer a need to try to be attractive, or to try to keep up with peers. Some mornings there are bags under my eyes and some wrinkles. There is beauty in an older person, and with acceptance there is a relief, and I embrace this. We are still attractive but in a different way.

When I was 42, I had my son and I decided to get the placenta encapsulated. I have a tincture, and I keep the capsules in my freezer, the idea being that they can be used instead of HRT. I'm not really sure of the exact truth of this; I think it's something to research further, but I have them if I need them. I'm not sure how much evidence there is, but we'll see. I'll definitely give it a go.

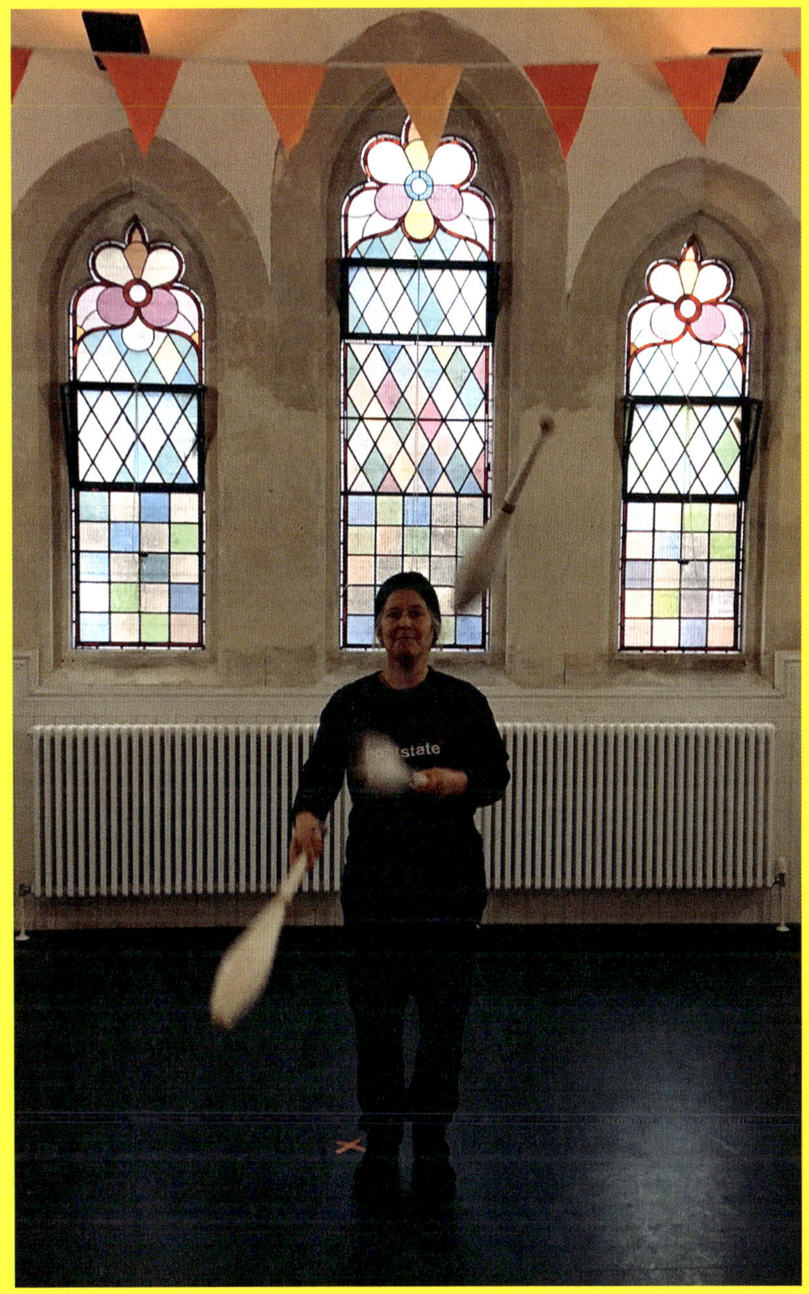

Rhian juggling with the NoFit State circus company in Cardiff

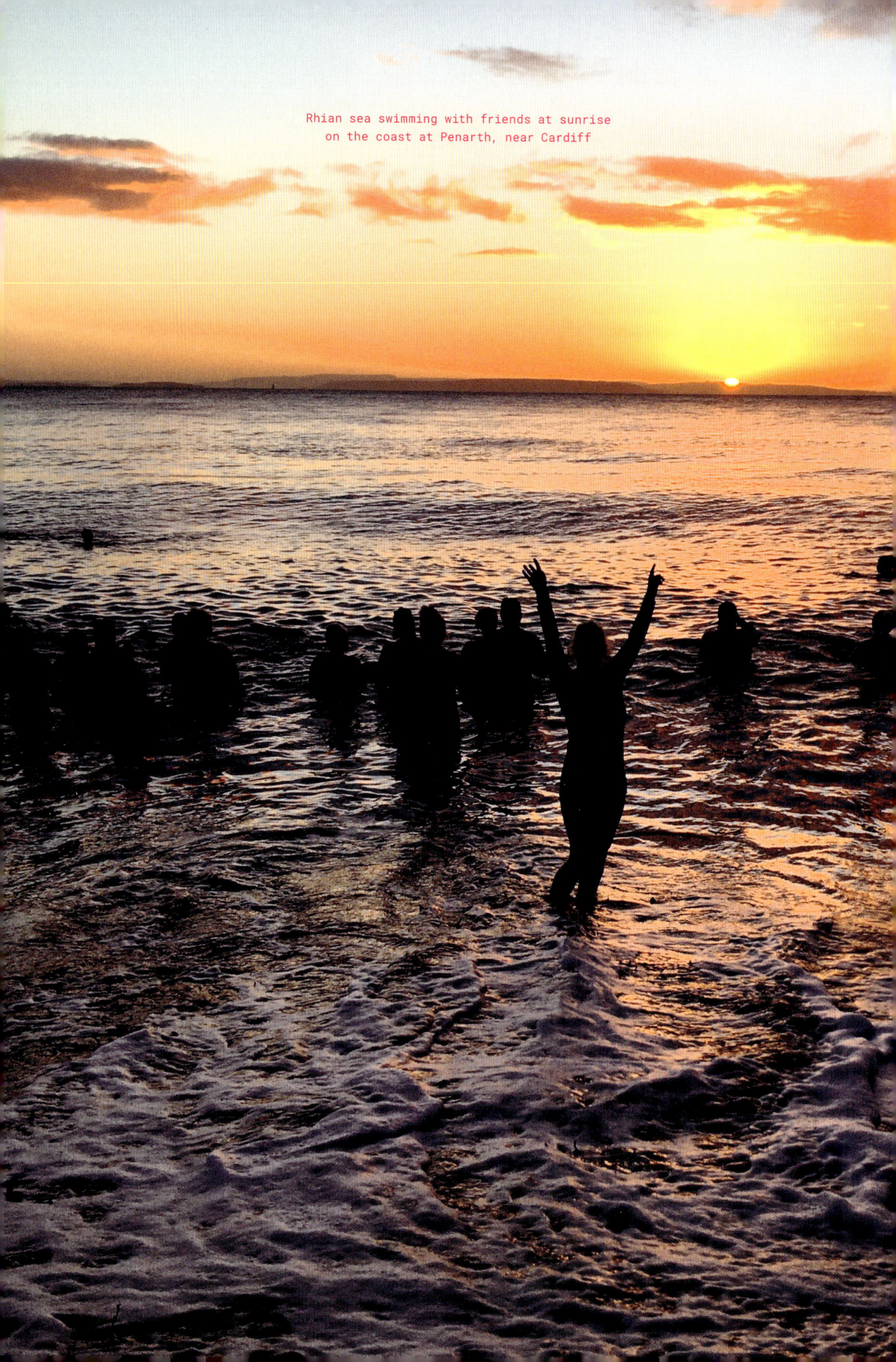

Rhian sea swimming with friends at sunrise
on the coast at Penarth, near Cardiff

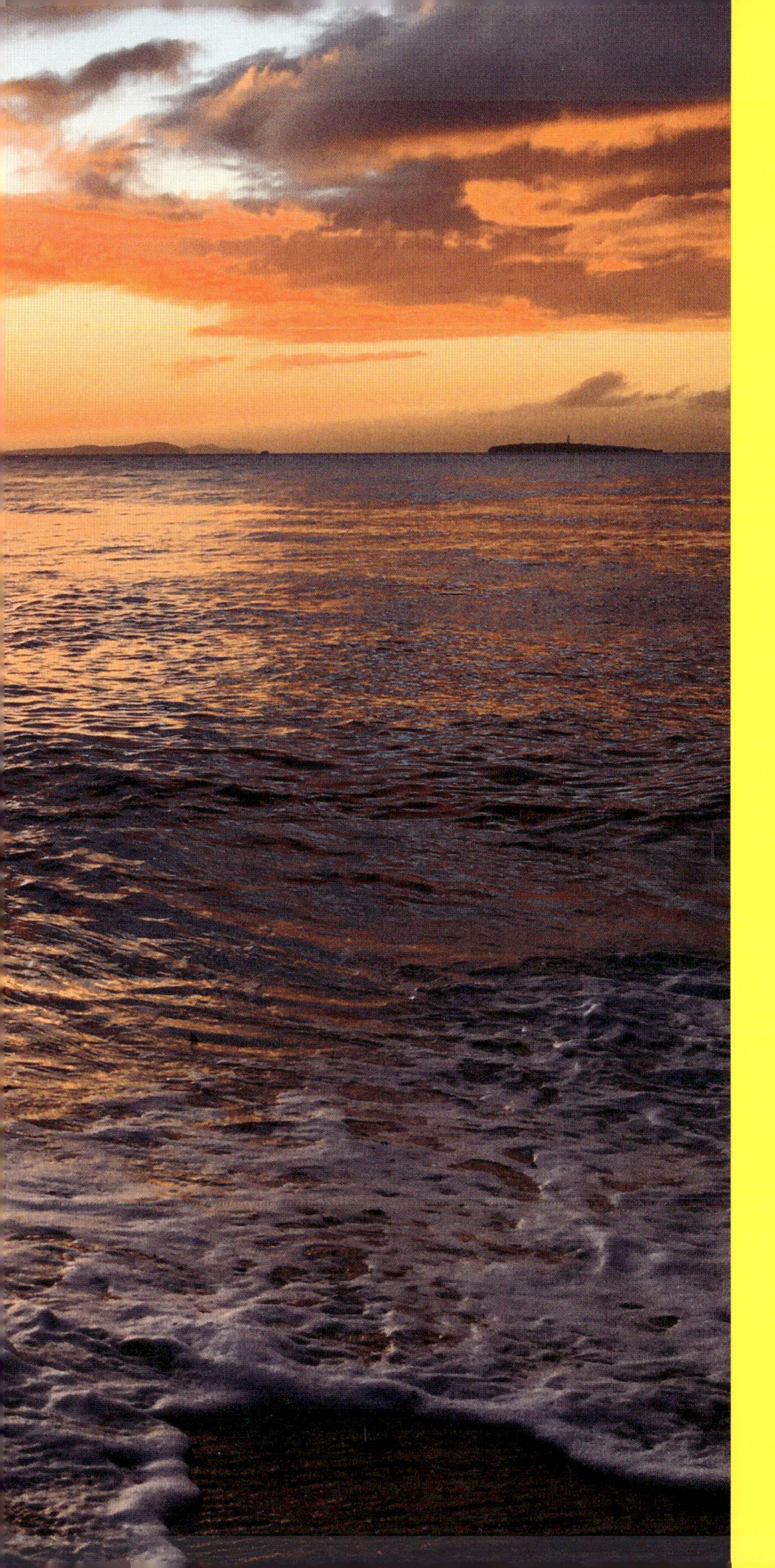

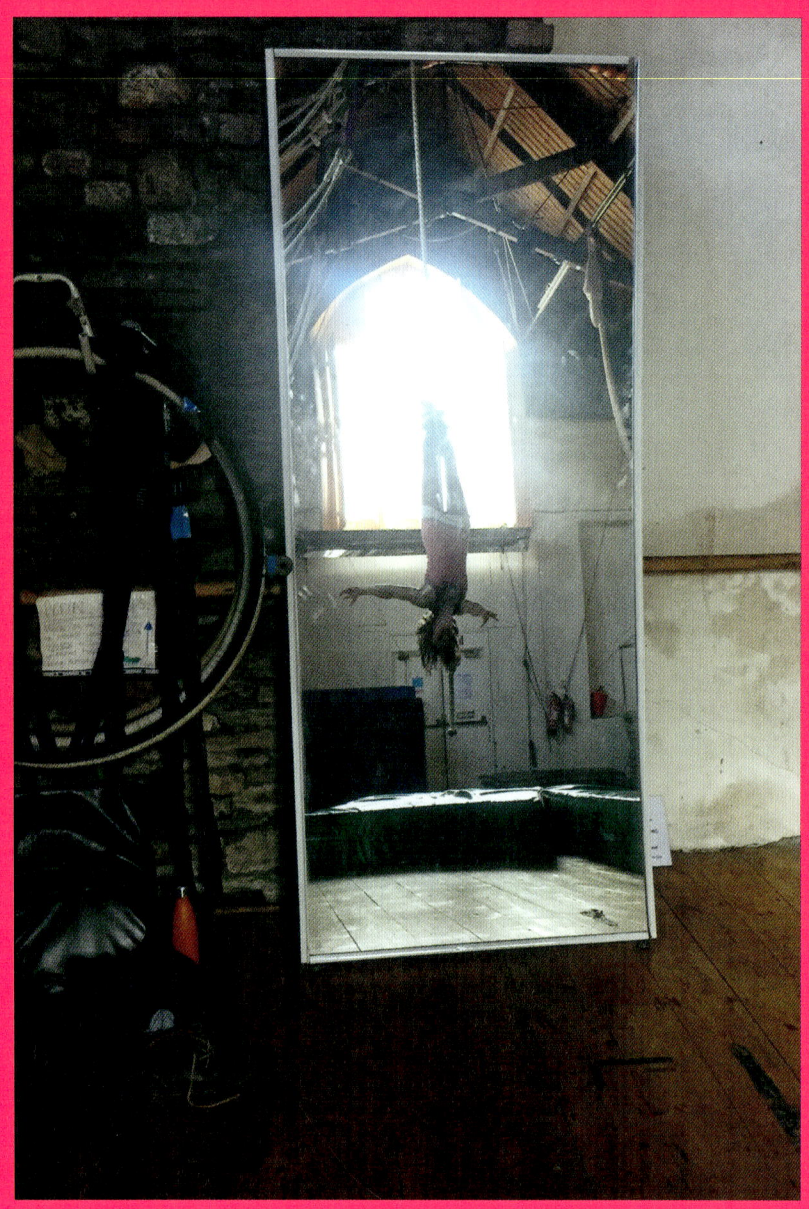

Terry practises aerial at the Albany Centre, Bristol

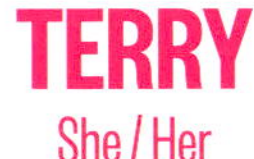

She / Her

Montpelier, Bristol
Age 59
Artist and office worker

It very clearly defines the end of child-bearing, in a way that's abstract because I didn't want children anyway; it's just that I have to think about where I am in my life. I haven't been through those obvious milestones that define a lot of people, like getting married and having kids. I got married later.

The menopause coincides with me being almost 60. I don't feel old, physically or mentally. I'm very lucky to still be active at my age. I took up aerial at 47 (an age when most people would be thinking about giving up!). Not having to use contraceptives anymore is a great thing. I haven't had mood swings, I've only had hot flushes. I take Chinese herbs and have acupuncture regularly – the herbs help with the hot flushes. It's the right combination.

I HAVE
MOOD
I'VE ON
HOT

'T HAD
SWINGS,
Y HAD
LUSHES

BEATRICE

She / Her

Lives on the river
Age 45
Seamstress, rigger, massage therapist, single mum, boat dweller and aerial artiste

I went cloud swinging last week and I just smashed it out. It felt the best it's ever felt. I'm doing cloud swinging for my mental health as I enter perimenopause and a sense of my life caving in on me and becoming overwhelmed with it all layering up. Unmanageable situations, eg family traumas, relationship breakdowns, multiple jobs, toxic people and raising a child all on my own.

[I'm] retraining as a massage therapist to get out of my life [and] feeling stuck. It's a challenge that's taking me in a new, positive direction.

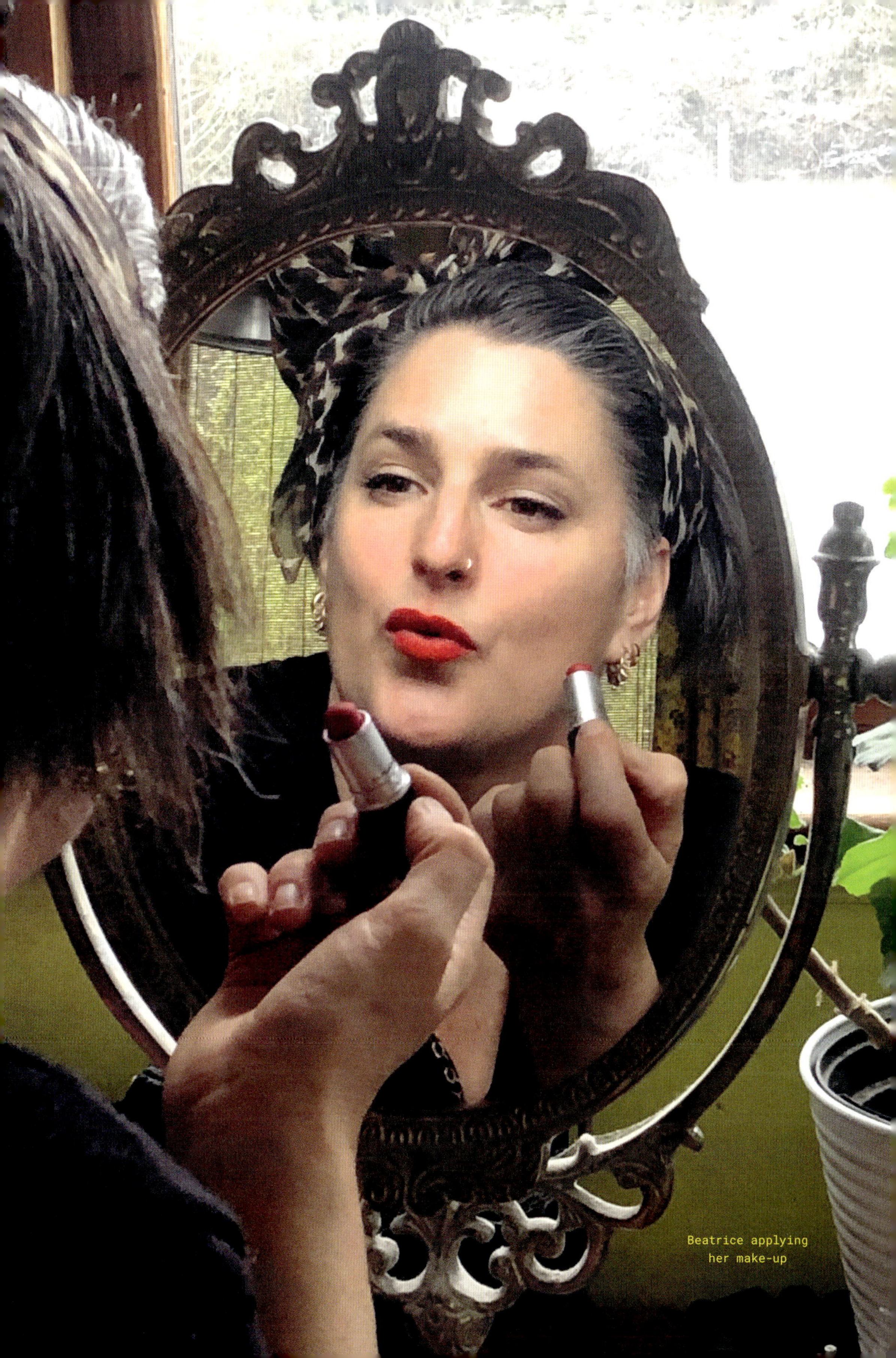

Beatrice applying
her make-up

Beatrice on the trapeze in her houseboat kitchen

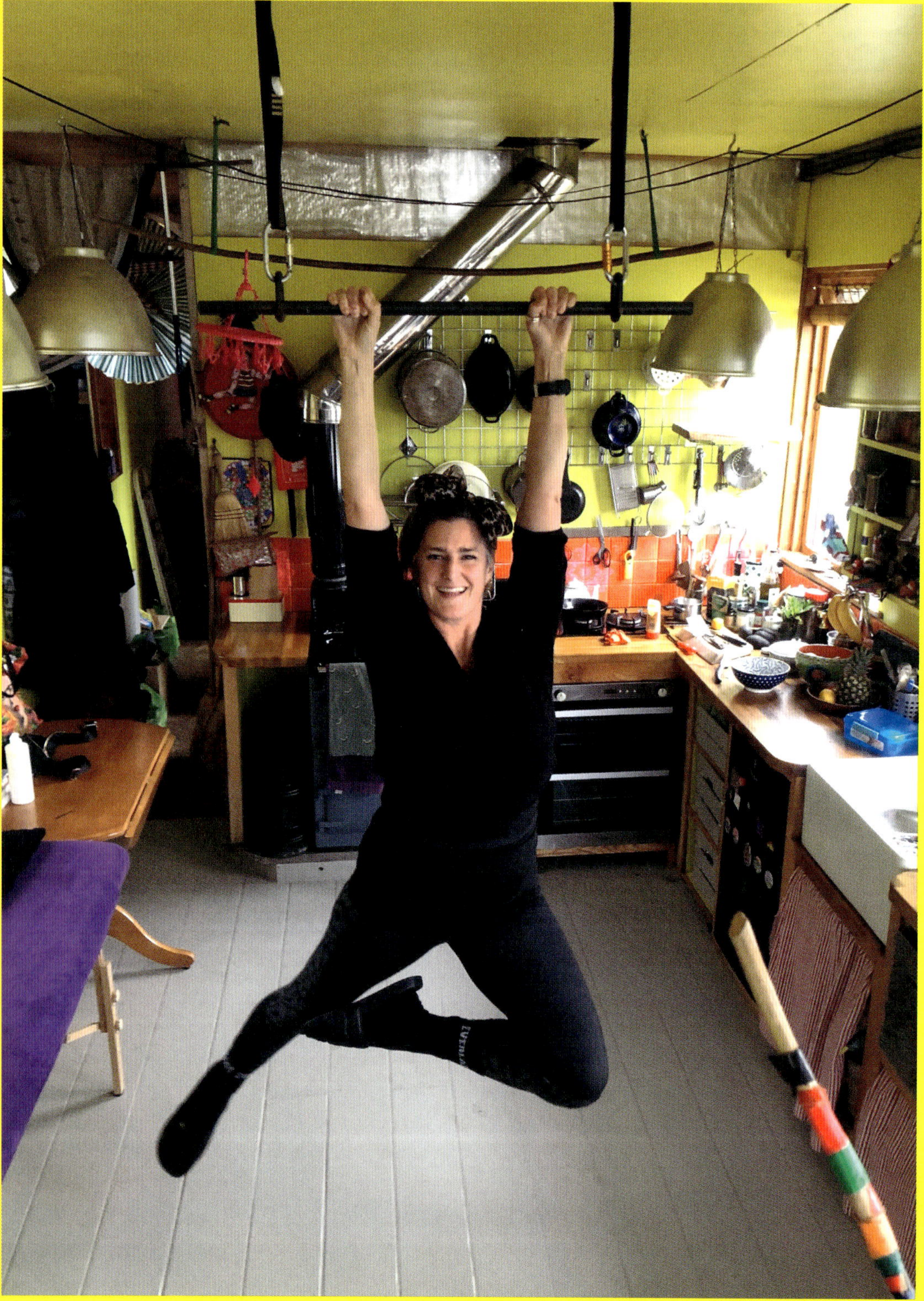

I went cloudswinging last week and I just smashed it out. It felt the best its ever felt.
I'm doing cloudswinging for my mental health, as I enter peri-menopause and a sence of my life caving in on me and becoming overwhelmed with it all layering up. Unmanagable situations eg family traumas, relationship breakdowns, multiple jobs, toxic people and raising a child all on my own.

Re-training as a massage therapist to get out of my life feeling stuck. Its a challange that's taking me in a new positive direction.

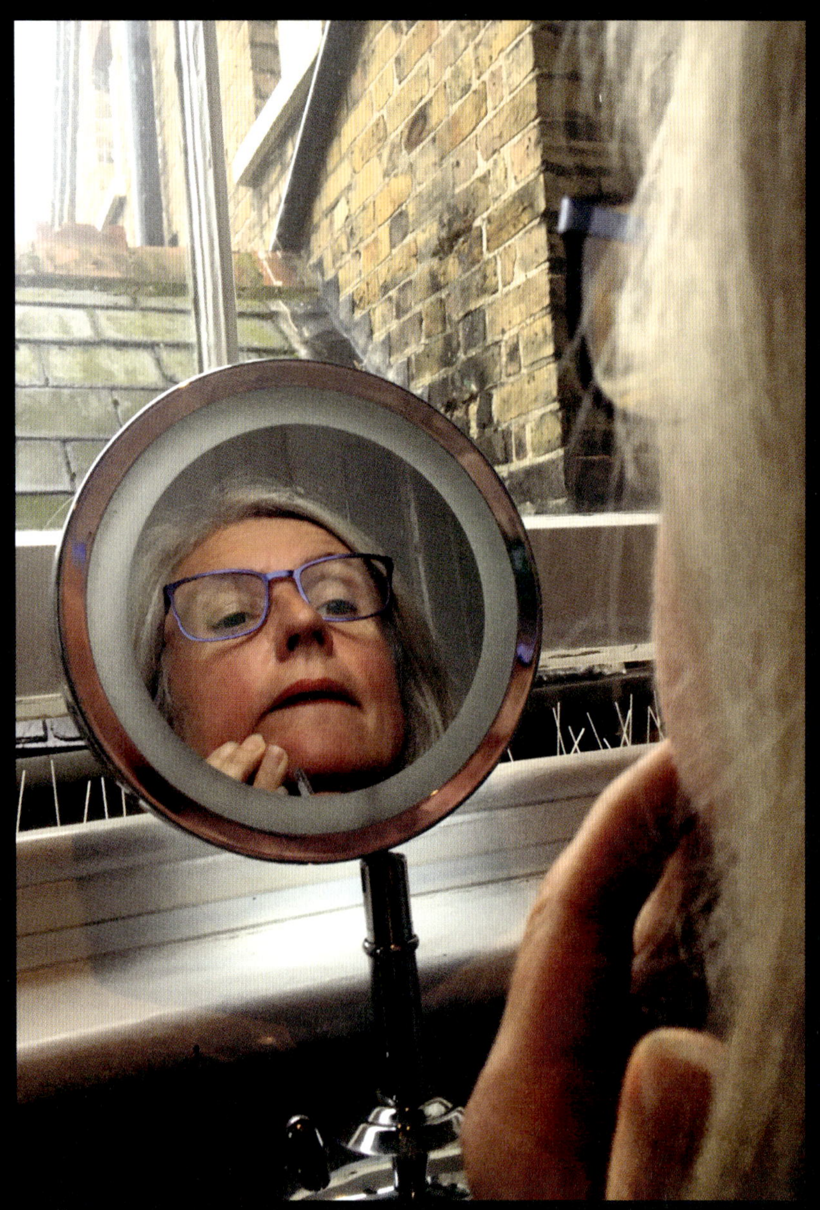

Anette tweezing hair from her chin in her bathroom

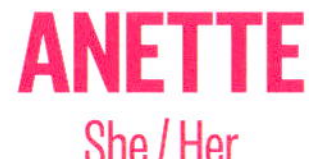

She / Her

Ramsgate, Kent
Age 53
Speech and language practitioner

I live with all men. It's quite nice to talk about the menopause to someone who wants to listen without feeling like I'm overegging it. I've got lots of friends going through it and we're like, "Could this be it and could that be it?"

I can remember the moment when I realised I had to let something go. I was 48 and in a yoga class; we were doing a breathing exercise and I just started crying and thought I had to let youth go. I'd just been doing a play in London and had to accept that wasn't happening anymore, I'm living here now.

Things happen at the same time. If you've got kids, they're grotty teenagers and your parents might be getting old. My mum went on HRT; she got dementia and I'm not sure if there's a connection there. My friend who got breast cancer was told not to go on it. So you wonder, don't you?

I met some friends last Friday and had a few glasses of wine. On Saturday, I was absolutely wiped out. I thought, "Well, I obviously can't drink anymore," and then Sunday my period started. You think, "Have I become this grumpy person?" or "Will it change?" You've got to hold on to the fact that it will change, hopefully, but then nobody talks about how much does come back after you've been through it. Do you still have short-term memory loss, or does your memory come back? Women need to talk about it more.

SYMONE

She / Her

Ramsgate, Kent
Age 56
A very proud, visibly changed gender woman. Out and proud. Illustrator and volunteer at Newington Youth Club

I spent a very unhappy part of my life not being able to be myself because of society's attitudes and conventions. My father should have been born in the 19th century because he had Victorian points of view.

I was sent to boarding school in Thanet up until I was 16. While I was a pupil at Laleham School, I was abused by one of the teachers. I think part of my trauma, and why I can't get any closure on this, is because he took his own life. What makes me angry is that I know for a fact that there would have been other victims who haven't come forward and will never get any justice.

Moving forward as a woman, and being myself without fear, now nobody can tell me that I'm not good enough.

Taking feminising hormones means that I suffer symptoms of the menopause, including hot flushes, aches and pains, insomnia, poor memory, a foggy brain, total mind blanks and headaches. Understanding how our brains function and how we behave makes us realise when talking to others that we're not the only one suffering from this.

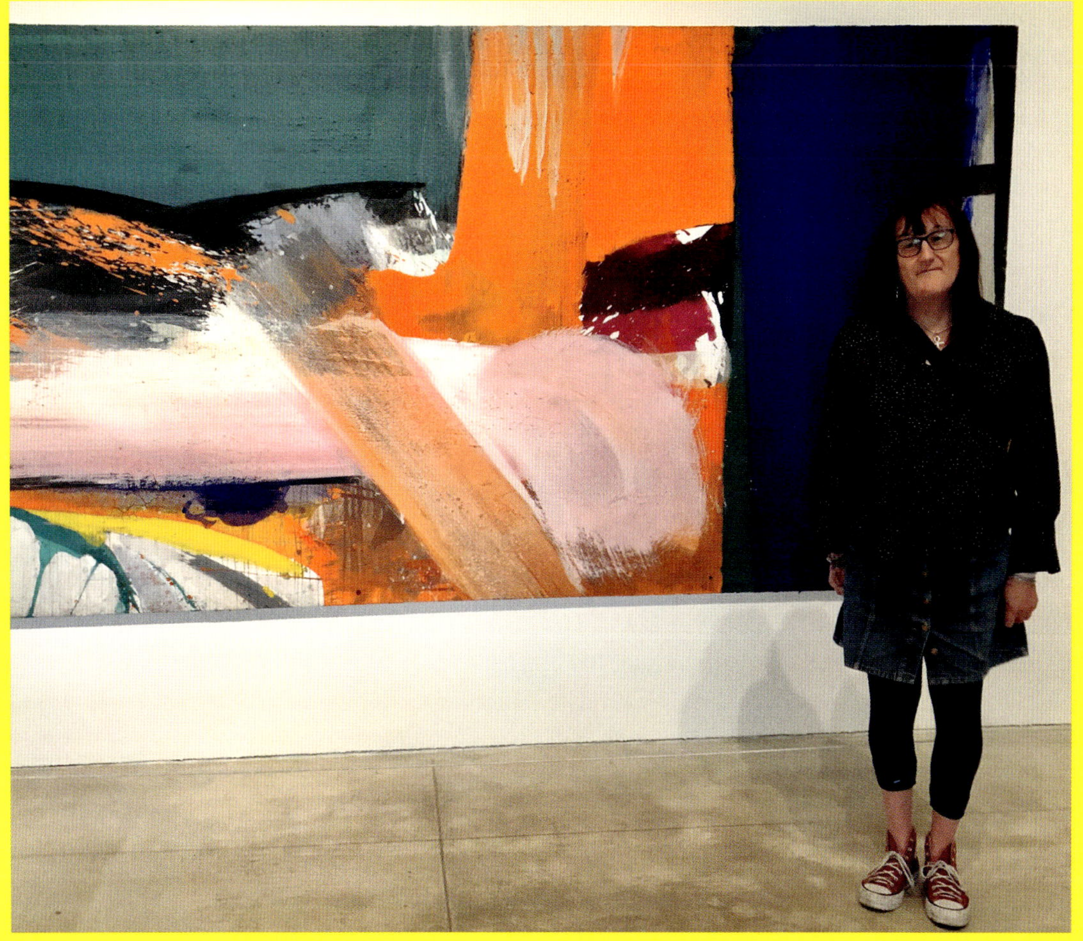

Symone next to a painting in the Ed Clark exhibition at Turner Contemporary, Margate

SPORTS

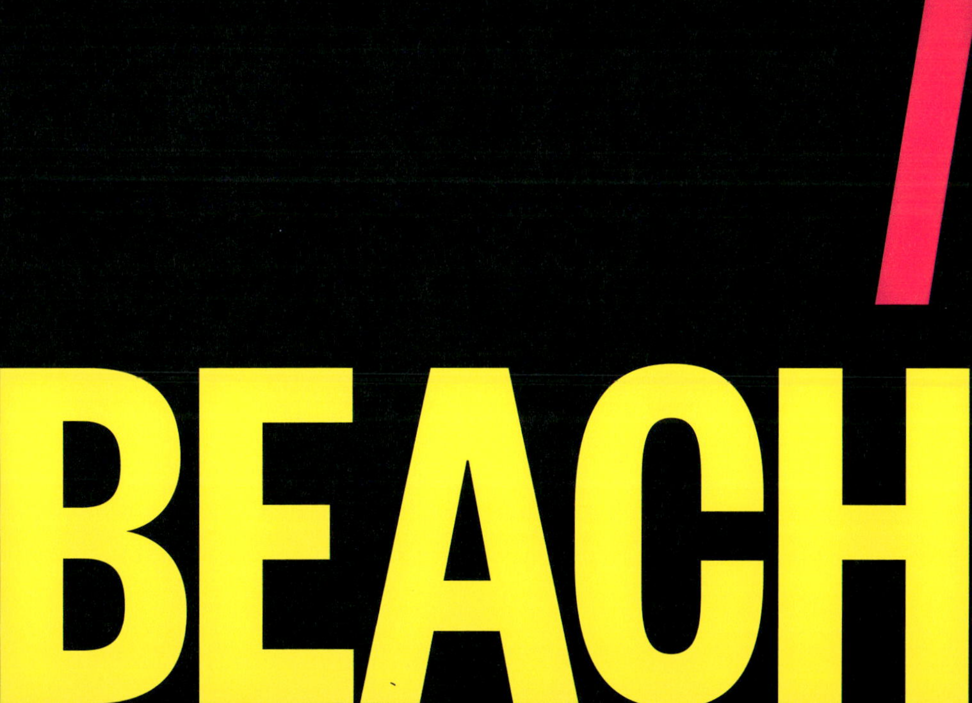
BEACH

Fay weight training at Foundry in east London

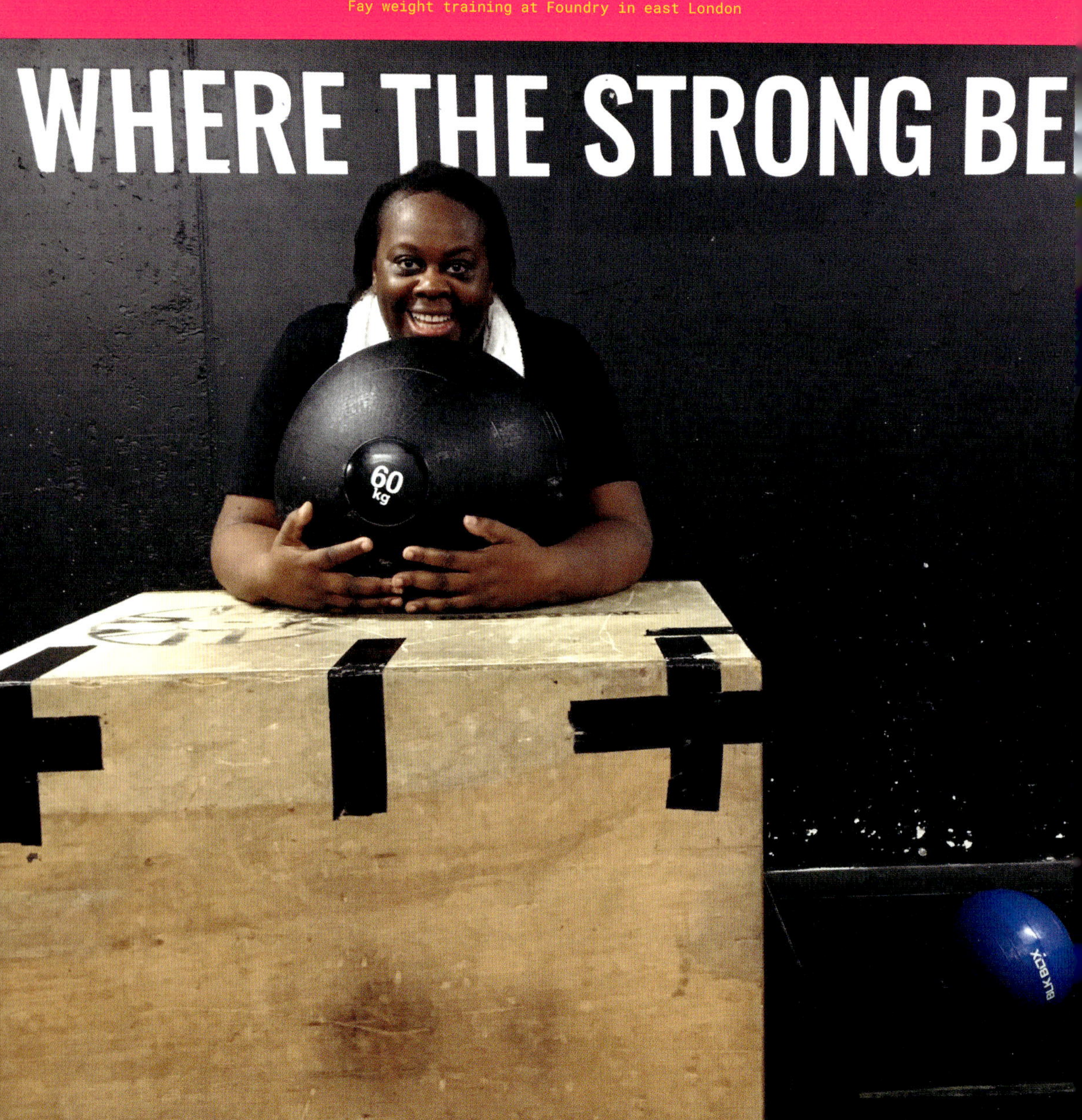

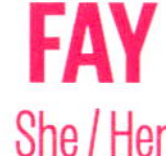

FAY

She / Her

Haggerston, London
Age 54
Personal assistant and menopause warrior at 9to5menopause

Certain life events cause stresses and triggers. My menopause coincided with my mum being diagnosed with terminal cancer and my job ramping up. That's when it fell off a cliff! I wasn't sleeping, I had night sweats and my anxiety was off the scale. I went to my doctor to get some help, as I was not coping very well. I basically hit rock bottom. My doctor prescribed HRT.

Exercise gets the blood pumping in the body and builds up bone density. So I started weight training; it was hard as I needed to really push myself, but I love it. I've massively stepped out of my comfort zone, but it's given me my confidence back and a zest for life.

I launched my 9to5menopause Instagram account two years after I started the menopause. When I first started, I did a lot of research and I couldn't find any women who looked like me – as in, black and had a job. The women I did find were all financially supported by their husbands and were suggesting things that were not financially or conveniently viable for me (private clinics, yoga in the day, a nutritionist).

People in work found me and started following the account. And I left my job, which was the best thing I've ever done, as it gave me some breathing space just to be me and to see what I wanted to do next.

My forties were a write-off; maybe this is why I've embraced my fifties so much. It's given me my confidence back to go, "That's what I like, and that's what I don't like. That's what I'm going to put up with, and that's what I'm not." I get quite emotional talking about it, as I've come a long way.

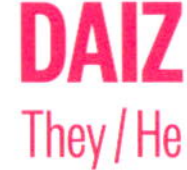

DAIZ

They / He

Margate
Age 25
Gender fluid skater, artist,
events manager, museum nerd
and Trans Club Margate founder

I started transitioning when I was 14; I always knew I was a bit different. People always asked if I was a boy or a girl, but I didn't know the language around gender at the time. I found out the term gender fluid at 14, and it felt like it fit, so I came out by baking a cake for my parents with "I'm gender fluid" on it in icing. After I'd left it in the kitchen, I went upstairs for a bit and waited for my parents to come home to see it. It was well received.

Around the ages of 16 or 17, I found the words "non-binary" and "agender", which means having no gender. At 18, I asked the GP to refer me to the NHS gender clinic, but the wait to be seen (it's usually around five years or more) was from 18 to 22. By the time I was seen I was 22 or 23 and I'd already funded my top surgery privately, as I couldn't wait any longer. I did a Crowdfunder, made a calendar with my friends which I sold and organised, and put on a big skate event to help fund my £9,000 surgery. I also did a lot of saving from the jobs I had, like backstage at the National and the Dominion theatres in London, where I worked as a dresser.

The surgery went quite smoothly. I had a few consultations beforehand, and then I got a call letting me know my date for top surgery. I was pleased when I got it, but it was strange having someone mark and touch my chest in a surgical manner. When they put the anaesthetic in, I was holding my toy dog, and then when I woke up, it was done. You have to wear a vest with foam to help the swelling and I had drains for a week as well. After the week-one check-up, I got to see my chest for the first time. Even with all the scans and discolouration, I was over the moon. I'm very healed now, but I still get a weird sensation around my nipples – numbness where they reconnected them and the nerves haven't reattached.

I'm part of a trans community online and in Margate, where I started Trans Club with another transmasc friend. We try to do it every month; we talk about doctors, medicine and hormones. But we also talk about things that have brought us joy, things that bring us together as a community.

I went to six sessions with a speech therapist. They gave me some vocal exercises. I started taking testosterone about a year ago. I didn't think I wanted it, I just thought I wanted chest surgery, but afterwards it felt like it wasn't enough, so then I decided to take testosterone as well. The first one I took was Testogel. I rubbed two pumps a day into my thighs. Within the first week, I definitely felt a change. It sends you into an accelerated puberty. Within the first month, I was having hot flushes and appetite changes. It made me more hungry and want to go out and exercise a lot. The smell of my sweat changed as well and I sweat a lot more. My legs and arms have got hairier (everything has got hairier).

I wasn't taught about menopause at school, and I went to an all-girls' school, so it feels like a topic we should have touched on, what with most of us experiencing it at some point. I didn't learn about it until my mum started going through it a few years later. We've had quite a few conversations about it, the similarities between our transitions; there are definitely a lot of parallels, especially with taking HRT and the hormone changes we go through. She said she felt like she was losing her identity when she went through it, whereas I feel like I'm finding mine.

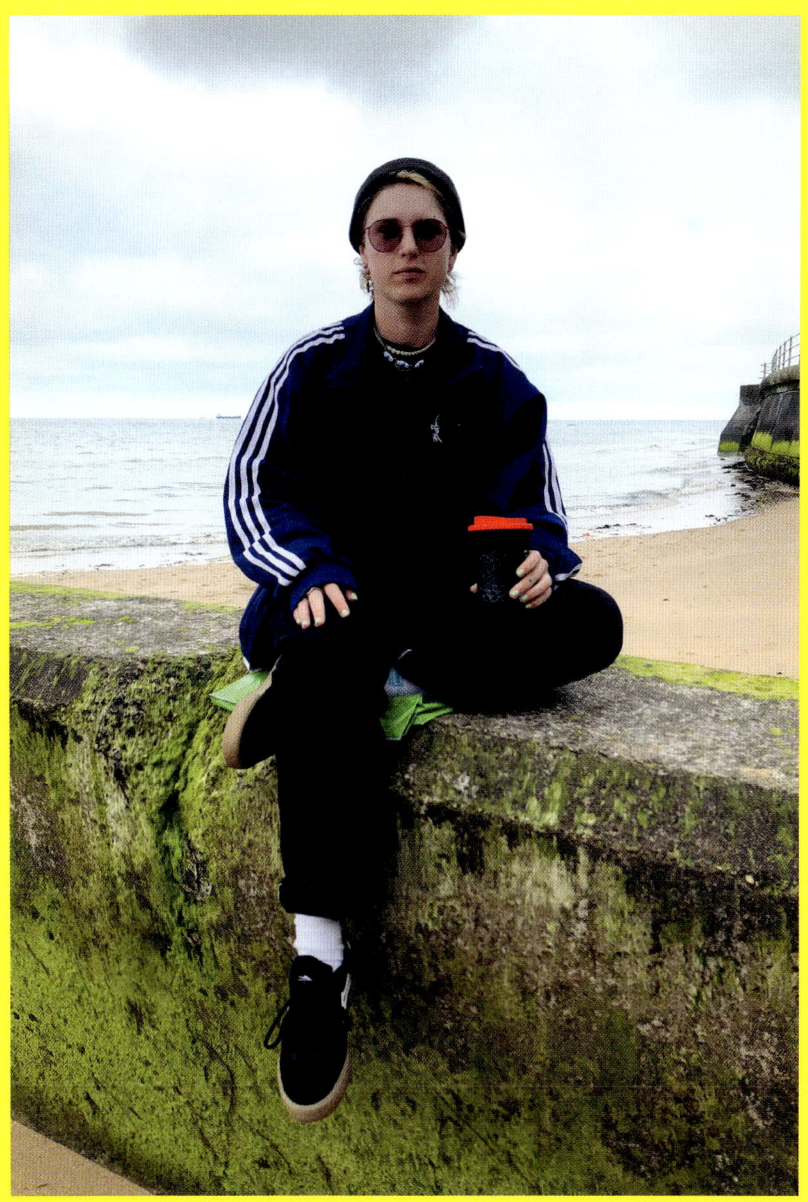

Daiz at Walpole Bay tidal pool, Margate

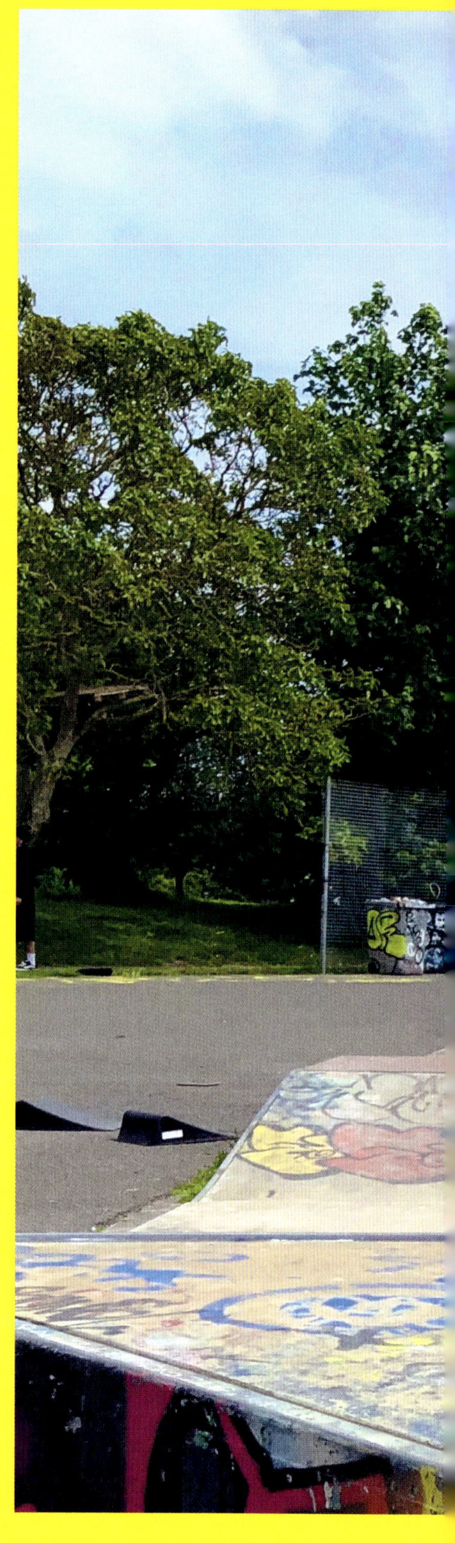

Daiz at a skatepark in Broadstairs

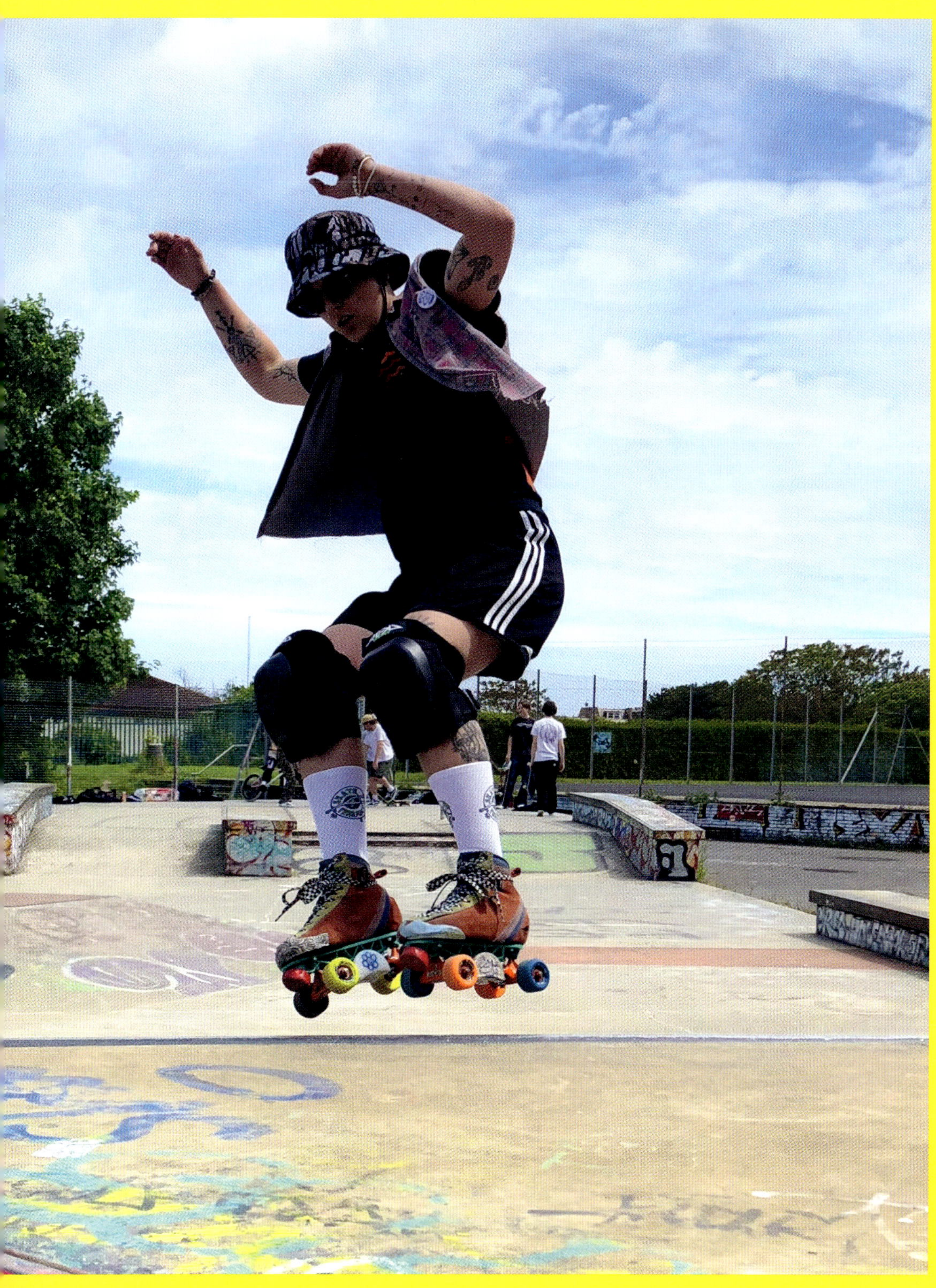

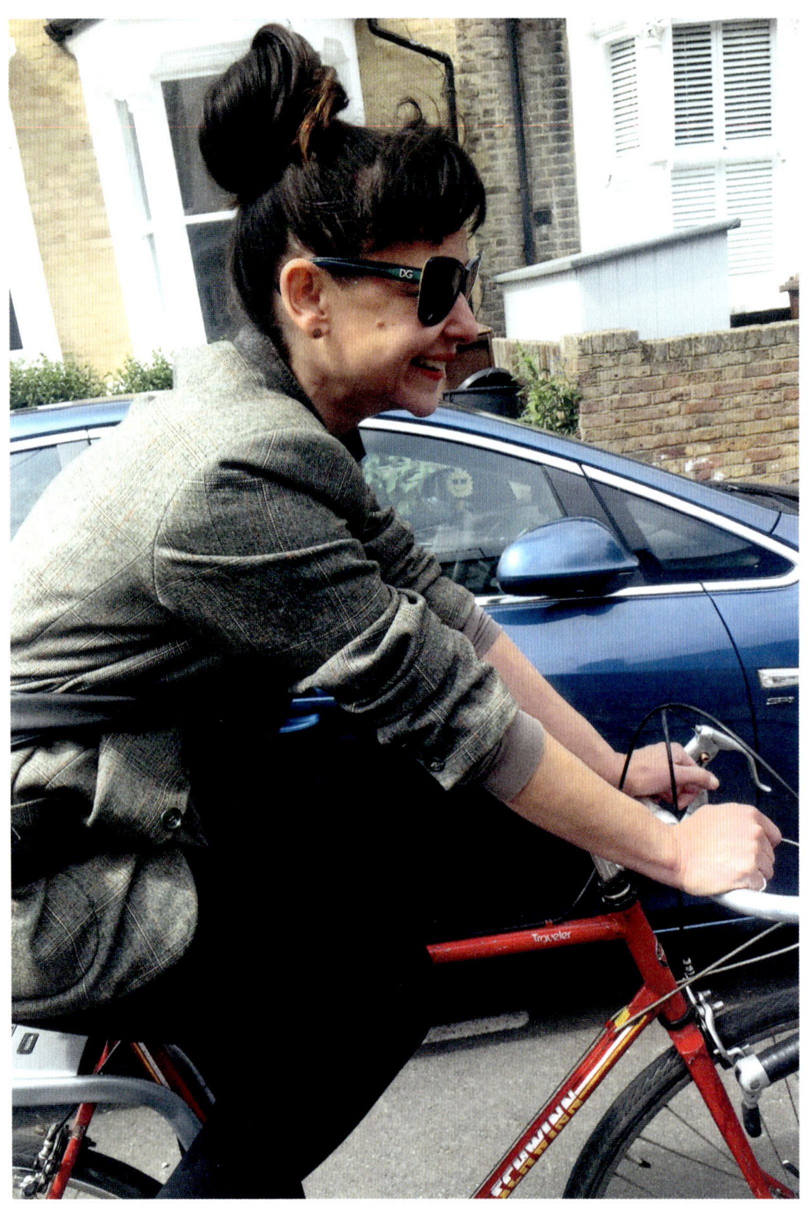

Serena riding her bike through Stoke Newington

SERENA

She / Her

Stoke Newington, London
Age 46
Artist and Pilates instructor

A deeper awareness of myself and the ability to create limits within my own energies. Better sex, great sex, since my forties, off the scale! A deeper listening into my own body, which is already deep. Stepping into myself as an older woman is empowering. And though I am a confident woman – I've always been confident – I feel like it's about helping to empower other women. I've always been a woman who's orgasmed, now I'm orgasming a number of times, and I think that's part of that empowerment. Noticing the imbalances, and then the challenge of trying to rebalance and how to do that in a positive way.

The acupuncturist said that anything that's going on is an imbalance. I knew that. Because I'm such a yang energy, I knew it was about balancing the yin with me. I need to feed my yin because my yang takes over. It's positive: finding the balance is a challenge, but it's a growth. I see it as an evolution.

A deeper awareness of myself and the ability to create limits within my own energies.

Better sex. Great sex, since my 40's, off the scale!

A deeper listening into my own body, which is already deep. Stepping into myself as an older woman is empowered.

And though I am a confident woman, I've always been confident, I feel like it's about helping to empower other women.

I've always been a woman who's orgasmed, now I'm orgasming a number of times, and I think that's part of that empowerment.

Noticing the imbalances, and then the challenge of trying to rebalance, and how to do that in a positive way.

The acupuncturist said that anything that's going on is an imbalance. I know that. Because I'm such a yang energie, I knew it was about balancing the yin in me. I need to feed my yin, because my yang takes over.

It's positive - finding the balance is a challenge, but it's a growth. I see it as an evolution.

NATASHA

She / Her

Hackney, London
Age 48
Midwife, mother
and grandmother

I enjoy being the age I am. I think it gets a really bad press. When I was 43, I had cervical cancer. I had a hysterectomy and that was all the treatment I needed. At the time the doctor said, "We'll leave your ovaries in, because at your age the advantages outweigh the disadvantages, but it might put you into menopause a little bit earlier."

Sex was "dry"; maybe people don't talk about that, but because I'm a midwife I'm used to talking about vaginas and telling women who've just had a baby to use some lube. Health professionals probably aren't very good at looking after themselves; I just dismissed it.

My mum had always said I'd never be able to have HRT because of our family history of breast cancer. I looked at the NICE guidelines to see what the risk factors were. I realised that because I have had a hysterectomy and don't need progesterone, I don't really have an increased risk of breast cancer with oestrogen only.

I called my GP who said, "I don't know if you can have HRT when you've had cervical cancer because it's a hormone receptive cancer and you've got a family history of breast cancer." I said to her, "I don't think it is a breast cancer risk, because I only need oestrogen." She said, "It's the oestrogen that's the risk." As soon as she said that, I thought, "You don't know what you're talking about and I don't trust you now." I ended up going to a private clinic. I feel annoyed that I had to do it, but am really fortunate that I could. Since I started on oestrogen gel I feel like a different person.

Natasha working out at the gym

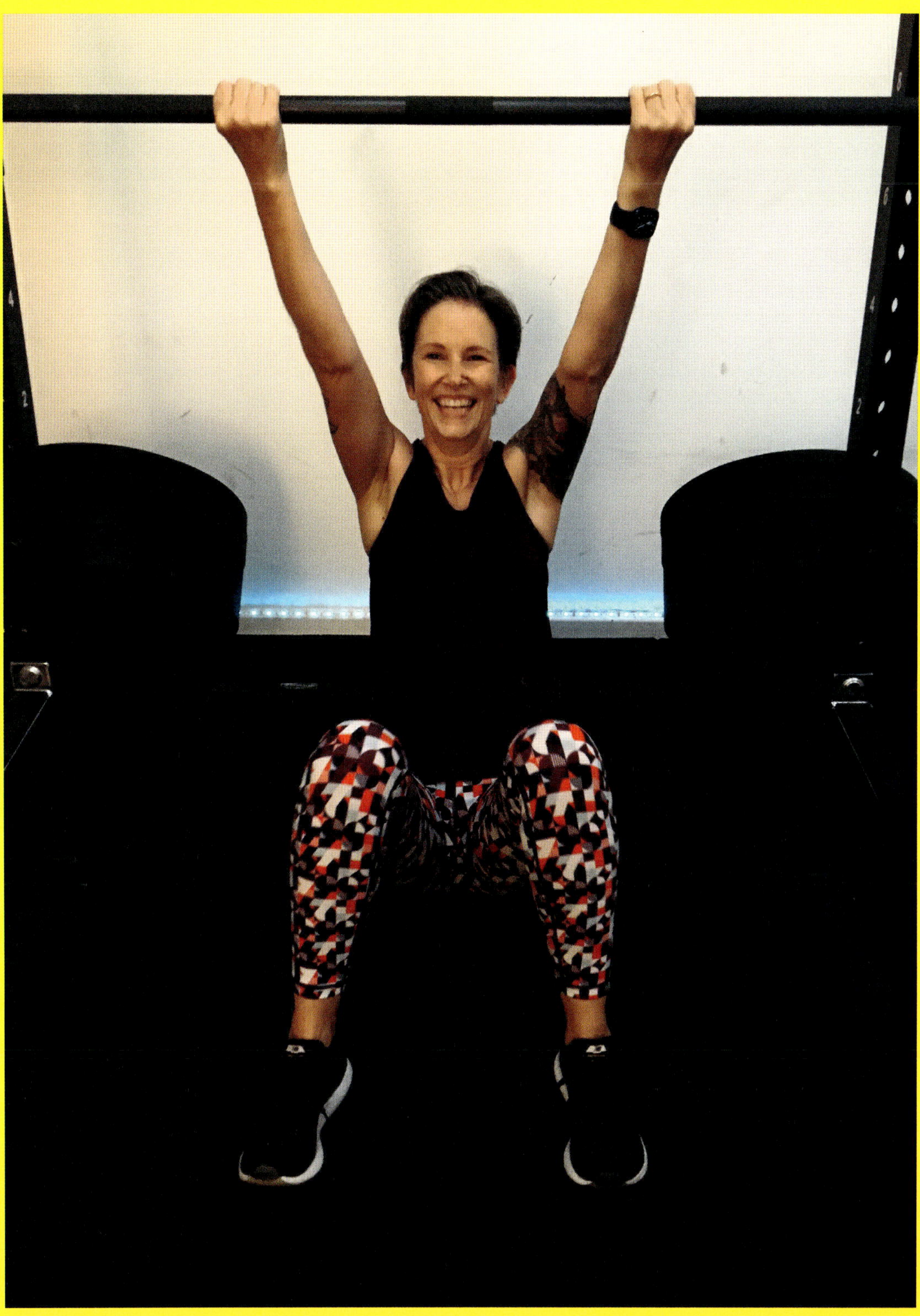

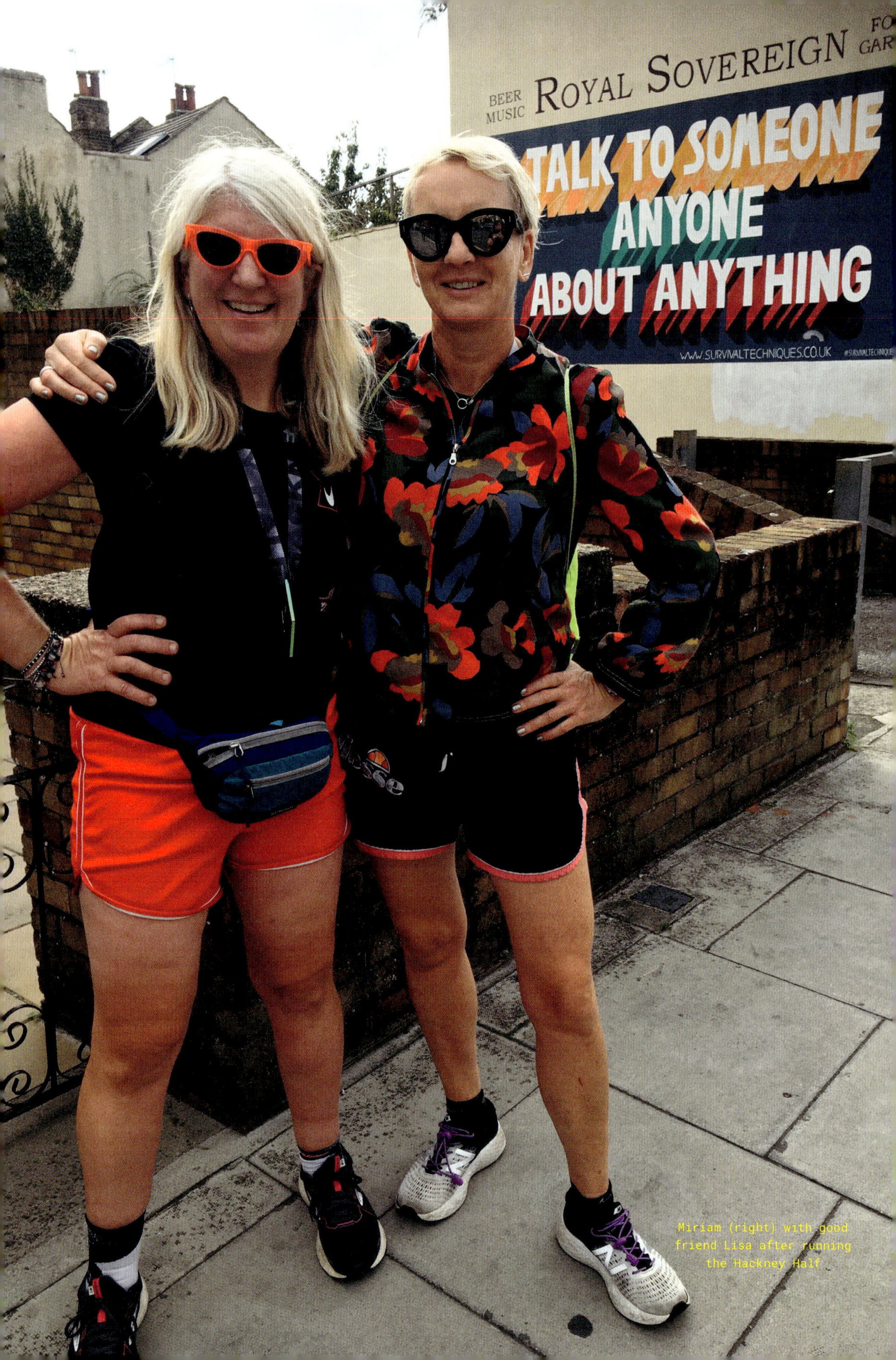

Miriam (right) with good friend Lisa after running the Hackney Half

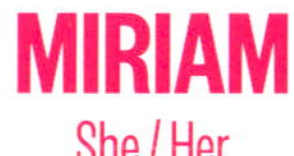

She / Her

Hernhill, Kent
Age 55
Caretaker, photographer and visual artist

There were only negatives until I got my HRT treatment. I've now got the gel, the best one that's compatible with your body. I was getting the hot sweats, feeling super-anxious, mood swings and lack of energy. I haven't had my hair falling out, luckily. I had really, really bad night sweats, so bad that the bed would be drenched. I was glad I was single, actually.

Menopause forced me to do a bit of self-discovery. I've got a water butt in my garden now; I've been in it at minus one and minus three, breaking the ice to get in. My sister comes along and, as she's "Miss Safe", she's shocked and amazed I have learnt to just get in the icy water as if it's a warm bath. I do Wim Hof breathing and get in there really slowly. This is a Miriam I thought I would never be. I read up a bit more about human beings; it's woken me up a bit, rather than just accepting it.

I also go sea swimming – I've found some friends and there's so much positivity. Regarding the sea, you cannot have an ego; it's nature, it's dangerous, you can drown. You have to be respectful of it, so it keeps you humble, keeps your ego in check. They do say, leave your ego on the shore.

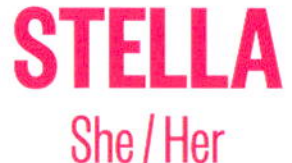

Ramsgate
Age 59
Mum, sister, lover of
anything sporty and that
brings people together

It didn't last too long for me. Not having periods anymore is a positive [and] being older means not being attached to anybody, so being able to do what I want when I want, without having to answer to anybody.

When the hot flushes did happen I was very uncomfortable, but I didn't get that many if I'm honest. [I'm] very much aware that the body depletes in certain vitamins and hormones, so I try to eat a very healthy and balanced diet.

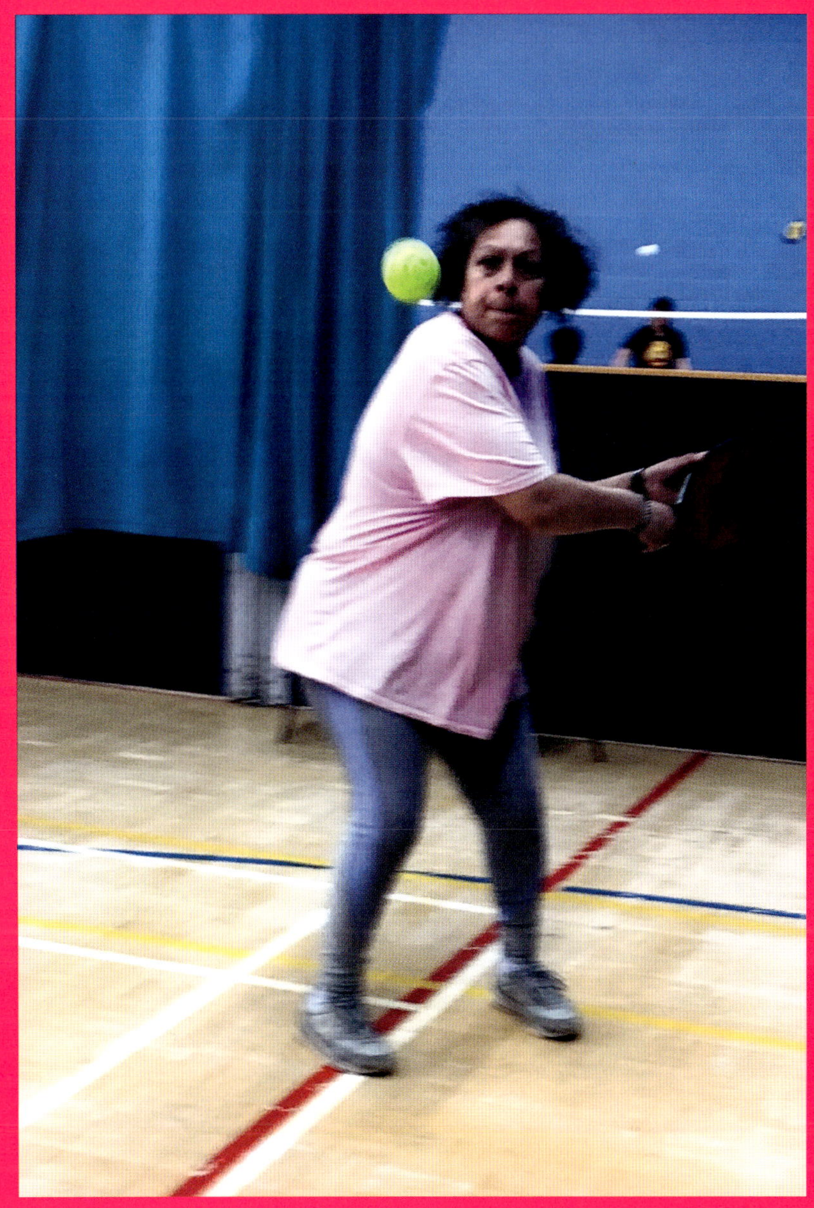

Stella playing pickleball

It didn't last too long for me. Not having periods anymore is a positive being older means not being attached to anybody. So being able to do what I want when I want, without having to answer to anybody.

When the hot flushes did happen I was very uncomfortable, but I didn't get that many if I'm honest.

Very much aware that the body depletes in certain vitamins and hormones. So I try to eat a very healthy and balanced diet.

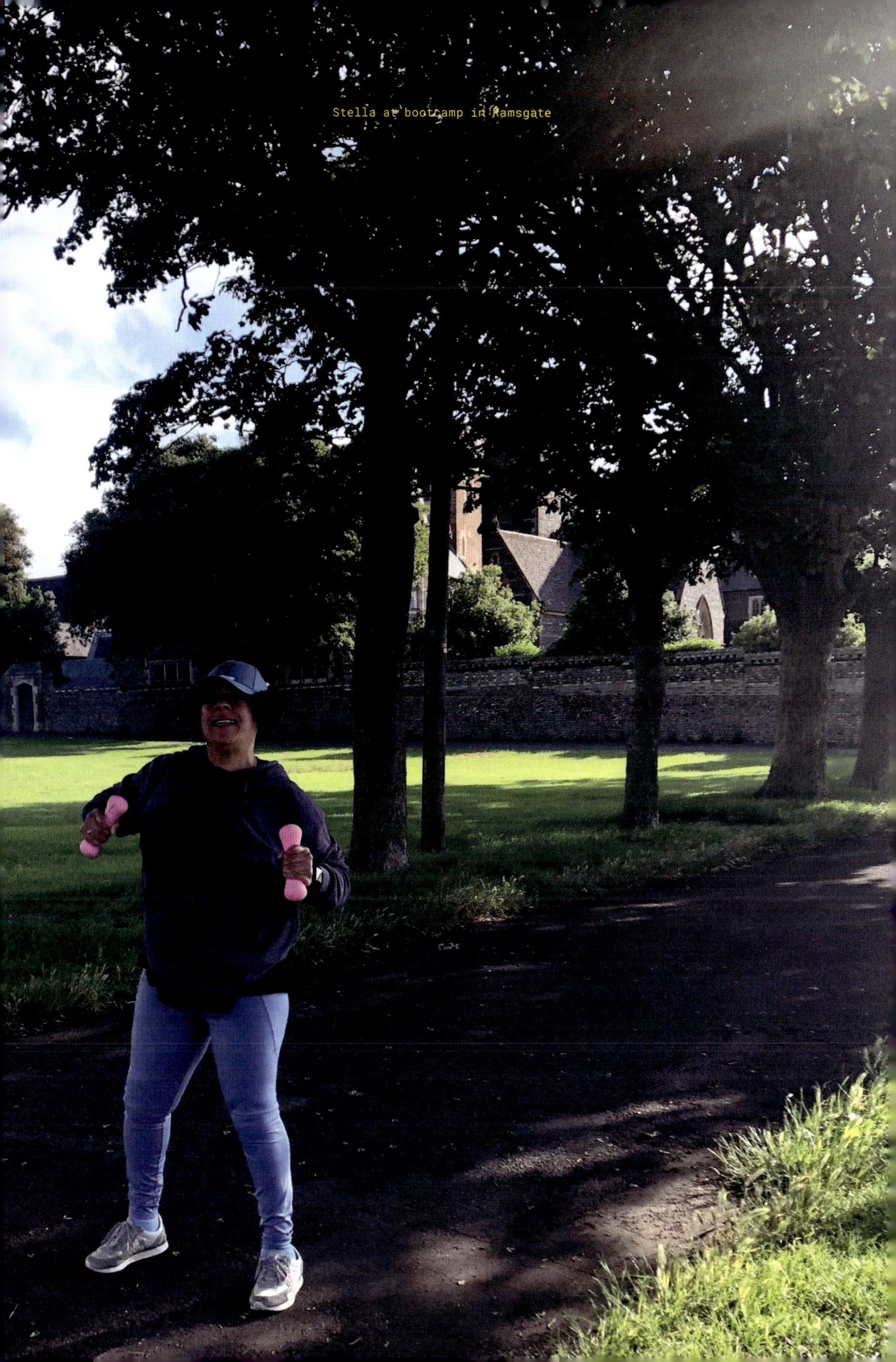

Stella at bootcamp in Ramsgate

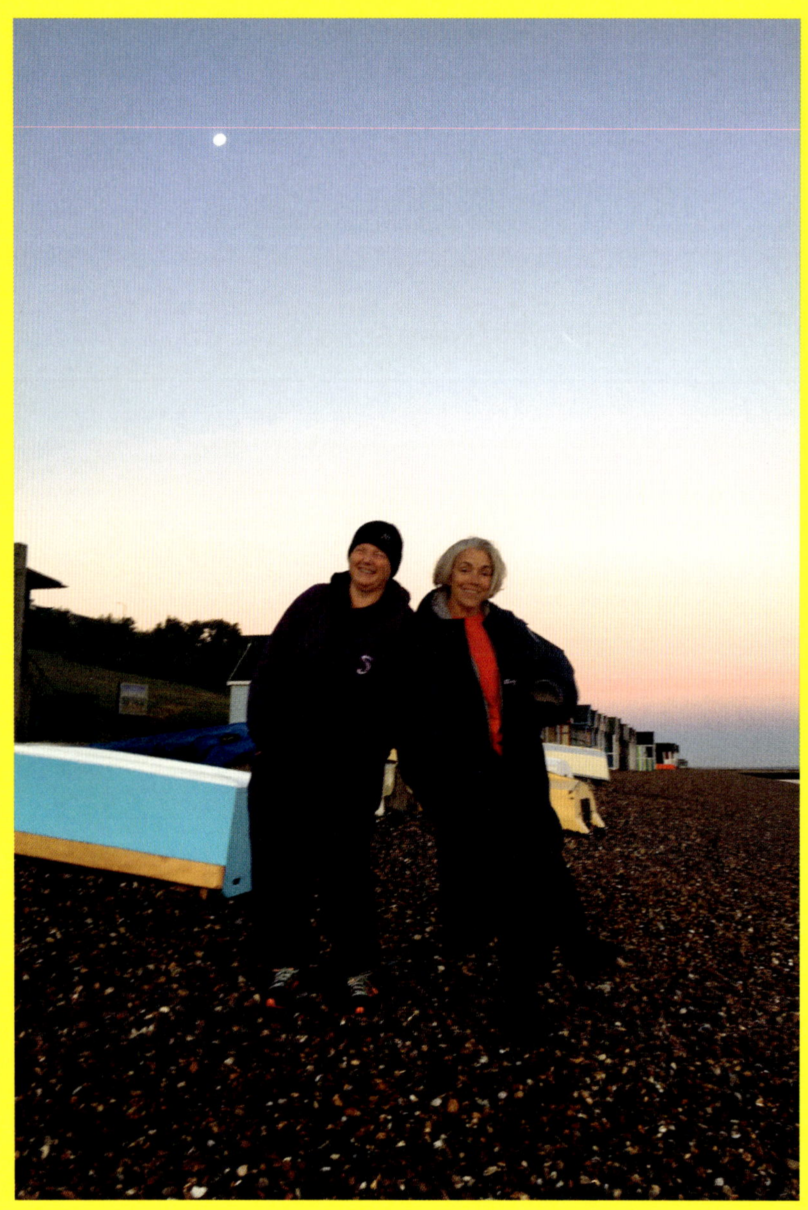

Sarah (left) with friend Mercy in Whitstable after a sunrise dip

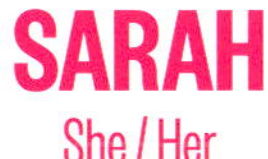

Whitstable, Kent
Age 53
Nurse

I had a full breakdown in February 2019. I've always been someone who's really liked stress and thrived on it, and I just became someone who couldn't cope with it. I was offered antidepressants and I had to do my own research to find HRT. I have to say, the best thing that a GP did for me at the time was give me a book about mindfulness.

I stopped drinking on 1 January 2020, just before the pandemic. [Laughs.] Good timing. Something to focus on. Not drinking has had a massive impact – for anxiety and inflammation in the body, I think. And I take HRT gel, just a little bit – one squirt – a day.

I often say to people that I'm not the person I was before the menopause. I'm a completely different person now, and at first it felt quite negative, but now it's been this massive positive shift in my life. It sounds a bit dramatic, but it's almost like I've been reborn – reborn into a different, calmer person. I manage my life differently and how I deal with things is now a positive experience. I've made so many new friends, not just menopausal women. Lots of them are from the sea swimming society and those little gangs. It's just been life changing.

CAT

She / Her

Rochdale, Greater Manchester
Age 36
Works at Rochdale Pioneers Museum,
mum and ultramarathon runner

In my late teens I was very poorly with a severe eating disorder and my periods stopped. I received a lot of treatment, but once I got back to a healthy weight, they didn't start back. That was attributed to me being quite sporty.

About five years ago, we decided to start trying for a child and received IVF treatment. I did one round of IVF and it didn't sit right. The consultant said I should take HRT; I carried that letter around without going to the GP because there is stigma attached to it. IVF turns your body upside down and I was exhausted with the fiddling. When I got on it [HRT] I felt better almost the next day. I still don't sleep that well and the night sweats are horrendous. I know I'm trying to juggle which HRT is right for me and a testosterone implant was recommended.

I'm so proud to live in Rochdale, but it is poor. We're a very divided community. There are so many people not getting help because they're not educated or confident enough to say, "No, you're wrong." It saddens and angers me. It's not fair on the community. The NHS is overstretched and there needs to be more training and awareness about the menopause.

You've got to be driven. Whether it's saying, "No, this medication isn't working for me," or coming out in the pissing rain and running 15 miles. You've got to have that inner drive. Some really strong women in my life have come through the menopause and it felt like an admission to say "I'm struggling". Actually, it's not a struggle, it's just what I am going through right now. If it wasn't for one wonderful woman saying, "You're not right, Cat, get a testosterone implant," I'd still be struggling now. Women support women, and the menopause has really taught me to celebrate women.

Cat on a training run in the South Pennines

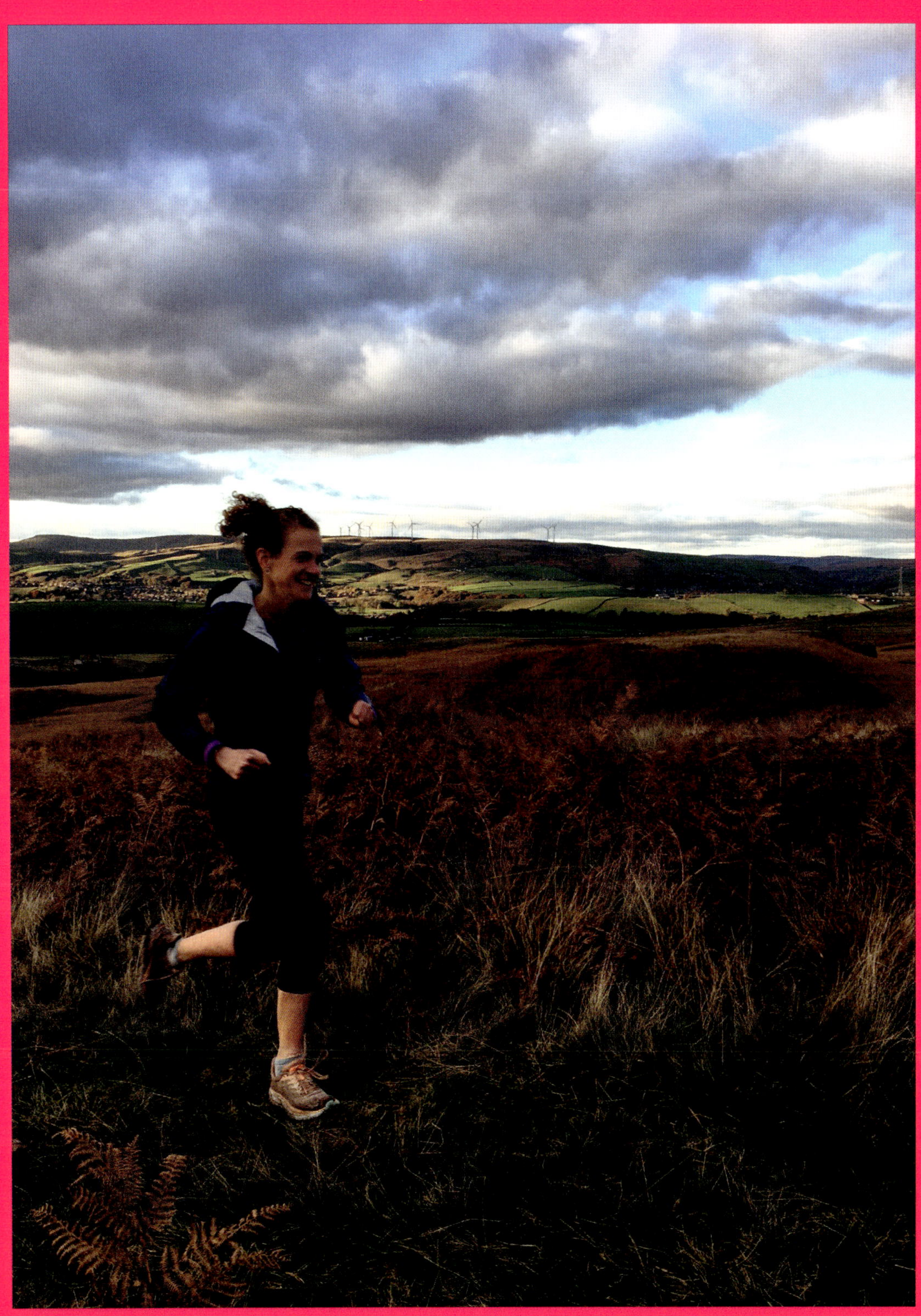

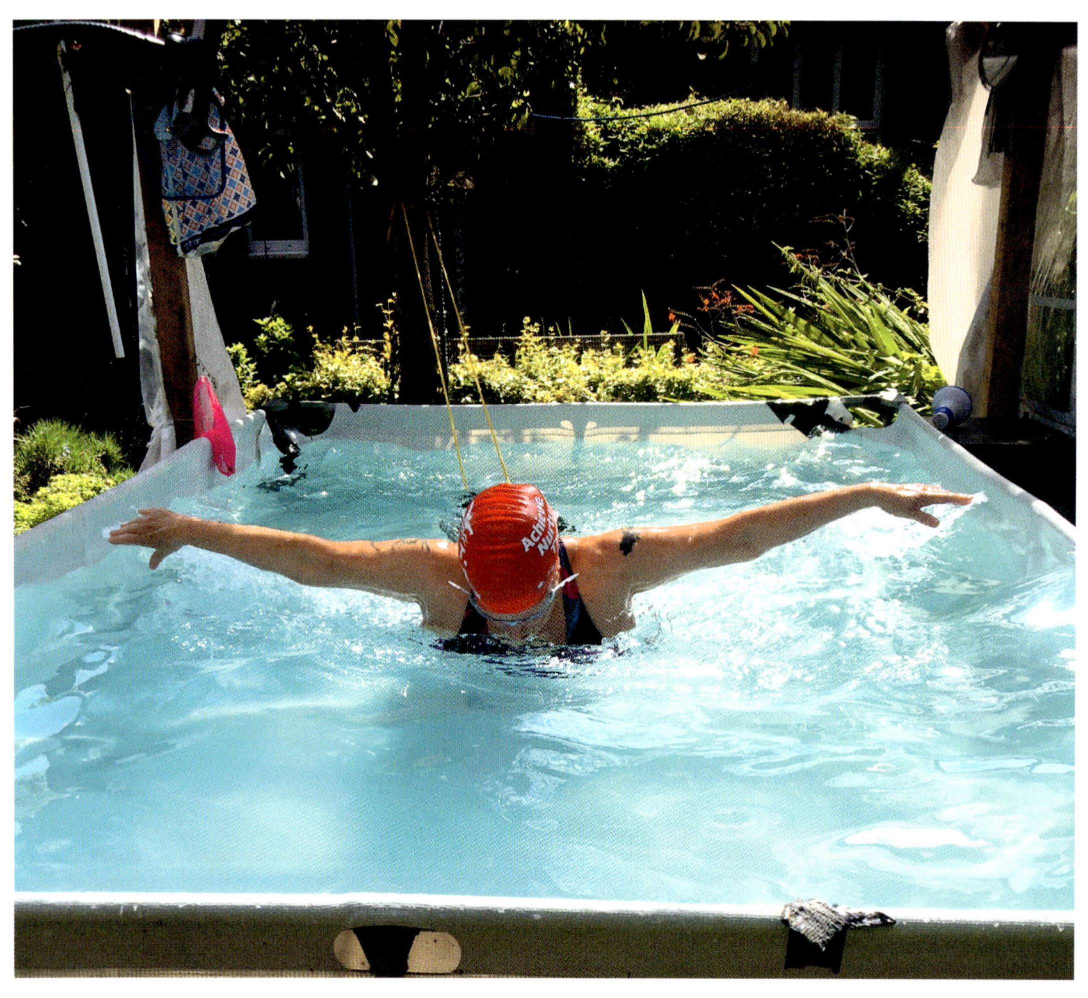

Cherie trains with a swimming tether in her garden

CHERIE

She / Her

Buckland Dinham, Somerset
Age 57
Competitive swimmer, sewing machinist and butter maker

I get continuous hot flushes. It's incredibly difficult when I work. Because I get flashing in my eyes I'm more at risk from stroke if I take HRT. I want to try anything on offer, but unfortunately I just have to go through it naturally.

I used to compete [in swimming] in my twenties. Watching the Olympics in 2016, I said to my husband, "I'm going to get back into competitive swimming," and I haven't looked back. I have competitions ahead of me and a string of medals. The only time I forget menopause is when I'm in the water. I swim three times a week. I'm also going to do my first long-distance lake swim. The training is pretty intensive: they put you through your paces, but I love it.

I get migraines and severe fatigue. I feel down a lot and like I've got nothing in my life other than swimming. I'm not coping with everyday life; you feel alien that you're the one that's changed and you can't help how you feel. I don't want to go out to pubs or out for meals anymore. I think a lot of that's to do with the menopause. I've been called a miserable bitch.

When I turned 50, I really started to notice the changes. It's like you've hit a brick wall. You're constantly down on yourself, you can't stand to look at yourself in pictures, you're desperately trying to lose weight all the time because you're not what you used to be, and you get paranoid about everything. It has made me look at my life and think differently.

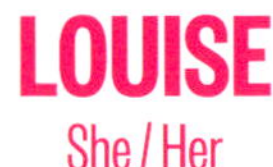

LOUISE

She / Her

Bolton, Greater Manchester
Age 46
Business Improvement Manager
at Southway Housing Trust

I find the subject matter really fascinating and I'm talking to other people about it, more than I did 12 months ago. I had my children young, so I'm going through the menopause with adult children. I can't imagine what it would be like if the children were a lot younger. I empathise with women who have younger children. Myself and my partner are excited about entering "phase two" in our lives. We are going to sell the house, rent in Manchester and ultimately move to a cabin in the woods. I also empathise with women who are entering the menopause and who couldn't have children and how that must feel.

The night sweats are something I've never experienced before. They are uncontrollable; there's nothing I can do to prepare for them, and I'm uncomfortable with that.

I wonder how much of my negative behaviour I put down as the menopause is actually that, or just me being a bit of a bitch. It's still an uncomfortable subject matter for a lot of people. I find it really challenging that it's still a subject to be ridiculed by men – and women.

Louise on a run at Walker Fold in Bolton

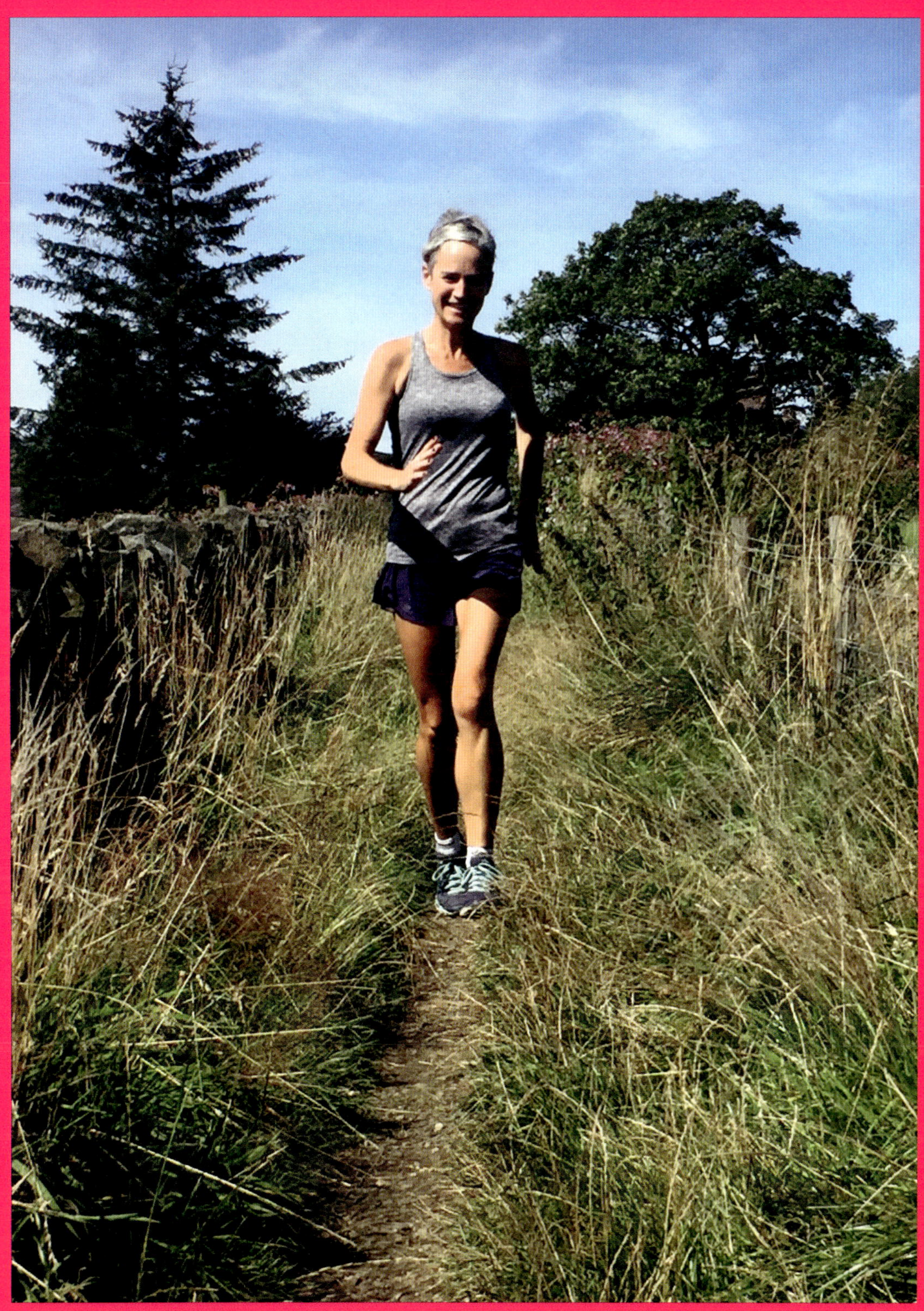

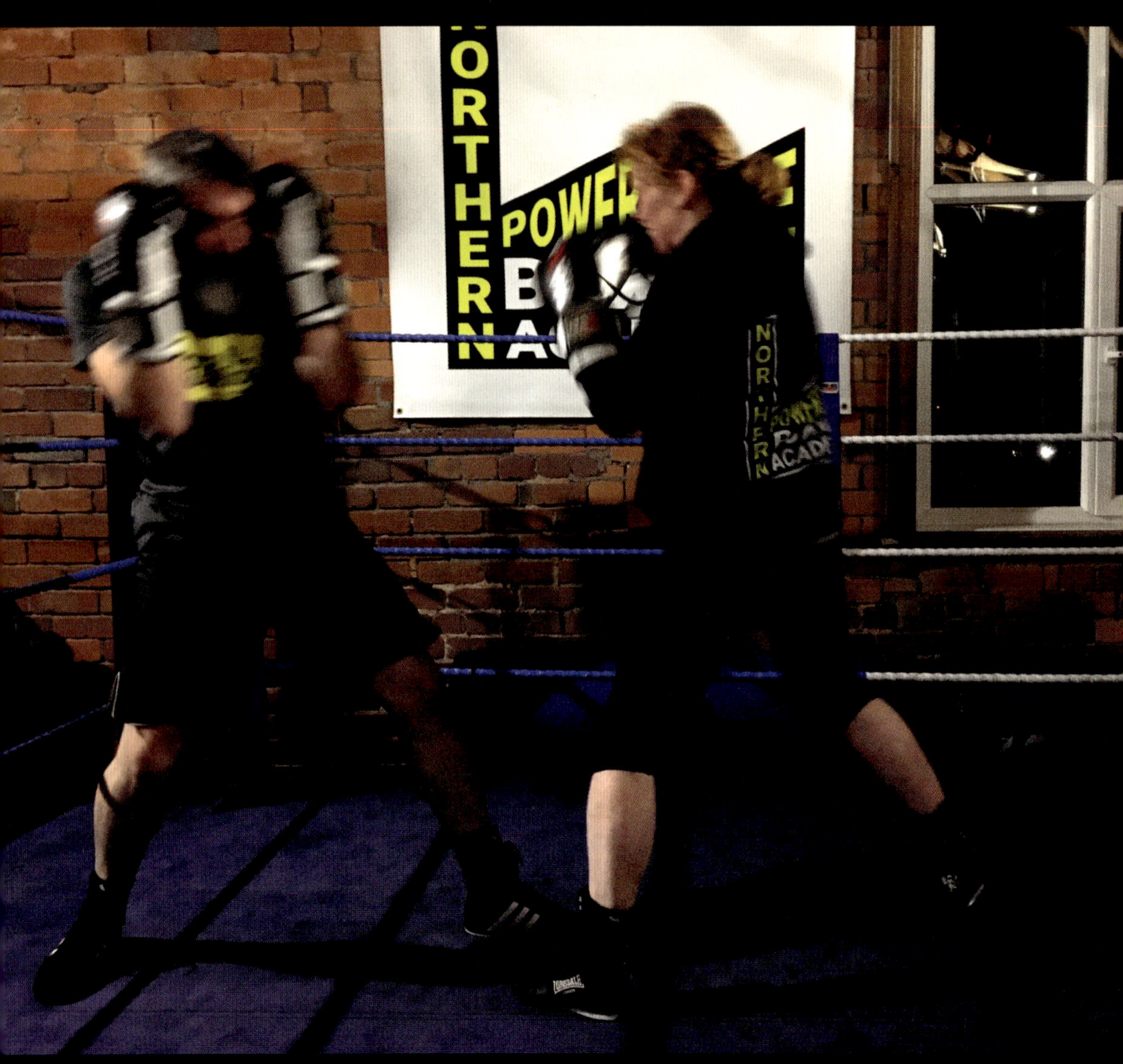

Rachel boxing at her local club

RACHEL

She / Her

Hebden Bridge,
West Yorkshire
Age 48
Textile Production
Manager

I work full-time in a good job and I was getting really narky. My family noticed and my boss asked, "Are you all right, Rachel?" I rang the doctor and was immediately offered antidepressants. I was not happy about the idea of having them and I thought I'd try tweaking them with herbal remedies. I didn't get very far, so I rang my doctor again and was offered antidepressants again. At the end of the course, I said to the doctor, "These aren't doing any good, give me some HRT."

I get so much support from the boxing club. A lot of the women there are about the same age as me or a bit older. We're quite open about the menopause; we're like a little family really. It's always been my release, my happy place. We're all different shapes, sizes and levels. We all train together and generally it ends up in fits of laughter. I wanted my picture to be at the boxing club because it brings me a lot of clarity; it helps me clear that brain fog. Everybody there has got their own experiences of life, and we share loads of stuff. There are lasses coming through that hear us talking about the menopause. There are blokes there as well and they're getting something out of talking about it.

We are all the same species, aren't we? Quite a lot of men still think that what goes on for women is some sort of mystery and secret. It shouldn't be like that. We're all human beings and we're living in a world that's not natural really. It's not working for so many people – that's my take on it.

VIVIENNE

She / Her

Ramsgate, Kent
Age 66
Ceramic artist, founder of Mermads swimming group in Ramsgate, and mother

In my early forties I wasn't aware of any perimenopause, and the day it started I was teaching in a school in Croydon. I was reading to a child and this heat started rising from my feet to my head. I was sitting there thinking, "What's happening?" It wasn't awful, it was just really weird.

That was all that happened. I don't recall that ever happening again. But I did get hot, and I did have to wear layers and sometimes take them off.

Not having periods anymore was a real plus. I was talking to my daughter Ellie about this, and I wasn't in touch with my body. Ellie and a lot of people I know are so in touch with their bodies – know when they are ovulating, etc. My mum had a hysterectomy, so I didn't know what to expect.

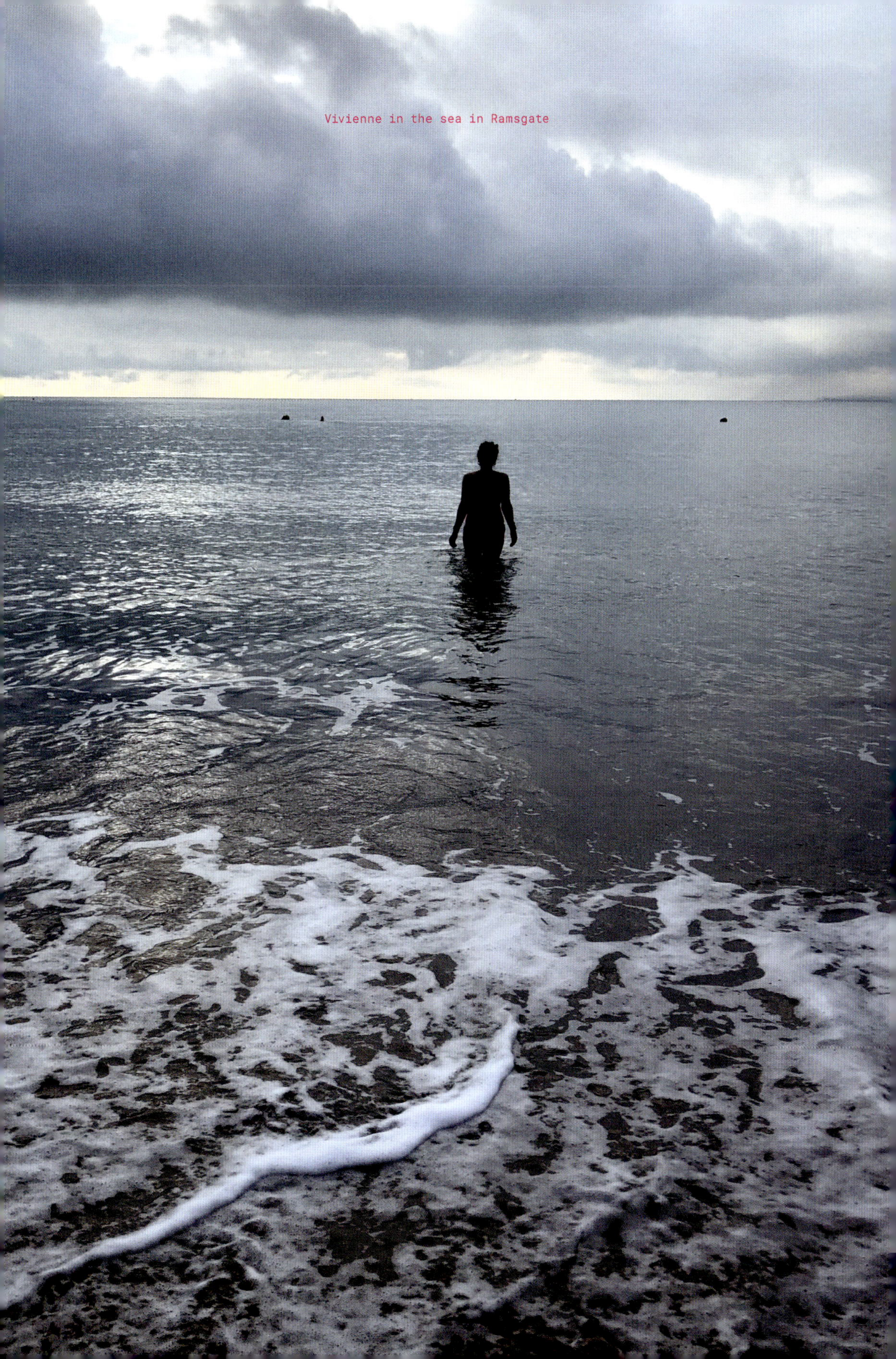

Vivienne in the sea in Ramsgate

A LOT OF
I KNOW
IN TOUC
THEIR

PEOPLE ARE SO H WITH BODIES

On the Western Undercliff beach, Ramsgate

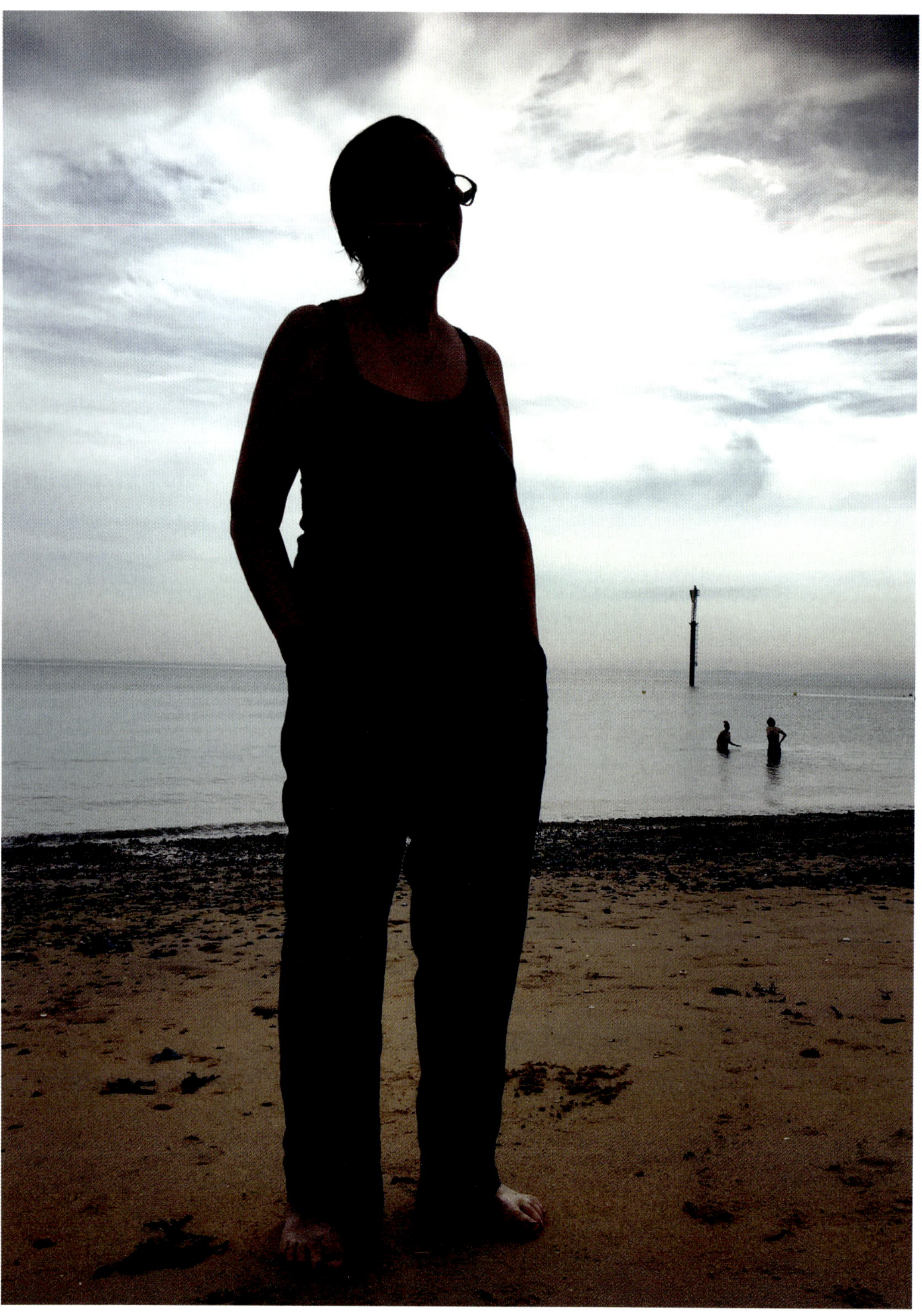

ANONYMOUS

She / Her

Ramsgate, Kent
Age 59
Visual artist

When I first saw the call-out to talk about the menopause I really was against it, but it kept bothering me why I didn't want to be part of it. I was quite embarrassed, ashamed. I decided that I did want to take part, but I wanted to do it anonymously. Not for a vanity thing; it's something that is hidden or not discussed – still one of the taboos, I think.

My hair's going grey, I'm getting whiskers on my chin, and when I see women my age it surprises me, and then I realise that's what I am. There's also a joy: I know myself better than I ever have and there's such a relief in that. I still wear lipstick, even for a dip in the sea. I like to think I can still be attractive, but I wonder if that's part of being a woman and society's expectation. I'm not exactly sure how I should be.

When I was 47, I left my then husband. We had a fantastic marriage. I do wonder now whether I was perimenopausal and I didn't know. There was something going on inside me that thought, "No, I just can't keep doing this anymore." I needed something different and, looking back, if I'd have known, somebody could've said, "Actually, it's the menopause, hang in there."

I was a graphic designer for 30 years during the '80s and '90s, when graphic designers were gods, almost. I recently embarked on an MA in Canterbury. I wouldn't have done that if I was a younger woman – I graduated when I was 56. The MA was the best thing I've done for myself; everyone should do it. Don't doubt, just do it!

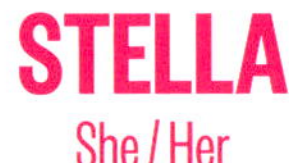

Lancing, West Sussex
Age 54
Ex-raver, road sweeper and nurse. Now a happily retired warrior bitch

What was difficult for me at one point was that I had a partial hysterectomy many years ago. My ovaries were left, but my uterus was removed. I didn't go into immediate menopause, because I was still ovulating at the time, but obviously my periods stopped because my uterus was gone. I was starting to feel forgetful with a foggy brain, and became very anxious at times. I didn't know if it was true menopause or something else going on.

I've probably got more positives than negatives: giving less of a fuck than I gave before; being sensible enough that when I was struggling in the workplace due to menopause I just handed my notice in and left my job. I had some unexpected money, so I thought rather than struggle on with work, dealing with the menopause, I'd just leave my job and live independently off my savings for a while. I don't have to worry about getting up early or remembering what I was doing. I don't have to make any lists because I'm just a free agent now.

This project is empowering. It's getting everyone talking about the menopause, not just menopausal women. It's a much less taboo subject than it was previously because of projects like this; that's a great positive. It shouldn't be a taboo subject, because half the population of the planet will go through it if they live that long. I feel privileged to have lived long enough to be a menopausal woman!

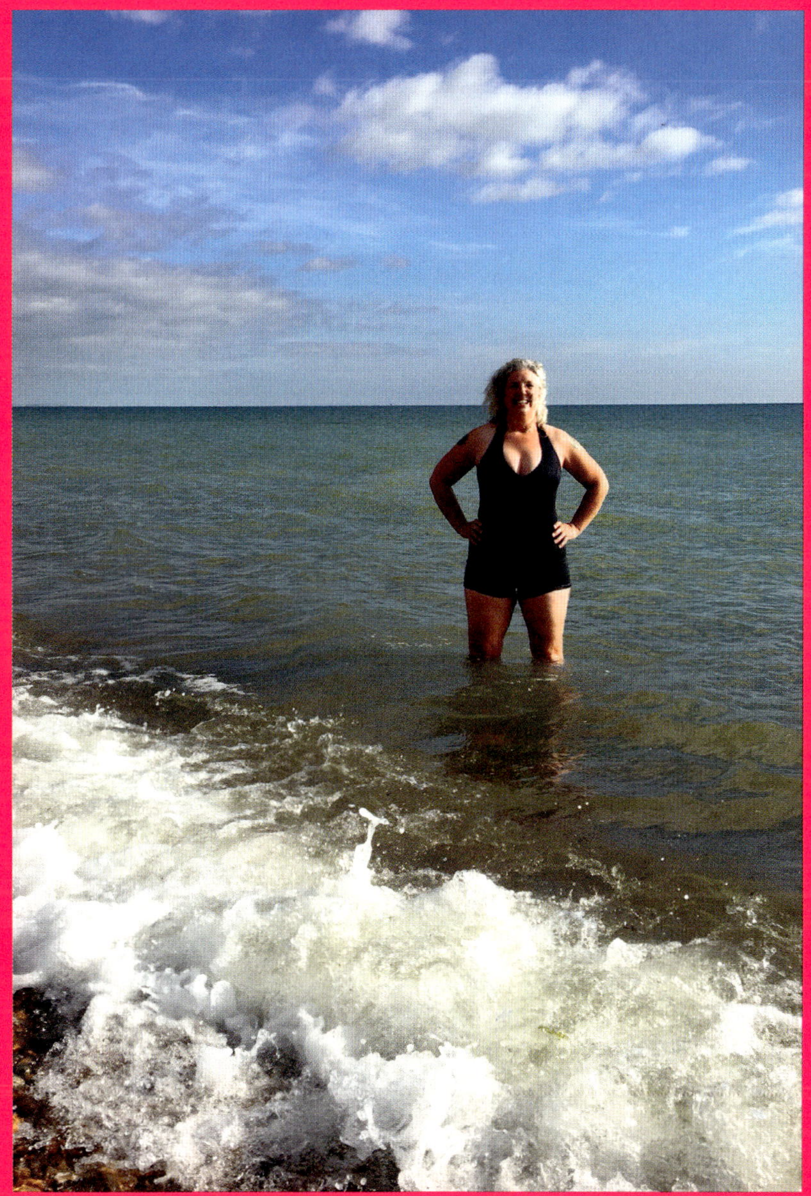

Stella in the sea near her home

Flick with her camera on the beach at Rottingdean, near Brighton

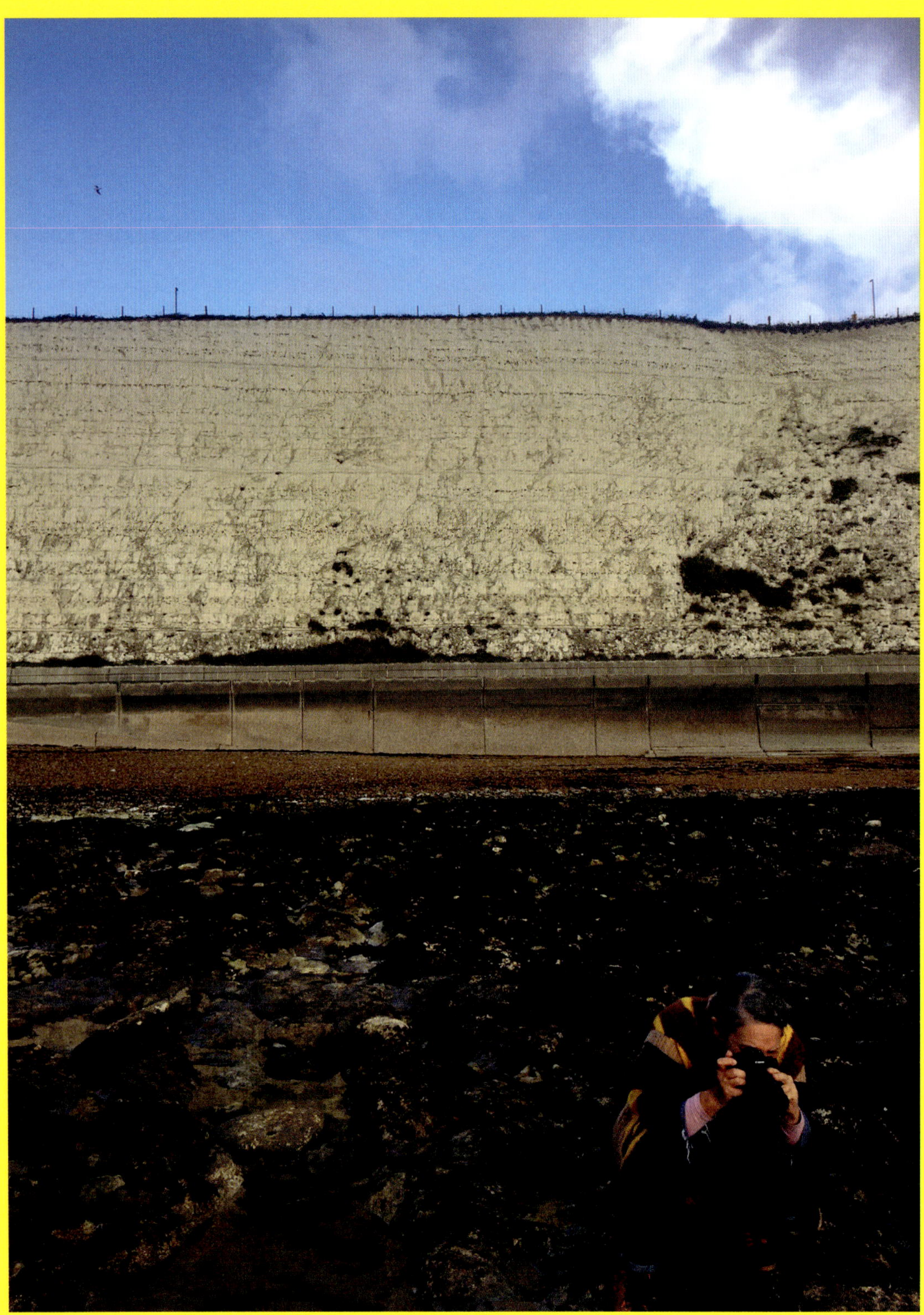

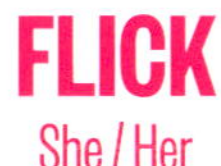

FLICK

She / Her

Brighton, East Sussex
Age 54
Artist, director
and performer

One of the hardest things for me was the fact that I don't have any children and the finality of that possibility that I was also dealing with. It became a kind of grieving. It's really good to acknowledge that there is a grieving process with the menopause.

It's called "the Change" because you're going through a change, which is about almost becoming a new person, a bit like a snake shedding its skin. You can embrace that new person, but before that you need to go through grieving the younger you, the vibrant you. It's quite easy to catch hold of what you see as something you're letting go of, thinking you're never going to have it again. Some of that is shit anyway, so it doesn't matter.

From that difficult part of navigating the menopause I've found a positive space to do anything and become anybody I want. Those hormonal changes that go on during menopause shift the other stuff and you're suddenly revealed. The anxiety was probably there before, but it didn't present itself until I started the menopause. I would have panic attacks where I just couldn't get off the sofa for days. I couldn't move; it was the craziest feeling. Anxiety is just a manifestation of something. I recognise that you go through this phase where you suddenly become really uncertain of things and scared of stuff that wasn't there before. You lose your confidence as a person.

It was harder for our mothers, but a lot of women of our generation are still working on having a value in society other than being a mother. When the menopause comes along, you've got to work twice as hard to bring your esteem back up.

WORK /
COMMU

NITIES

Louise services a boiler

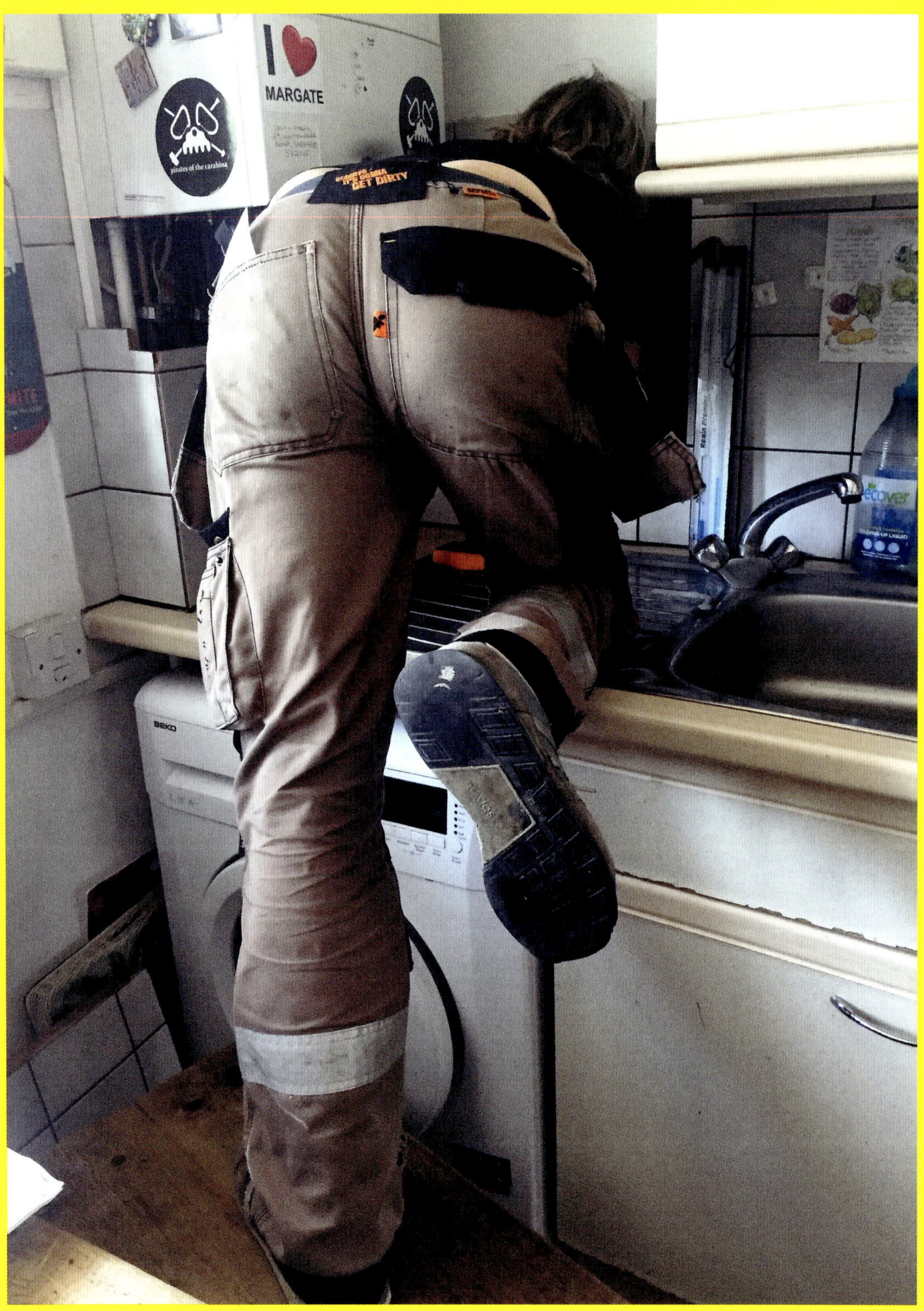

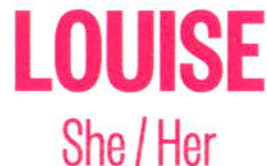

Highbury, London
Age 54
Heating engineer

My perimenopause began around 45. Night sweats, insomnia, rage, anxiety, brain fog. I stopped bleeding at 49, and it was around then that I became intimate with a deep sense of unease. It had always been there – a lifetime of stress and confusion hidden beneath the surface of things.

Plumbing turned out to be a strange kind of sanctuary. It allowed me to “be” with my aloneness, without needing to explain it to anyone. It kept me busy and distracted. It was physical, practical, unpredictable and gave me a way to disappear a little, even while showing up in other people’s homes.

Hormonal change can crack open the structures you’ve built to hold everything in. For me, menopause brought with it a long, slow breakdown and the eventual breakthrough I so badly needed. Years of coping, masking, pleasing and surviving all rose up, demanding to be felt. Yoga and meditation became anchors, untangling tension, listening inward, helping me be with everything as it surfaced.

Looking back, I think starting my business was as much about self-protection as it was about empowerment. I needed to work in a way that felt safe, in my own rhythm. And as hard as it was, I built something that gave me stability and autonomy, and the space to fall apart when I needed to.

This stage of life – menopause, reckoning, recovery – stripped me back to the bone. It wasn’t pretty, but it was real. It gave me back a kind of freedom I didn’t even know I was missing, and a way to come home to myself.

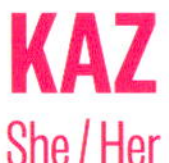

She / Her

Roundhay, Leeds
Age 52
Project Manager, third sector mental health

I'm more aware of how much energy I've got and able to be more discerning about where I spend it, and who I spend it with. [Menopause] is being more authentic, learning to actually say that I need things, and being aware that I can ask for help. Not taking any shit. When you're younger, you have time to worry about other people's problems, but managing my own emotions means I can't micromanage others, so I'm less reactive: not worrying about things you can't change, not overthinking what you've done or what others think. Having a sense of "turning within" makes me feel calmer. Learning to "be", not "do", is what changed in my life.

My life has been so focused on me as a sexual being, so not to be driven by sex is a relief; the loss of mojo, having relationships on a different level, that aren't based on sexuality.

Health issues. More pain. Body image. Weight gain. Lack of energy to motivate myself. The final acceptance of having no kids. I just feel flat and a bit empty.

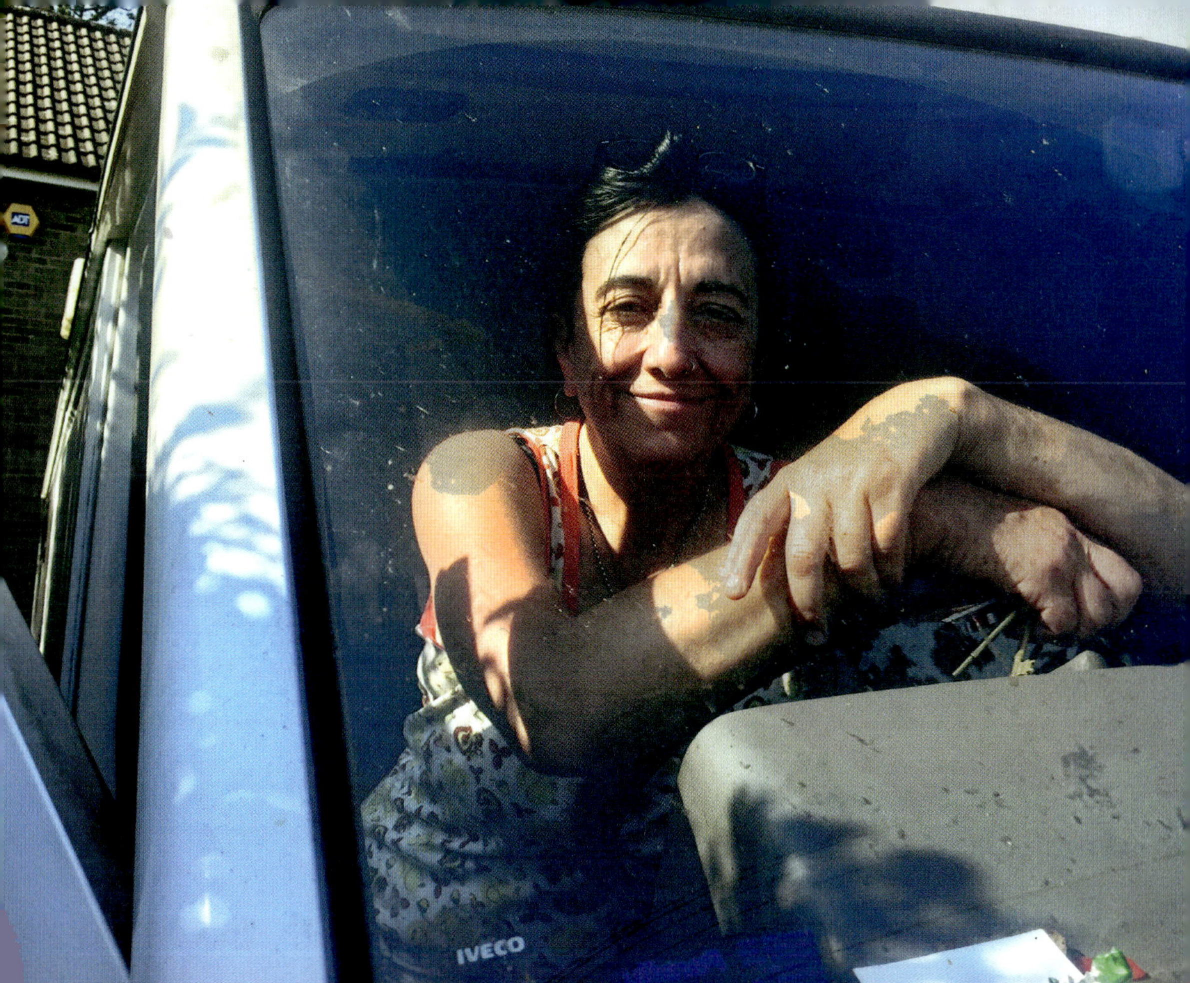

Kaz at the wheel of her van

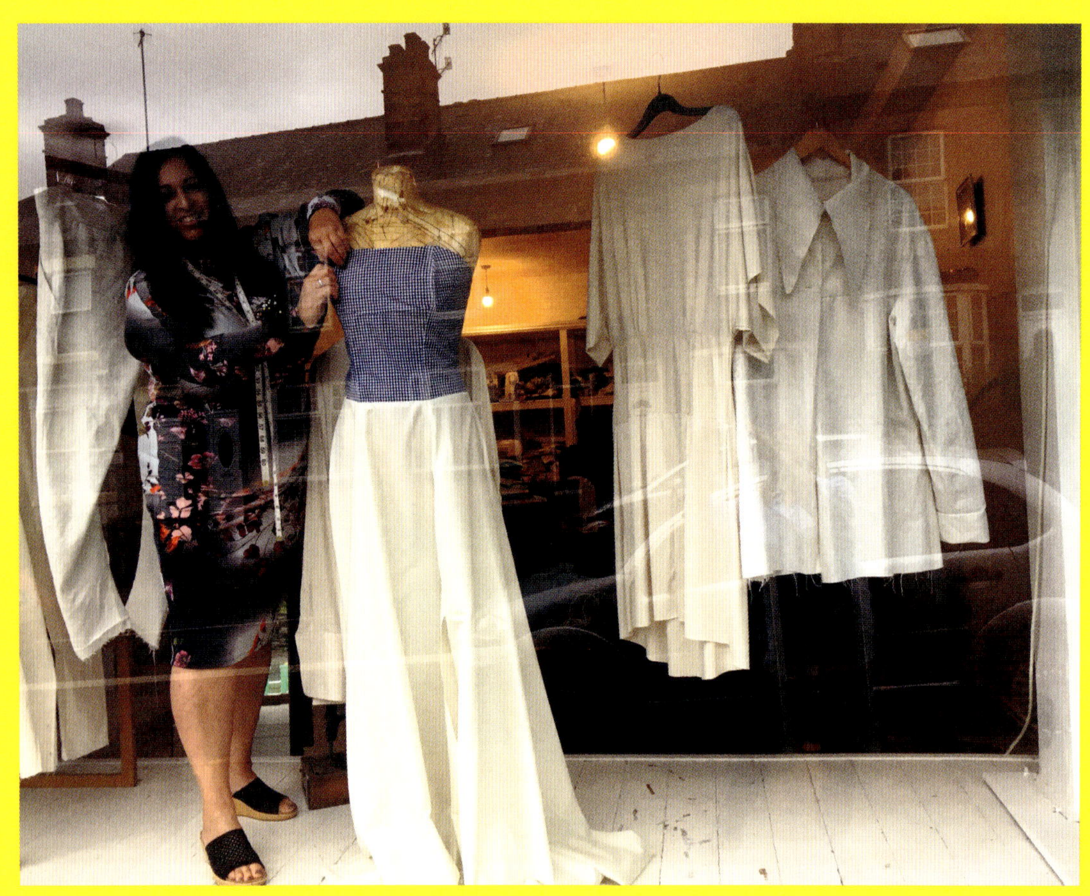

Anna in the window of her studio

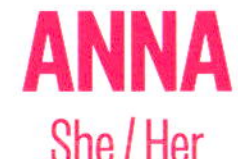

ANNA

She / Her

Sheffield,
South Yorkshire
Age 55
Fashion designer

As a fashion designer I have to look the part, but have been having menopausal symptoms for the past few years. People don't really know or see that side of me; it's all about the image.

I feel like I've got to own it, and the real defining factor for me was having a conversation with my daughter about this project, and her saying to me, "Well, you're not going through menopause are you?" I said to her, "I'm 55, what did you think, that I was just going to skip it?"

One minute I can be on top of the world and the next I can be at rock bottom. I think if I go and talk to somebody about it, they will just give me antidepressants, but I know it's not depression.

I've still got the responsibility of my business and I make sure I meet all my deadlines, so people would never know. But people should know. I think if it was a male condition, it would have been recognised. We are living very much in a male-dominated society.

I don't take any nonsense from people; I've gone through all this life experience and I'm still holding my own. I feel I get a lot more respect than I ever recognised before.

Because I work for myself, if I do feel terrible I can start late or come home early, and I don't actually mind saying, "Can we move your deadline?" I like that side of me, that I'm not afraid to say that now.

My happiest place is when I'm dancing, that is my therapy. I have been a dancer all my life, so finding salsa and kizomba again four years ago was one of the best things I've ever done.

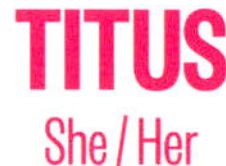

Stoke Newington, London
Age 63
Cabinet maker

You just have to tough it out and not give a shit as the world is not on your side as an older woman. As I get older I'm appreciating what I've got and valuing it, as I know it's not going to last forever. I also feel less tired; my energy is better.

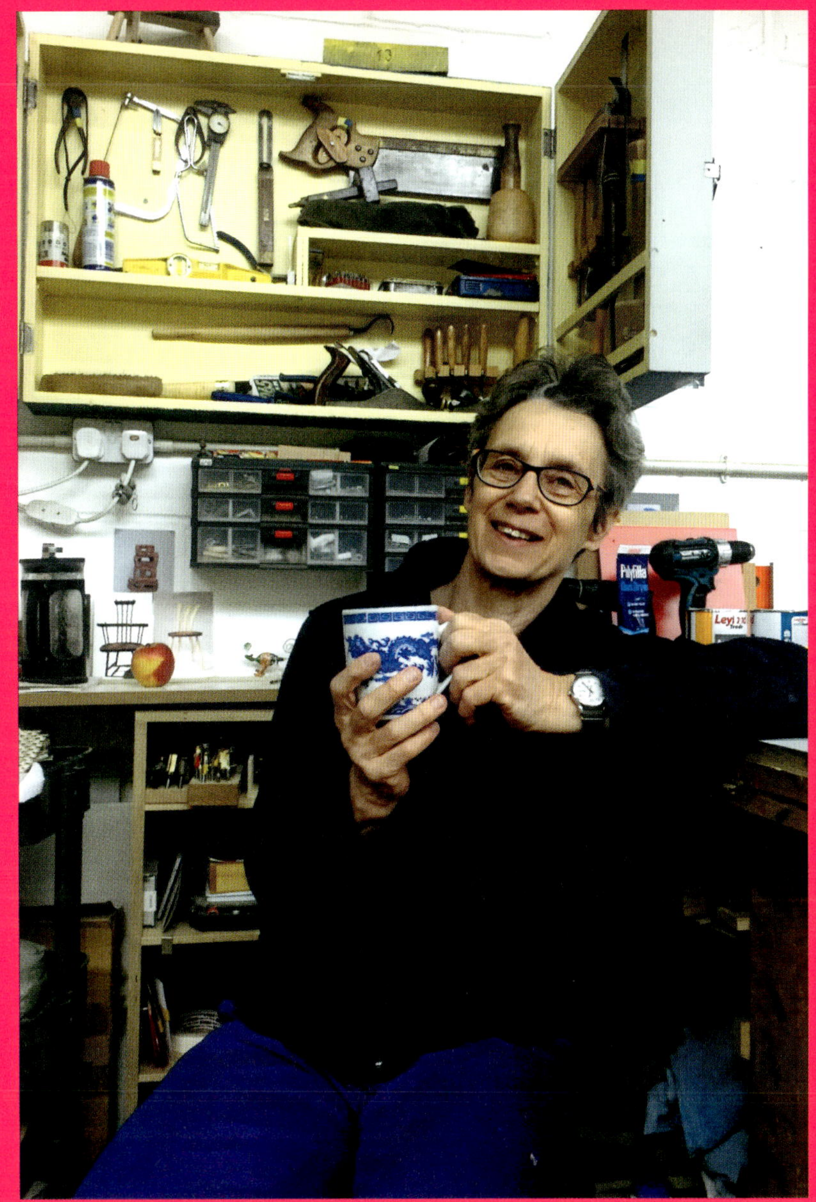

Titus relaxes with a cup of tea in her workshop

Claire uses a dimension saw in her workshop

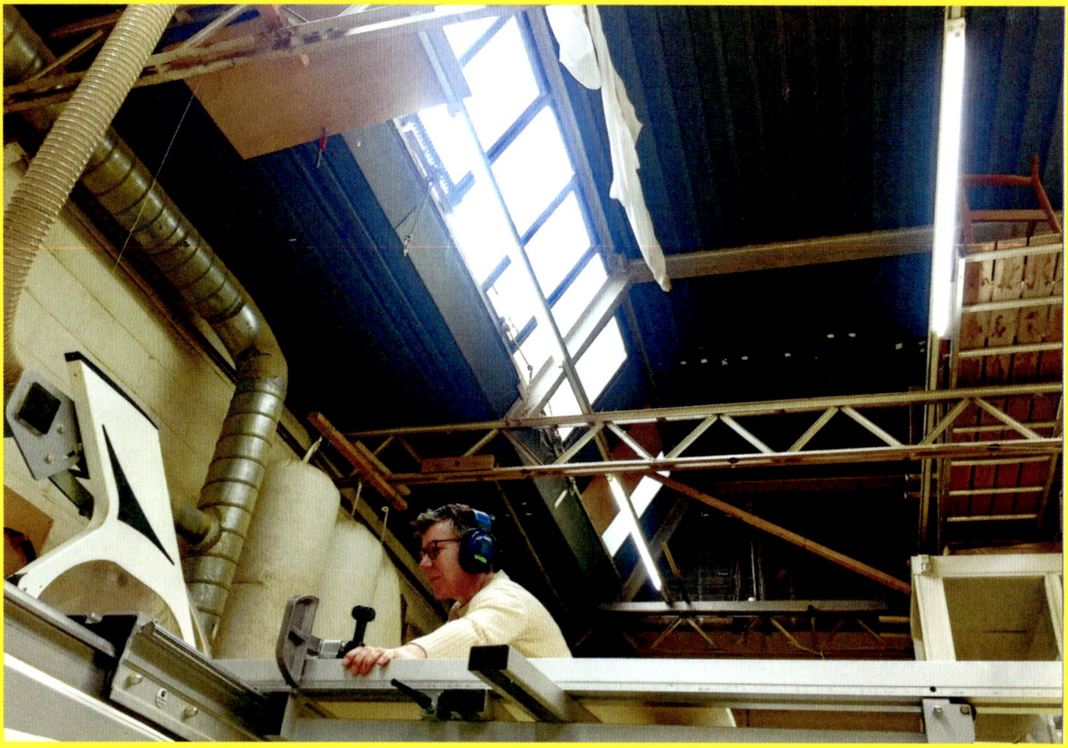

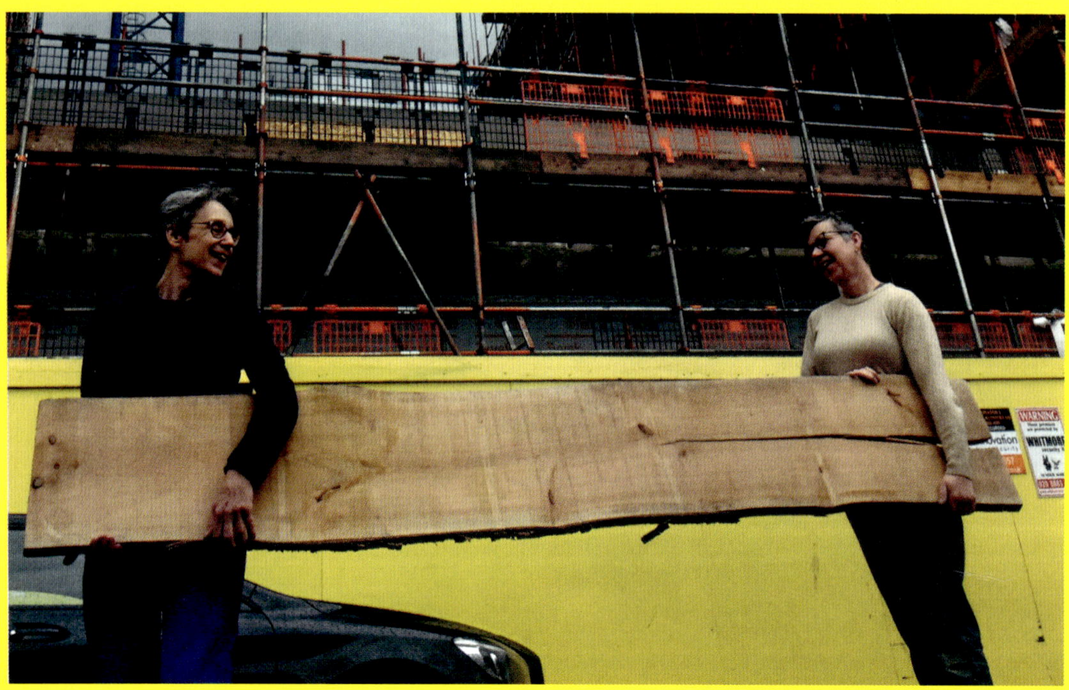

With Titus (left) carrying a piece of timber

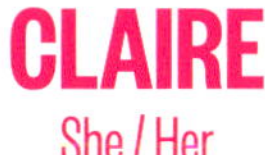

CLAIRE

She / Her

Bethnal Green, London
Age 53
Furniture maker

I'm prioritising more around work, saying "no" to jobs that don't work for me. I feel tired, but this has made me better at self-care.

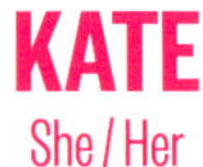

Highbury, London
Age 60
Librarian at
The London Library

For me, the menopause was a very positive thing. I had a pretty easy time. A few hot flushes, but I normally feel the cold, so they were positive. I looked forward to them in bed as they kept me warm! The only negative thing for me was having fibroids grow in the years leading up to my menopause – I think this is a common time for this to happen. It made my menstruation excessively heavy to the point of getting anaemia and having to stay at home and tough it out.

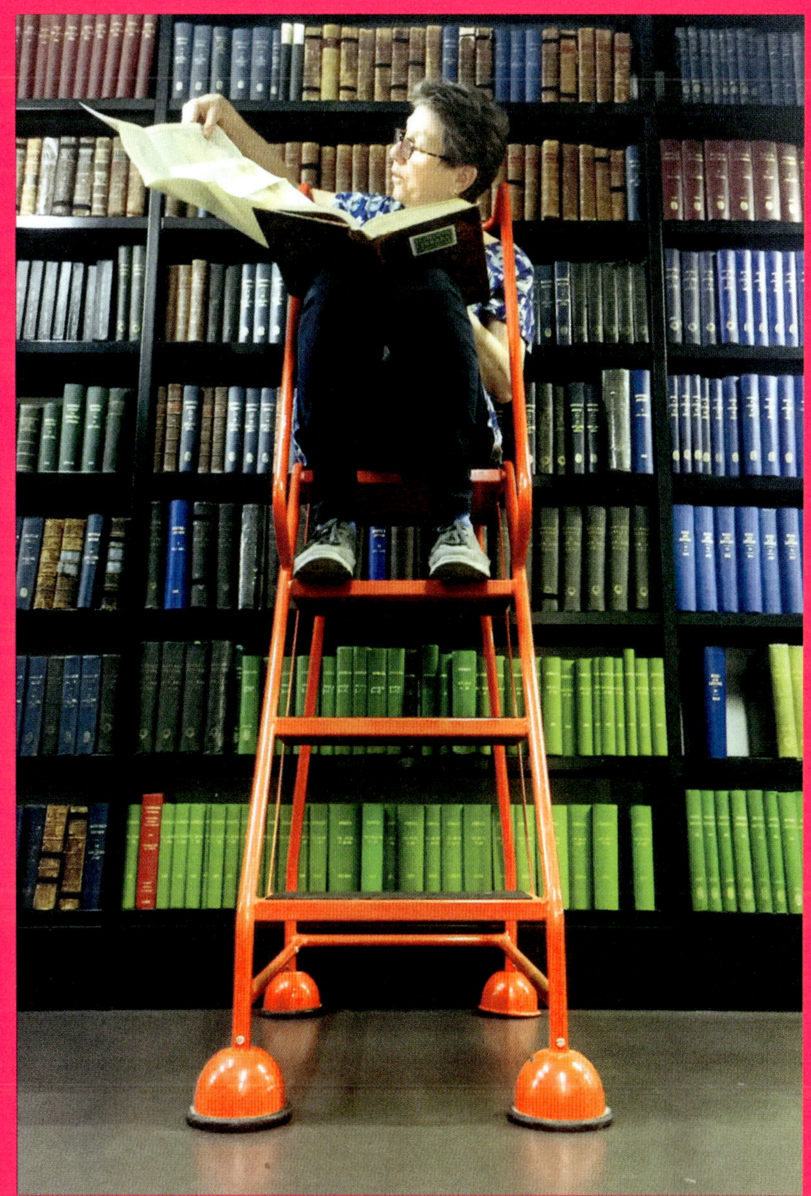

Kate looks at a book at The London Library

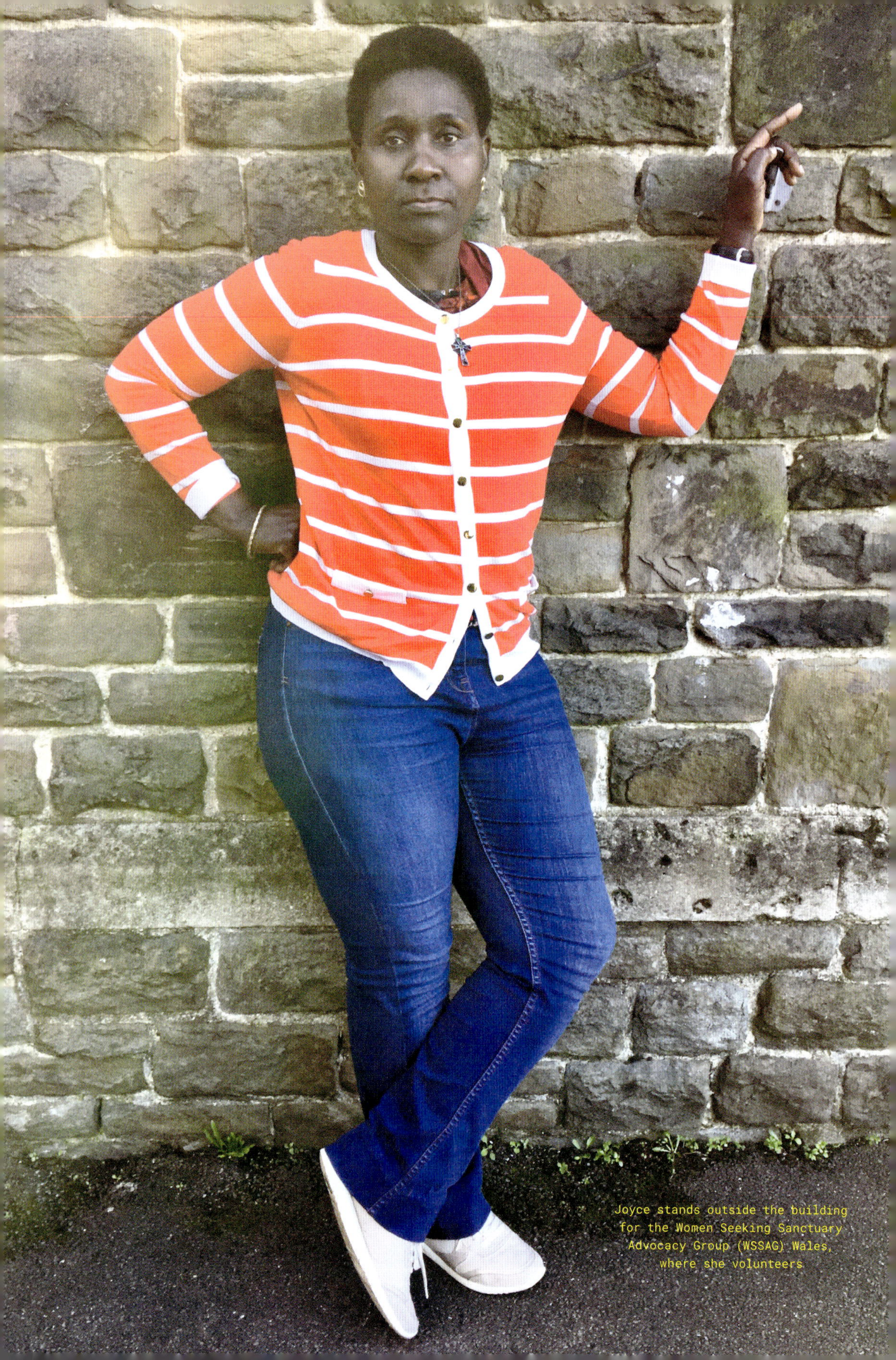

Joyce stands outside the building for the Women Seeking Sanctuary Advocacy Group (WSSAG) Wales, where she volunteers

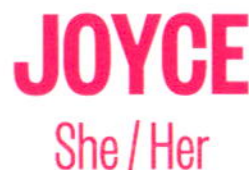

Cardiff, Wales
Age 50
Former grocer in Uganda,
mother and volunteer

I'm originally from Uganda. I've been living in Cardiff for almost 16 years. I'm still an asylum seeker. I'm awaiting my status.

I had a hysterectomy ten years ago, so I was thinking I might not go through it [the menopause], but because they left my ovaries in, my hormones are still active and working like any other woman's.

When it comes to relationships, you don't want your man to touch you. You are still a woman, but you feel really bad. Sometimes I think it breaks relationships. A man might think, "This woman is no longer interested in me; this woman might be cheating on me."

Uganda doesn't have healthy hospitals or healthy equipment. Women normally have their own treatment using herbs. In Africa, when women become that age, they try to hide. Instead of coming out and asking for advice, they just suffer. Back home, if you express your problems as a woman, they say that you are shaming your husband or your partner, so you just keep quiet. When you talk to someone, they may open up to you; but they might say, "Don't tell anyone, I don't want anyone to know." Society sees it as shameful, but I don't.

When you get older you are relaxed, because you don't have to worry about this and that like a young person. It is a time to look after yourself and talk to younger women about it.

IT IS

TO LOO

YOURSE

A TIME
K AFTER
LF

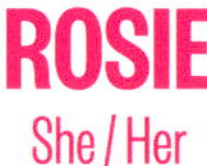

She / Her

Todmorden, West Yorkshire
Age 53
Funeral director

Crushing insecurity and the rage. Not being able to do natural family planning anymore. Decline in cognitive functioning, which was frightening and made work harder; I was worried something was seriously wrong with me. With regard to ageing, it's a privilege to age – I lost my mum when she was 47. With my profession I see people losing their partners suddenly all the time. At 21, I wouldn't have had the ability to handle the menopause; now I have.

My life is really good and I'm comfortable, happy and content compared to when I was younger. I've got maturity and I understand how to get my needs met, communicate in a straightforward way and [show] a better understanding of other people than when I was young. I'm much more resilient with maturity. In Chinese medicine, the menopause is called "the Second Spring"; it's a time when you reappraise what's important, what you want to do, and you're forced to look after yourself better. For me, "these are the days", not "those were the days".

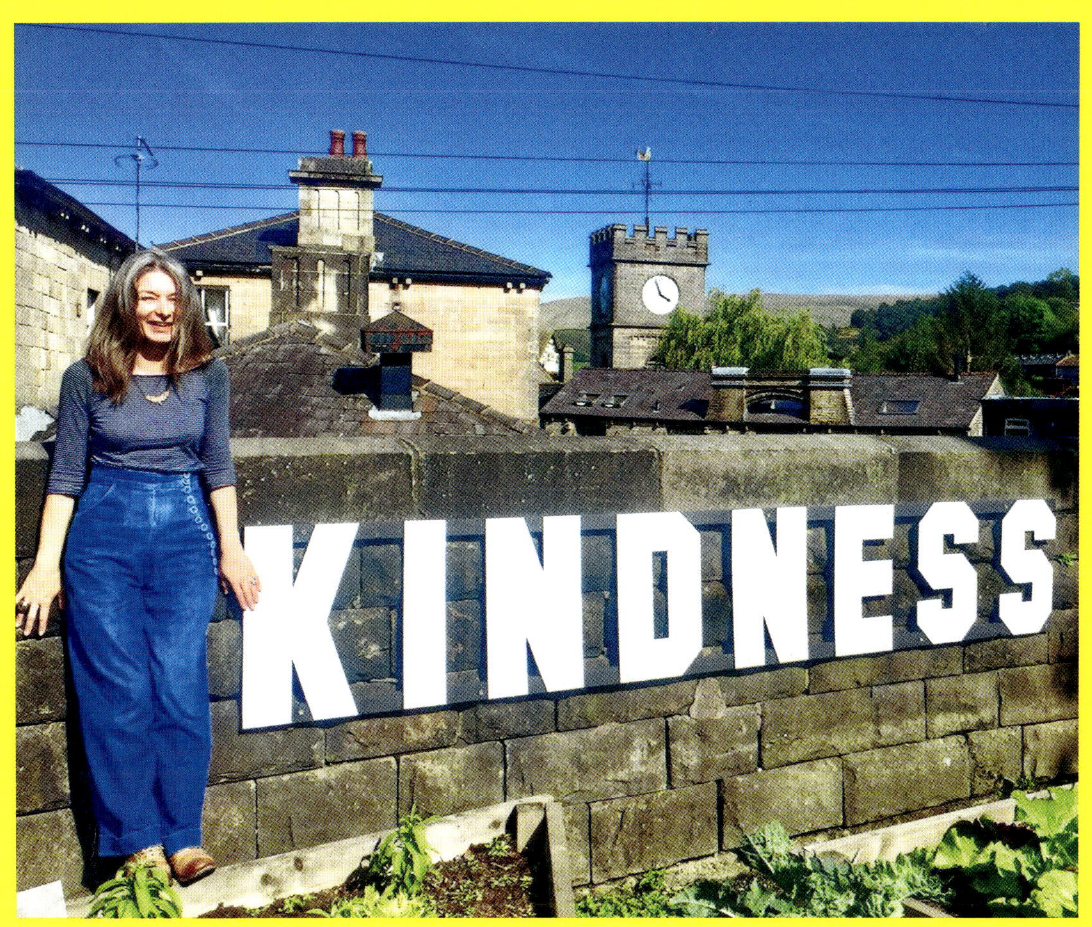

Rosie next to a "Kindness" sign in Todmorden

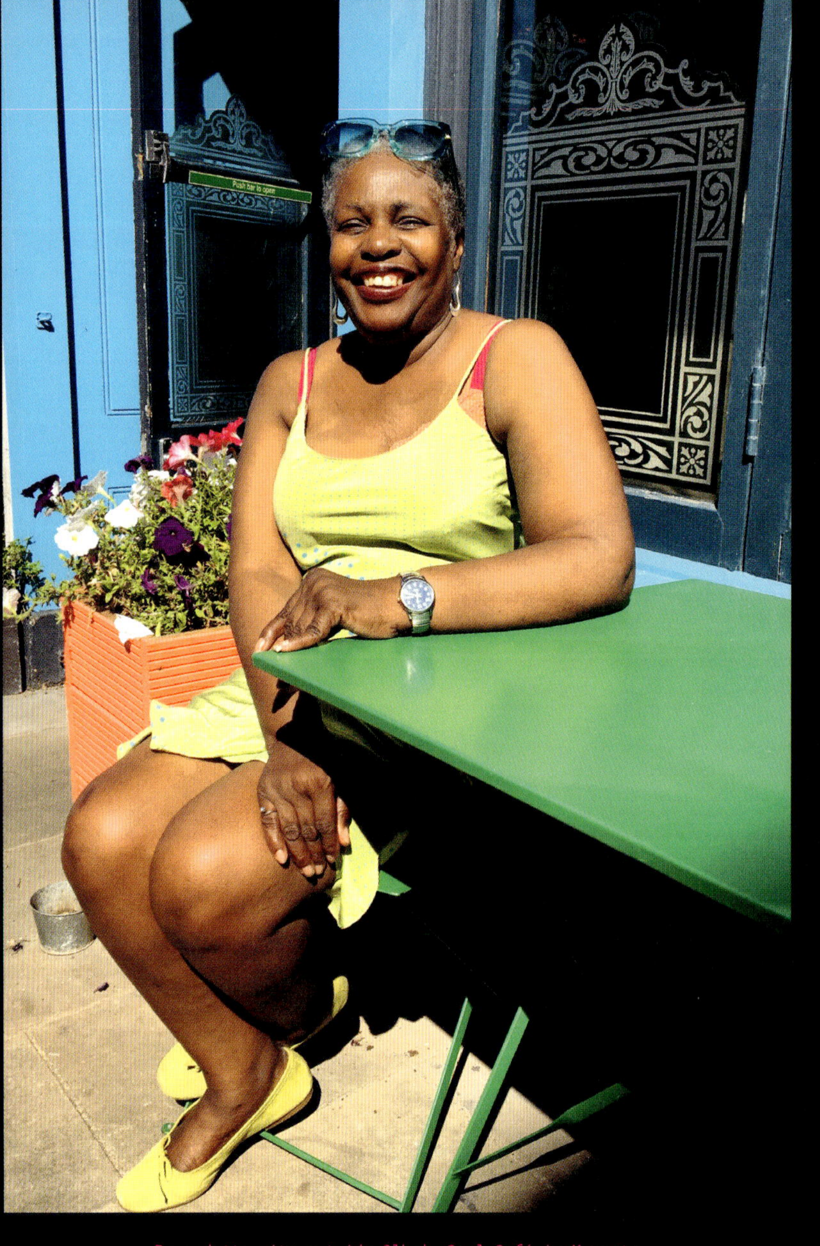

Bernadette sits outside Olby's Soul Café in Margate

BERNADETTE

She / Her

Margate, Kent
Radio Presenter/DJ and
unpaid community worker

I had my first flush when I was 41, sitting at the breakfast table. I thought I was too young. Fast-forward to April '98, when I had a confirmed diagnosis of breast cancer, which required a full mastectomy, months of the wound healing, followed by intensive chemo. The nurses did confirm that the chemo would put me into a "chemical menopause".

I started having hot flushes again, around 2000. I thought, "This is weird, this is meant to be all over." Then I was told that the flushes can go on for years and years after you actually stop producing eggs. I noticed I got them when I was anxious or stressed. I had a major life change around 55, when I left London and came to Margate. And I thought, "I'm going to settle this once and for all." I got my GP to get me tested to see where I was in terms of the menopause, and it was duly announced that I was postmenopausal. But that took about nine years really, to be fully well.

To be honest, I was fed up reading books about it, so I just relied on the experiences of other women. I hear things on the radio, like on "Women's Hour" and places like that, but I can't recall sitting around having chats with my friends, unless somebody was having a really bad menopause. Is it one of these forbidden subjects that we don't talk about? Or secret – we only talk about it in whispers?

BOZENA

She / Her

Margate
Age 62
Grandma, mum,
translator and Roma

I used to volunteer here [Cliftonville Community Centre] in 2011. I translated for other Czech, Slovak, Russian and Polish women. I speak five languages.

When it started I suffered from anxiety, depression, panic attacks and severe pain. I got migraine because I've had chronic headaches all my life. I spoke with the doctor and she said I was not allowed to take HRT tablets because in the past I had an embolism in the lung, so I have to suffer with the menopause. It's not nice; I feel sweaty a lot and it makes your body freeze – hot, freeze, hot, freeze.

I have one positive. My son is 42 and I have my grandchildren: two adult boys and one girl who is 14.

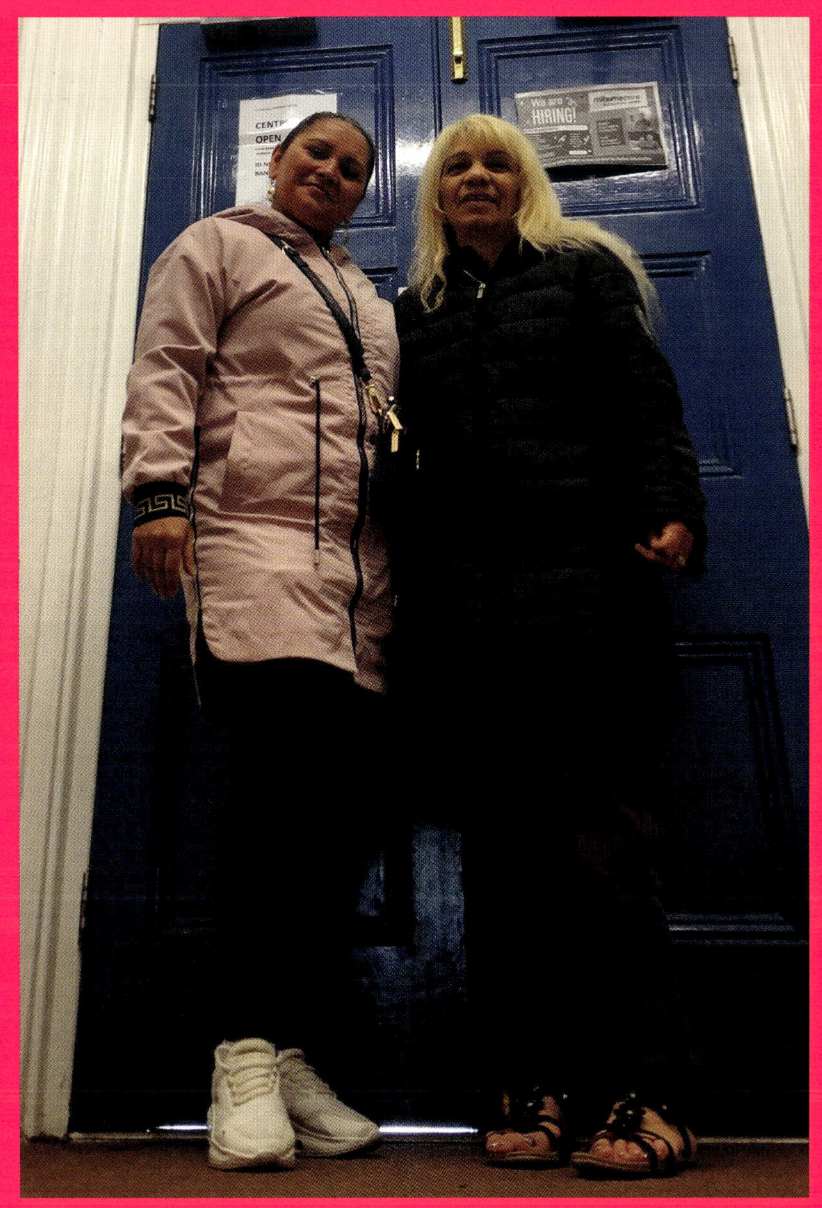

Bozena (right) at Cliftonville Community Centre in Margate with friend Adriana

Adriana inside Cliftonville Community Centre

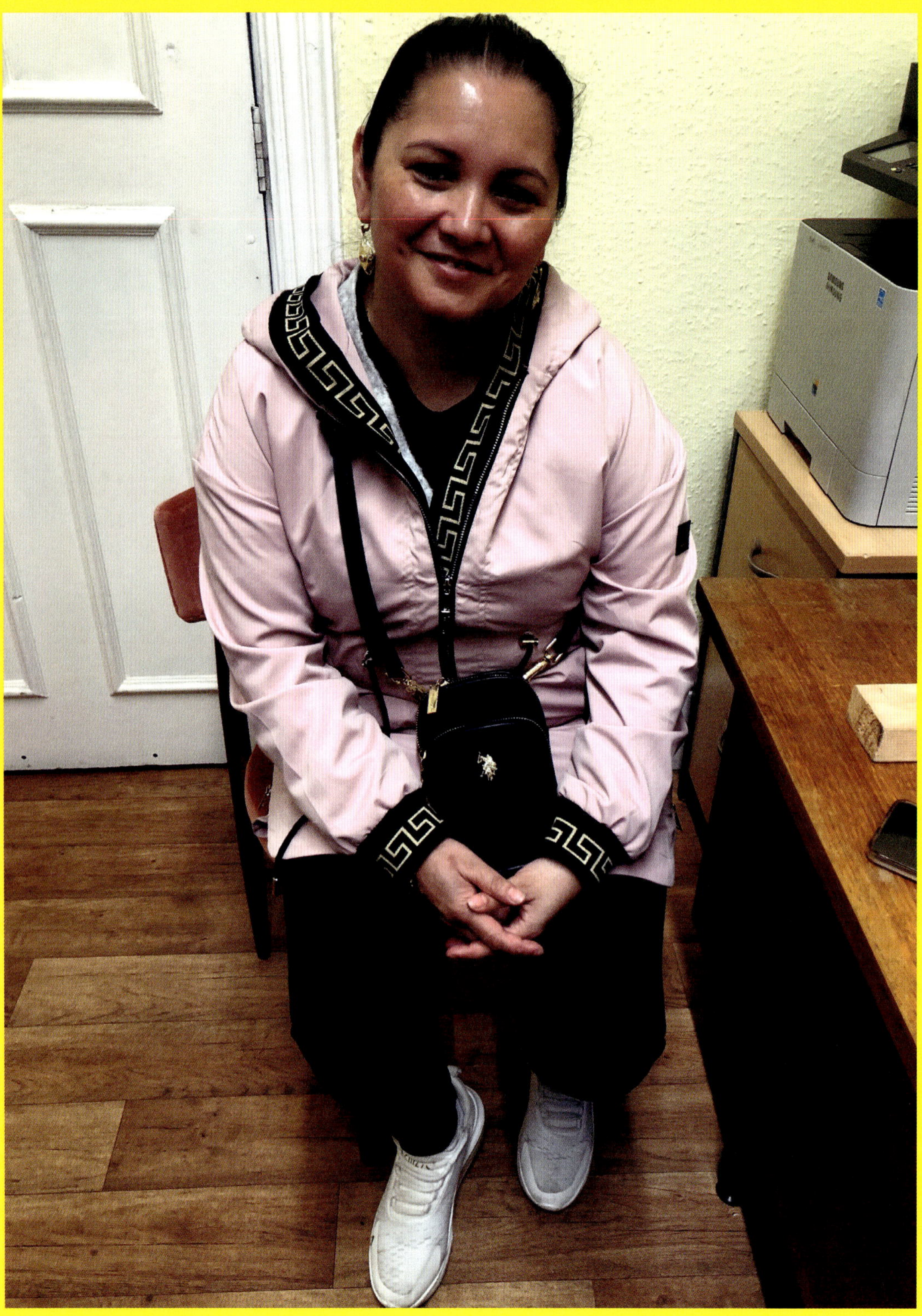

ADRIANA

She / Her

Margate
Age 42
Mother, kitchen
worker and Roma

I have four children. I've been working in the kitchen of a care home where old people live. Menopause doesn't feel good because I don't sleep. I'm very hot and my tummy feels swollen all the time. I started menopause young, at 38. The doctor told me I'd started it then because I had too much stress, and it was genetic. I go to Margate gym to exercise – this helps.

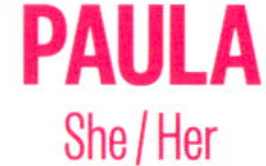

PAULA

She / Her

Margate, Kent
Age 44
In recovery, bubbly,
kind, doesn't like
solitude at the moment

I'm not a confident person, because I've been very neglected. I'm just very negative about myself. I've not really spoken about my past, I'm very closed in. I have a lot of trouble trusting people.

Since menopause I'm up and down with my mood swings. I get hot and cold; a hot prickly feeling and then it goes cold. It starts at the base of my spine and rushes upwards. Can you see me going red? I've got such a mop of hair it gets very hot and sticky.

I've turned my life around since I've found a roof over my head. I've been homeless for some time. I moved down here with my mum; she died of womb cancer. Luckily, I went for a scan and they saw a shadow. The next thing I knew I was having a scan to get lasered, and then I was in the operating theatre and they took the whole lot out. I'm starting to feel like Paula again. I've not felt like her for a while.

All my problems have come from being abused when I was younger. I think if I'd been able to speak about it when I was a child, I would have been able to move on from it and look after myself better.

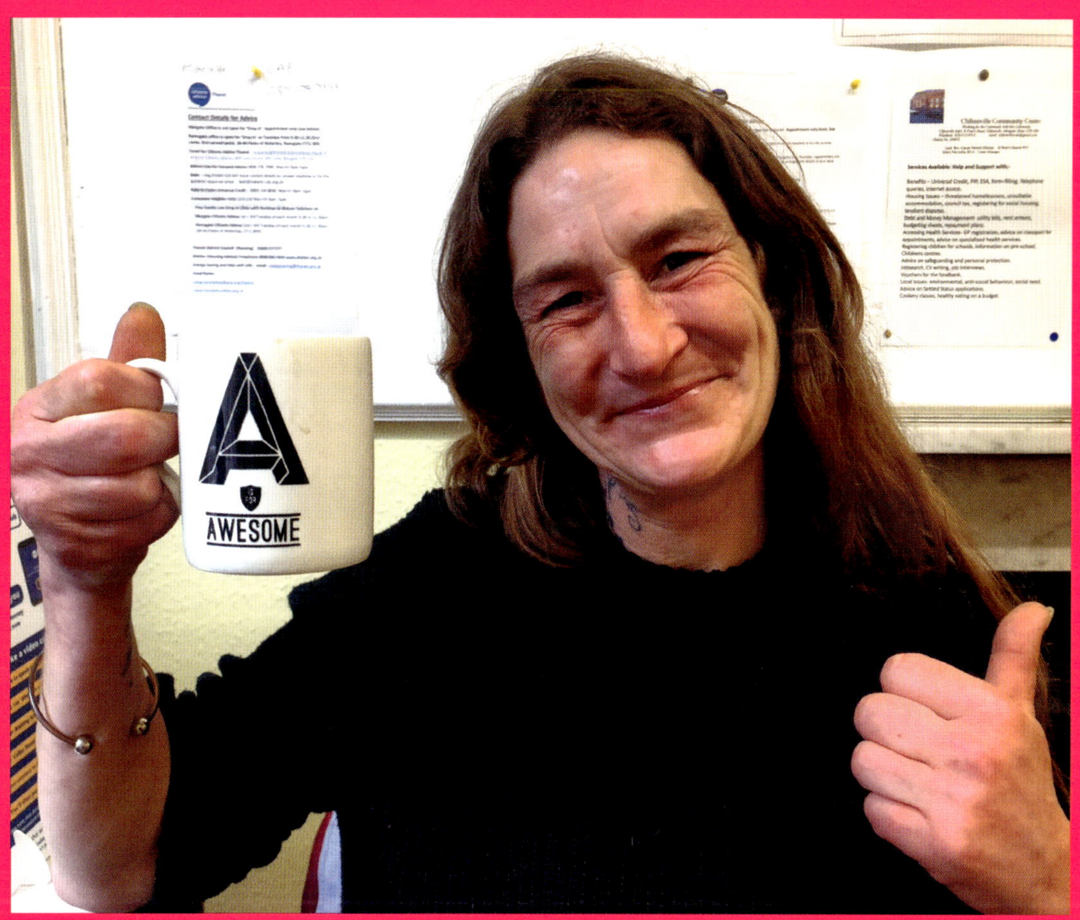

Paula enjoys a cup of tea inside Cliftonville Community Centre

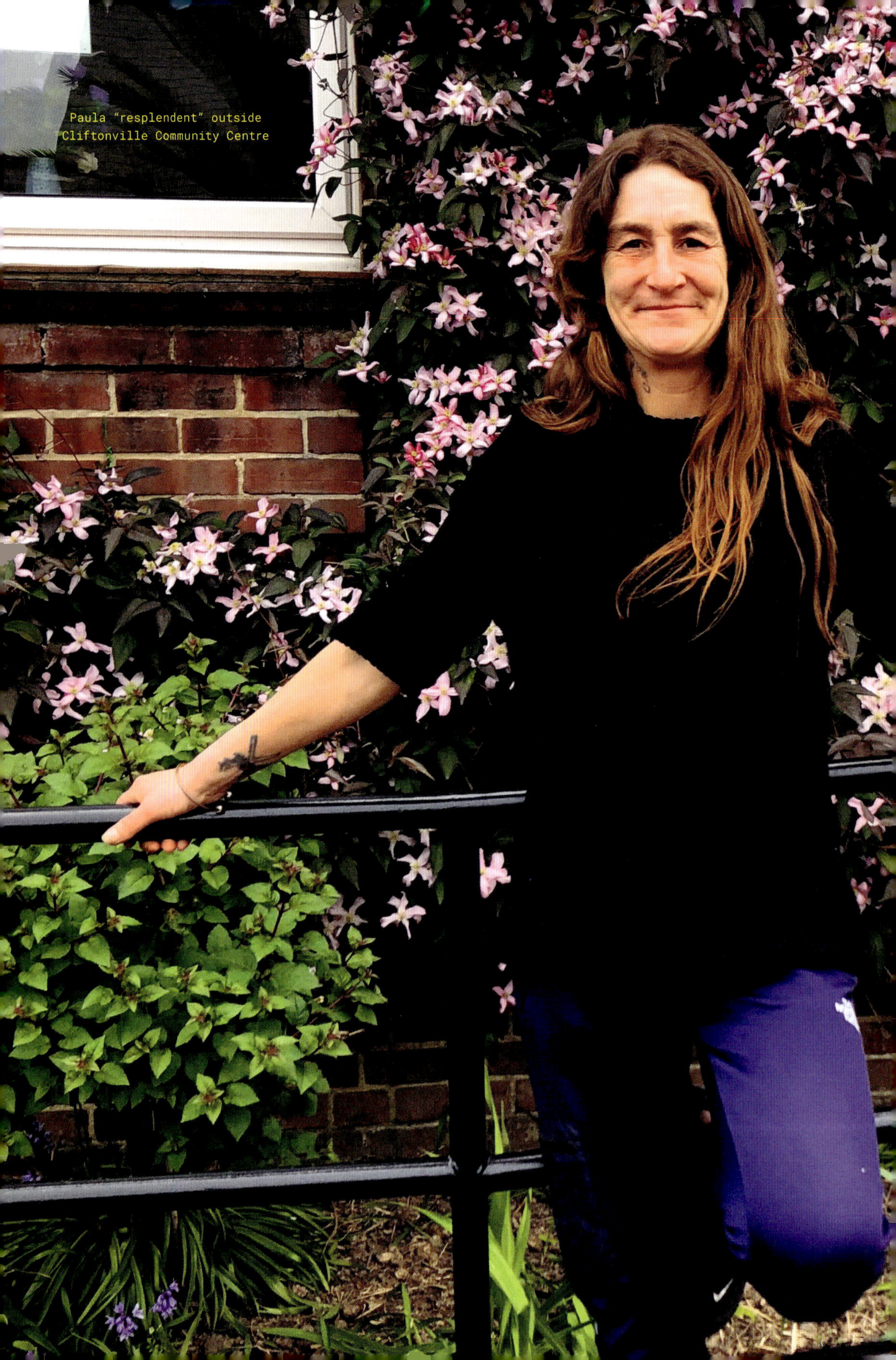

Paula “resplendent” outside Cliftonville Community Centre

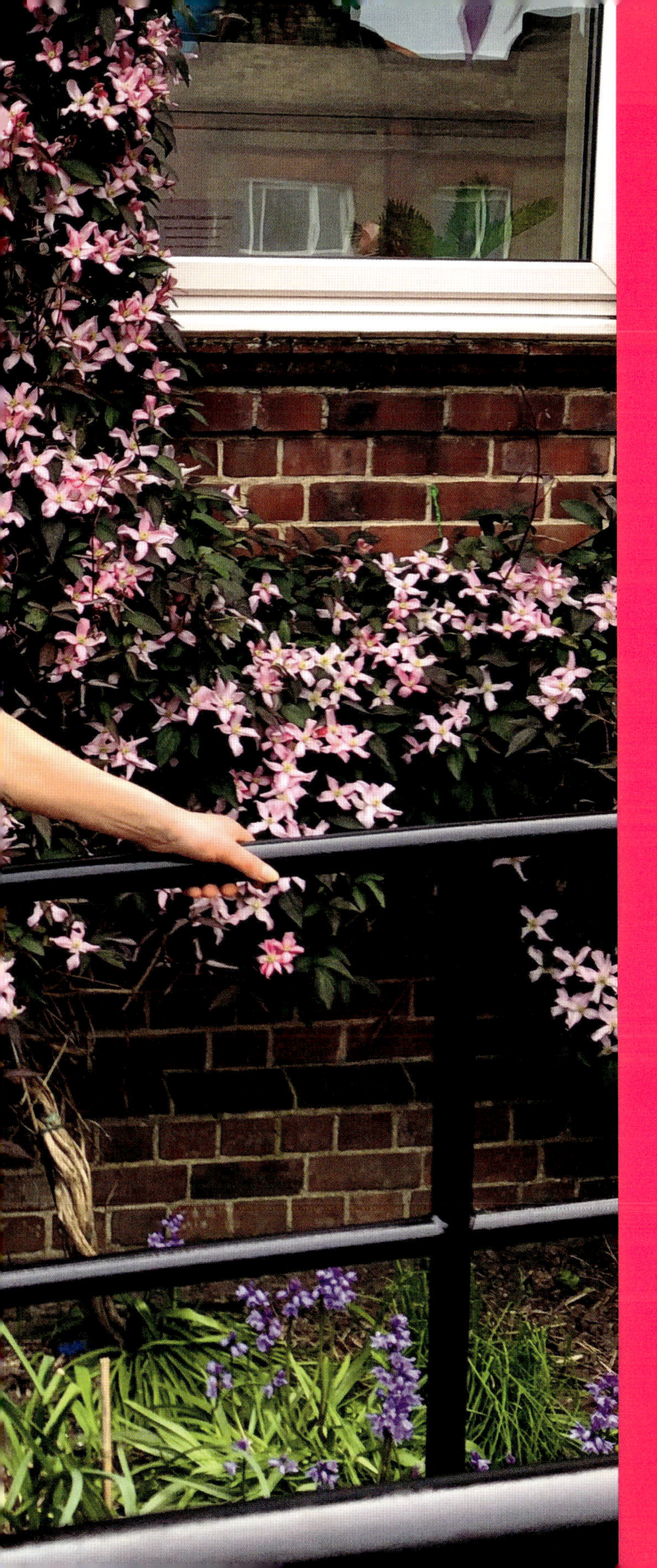

Fatima outside her favourite supermarket

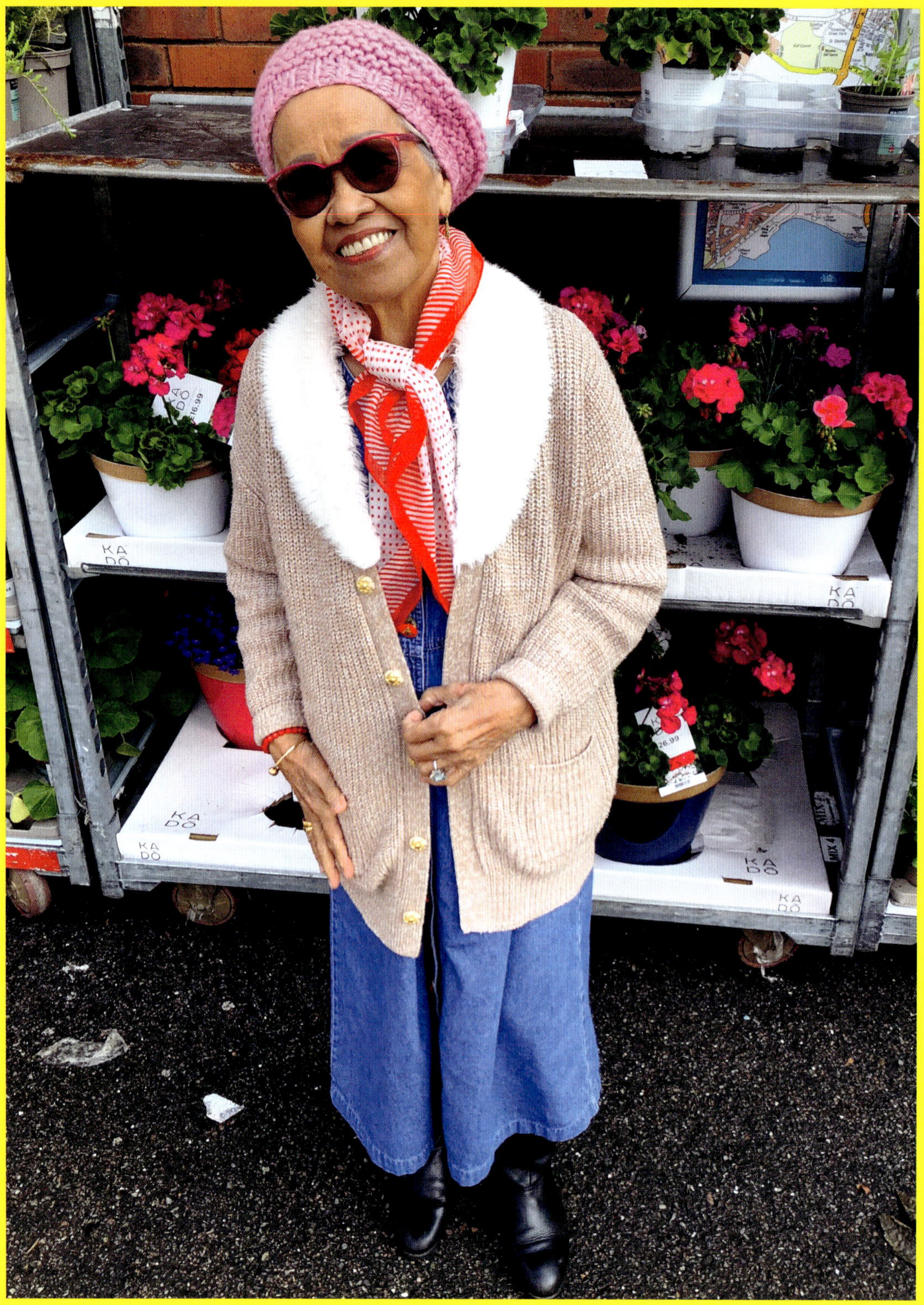

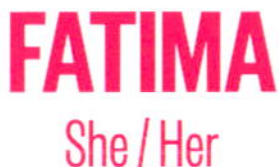

FATIMA

She / Her

Ramsgate, Kent
Age 85
Mother and
retired carer

Menopause was very easy. When I got mine I was 68. Very late! I was jealous of my friends who stopped their periods at 50. Around that time, I moved to Ramsgate. I've been here 16 years. I was advised by my doctor to live by the sea because of my lung problem – the bronchiectasis in my right lung. I was advised to only lie on my left side and sleep "upside down". I ordered a mattress in order to raise my legs up; it drains my lungs when I'm sleeping. There's no medicine for the condition.

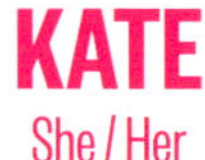

KATE

She / Her

Littleborough,
Greater Manchester
Age 51
Advice worker and menopause
peer support worker

The perimenopause forced me to make connections. I started off in work feeling quite isolated. I'd always been in a helping role and was very much a go-to co-ordinator and problem solver. Suddenly, I couldn't do those things. So I left that job.

Being out of work was a really negative experience. I'm now back in part-time work. I eventually started to support other women. HRT has helped with depression and anxiety. I've gone through being on antidepressants, which was the more negative side. They do work for some issues, but they don't work for reproductive depression.

Being perimenopausal and finding out I was neurodiverse collided when I was 39. I had dyspraxia. The oestrogen inside the body is like a scaffolding that holds things together. When that dropped I may have seemed together outwardly, but inwardly I felt very chaotic, like my head was a messy ball of wool. When I look back ten years later, it was the collision of the dyspraxic brain and the menopausal brain.

I would probably fall under being "involuntarily childless". I should've really thought about my own fertility in my early thirties rather than reflecting on it now, at 51. I don't feel it's a miserable existence, but I do think it's important to talk about it. It's a hope and a loss that I and other women have had, and it matters. Childless people and those who aren't childless should just support us and listen. That's all we need; we don't need you to put a silver lining on it for us. I think it's about light and shade, isn't it? We really will have shifted when society can say "not being a parent is an option". We're not there yet.

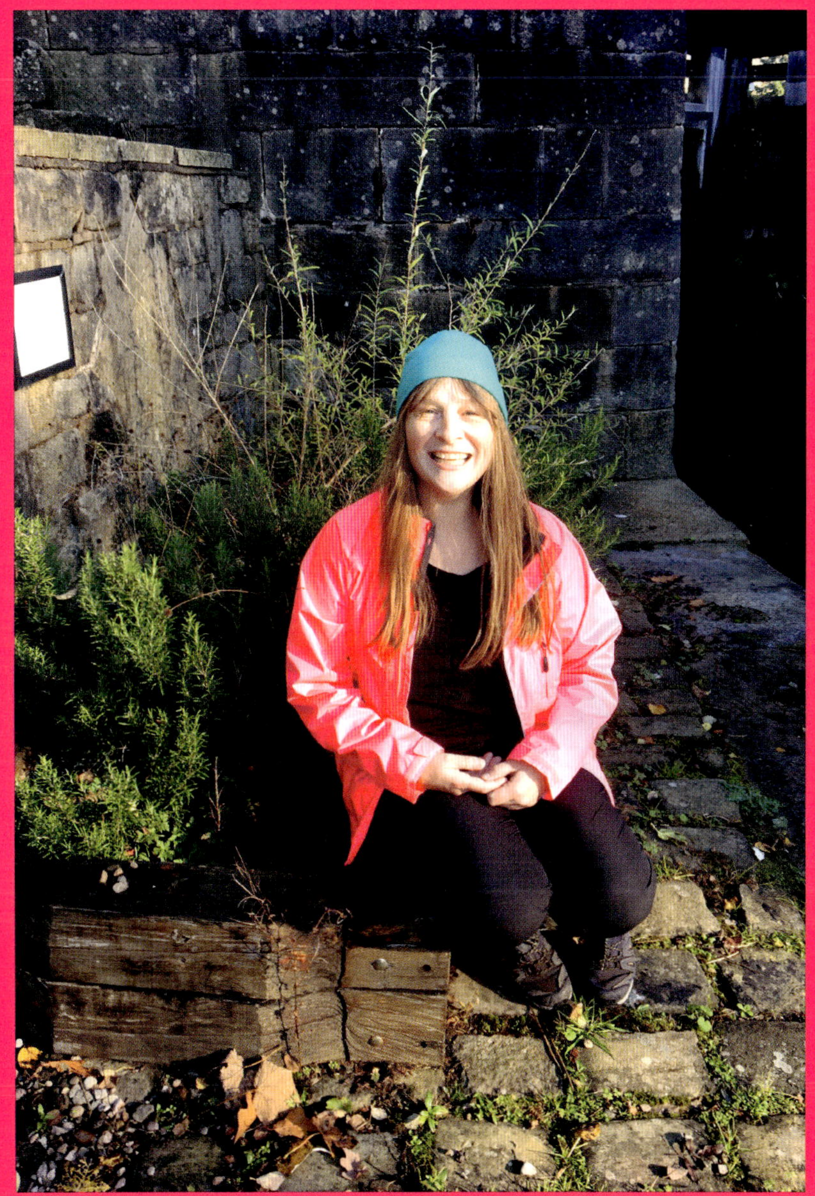

Kate sits by Rochdale Canal

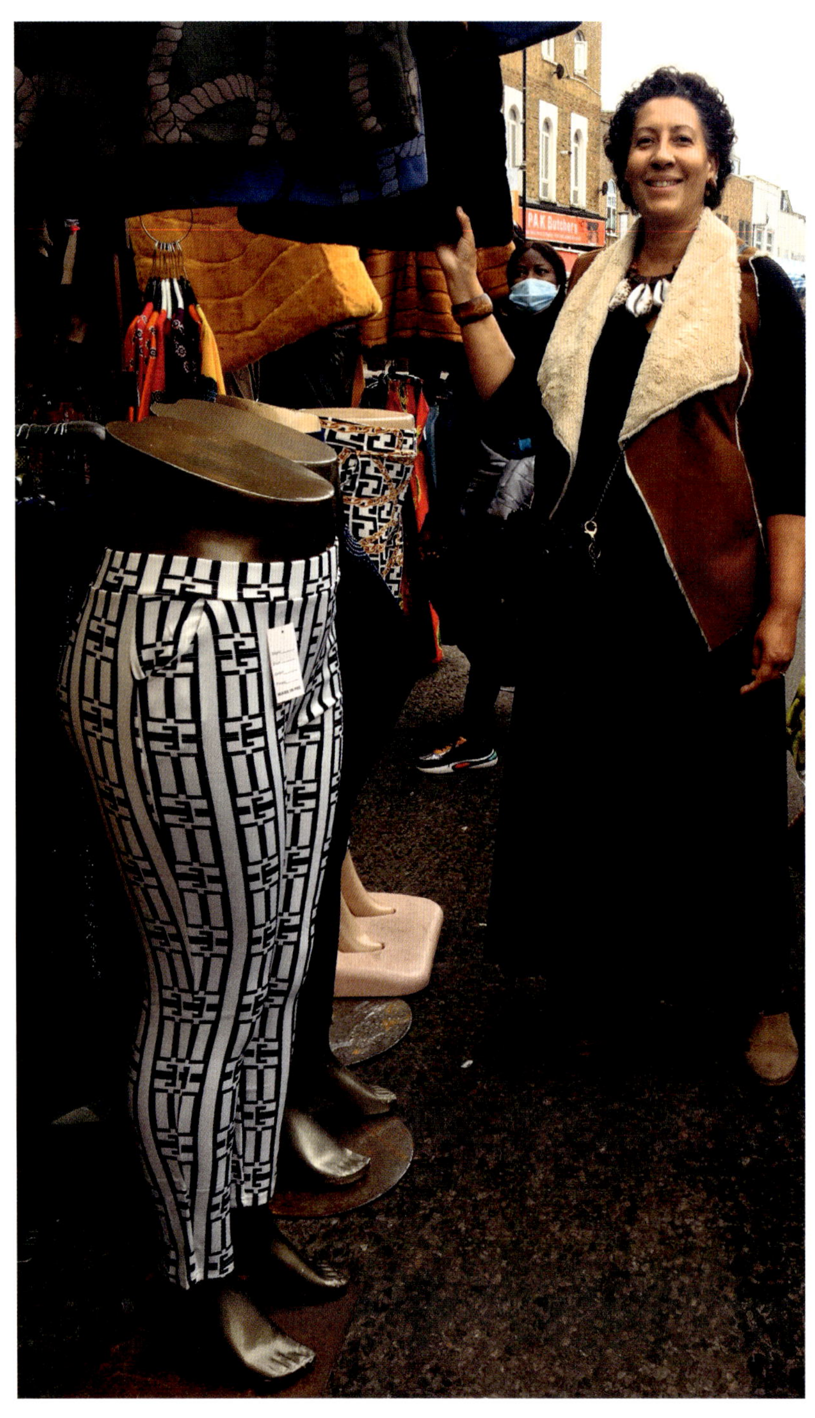

Hyacinth at Ridley Road Market, Dalston

HYACINTH

She / Her

Dalston, London
Age 49
Author and
empowerment coach

I started my perimenopause at the age of 42. I decided to go to my GP. I kept going back with other symptoms, like urine infections. The doctor just kept on testing me for sexually transmitted diseases! At that time I wasn't even interested in having sex with my partner.

I've found out this happens to other women. It's really quite disgraceful. I didn't realise that when the changes happen down there, you are prone to getting infections. After insisting I see a gynaecologist, they ran loads of tests and said I was definitely perimenopausal, and had been for four years. I was offered the HRT oestrogen gel just to stop the infections. I really believe in holistic therapies, but as nothing was working I used it for five months, and it was brilliant. And then that was it. I've never used it since; I didn't need to.

I haven't had a menstrual cycle for about ten months, but they wait until it's 12 months and one day to diagnose actual menopause. Last year, I think it was 11-and-a-half months – and then I got one! That was probably the end of it last December, but it'll take a few months for them to formally diagnose it.

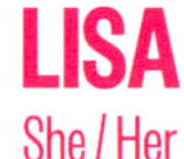

She / Her

Archway, London
Age 51
Social worker (anti-human trafficking) with women

I started noticing my periods were irregular at 49, and I was becoming irritable and having night sweats, which I thought were related to work burnout. I had to face up to the fact that it was the start of menopause. I thought, "Not me, not yet." In the back of my mind I had this fear that all of a sudden I would become this wrinkly, invisible woman. I thought I would slip into frailty. Being single as well, I thought, "That's it." You consider your sexuality. Am I going to be this unattractive woman on my own? This lasted about six months – wrangling with my sense of being attractive and sexual – and I struggled with it. But then I got sick of my own bullshit and thought, "This is an emotional form of self-harm" and "You're the only one that thinks that." I realised there were lots of mates going through it. I had this "how dare you" moment, where I thought my value isn't weighed on my looks. I love body art, tattoos – my value isn't external – it's what do I want to look like?

I've always expressed myself in my own way and for those six months I thought maybe I should start toning it down, but I've come out of that now and thought "no, bollocks". From that point, I've grown and become stronger in myself. I don't feel like I need anyone's approval anymore. I really don't give a fuck what anyone thinks. I feel like I've been released from a societal mindset that says "at this age, you've got to do this or that". I've realised it's all about being yourself, and I don't want to be a miserable, unhappy old lady. I feel more confident in myself as a person. My mind has been opened and I'm far more accepting. I've got an increased sense of fun and grab opportunities and life: I just go for it. I'm much more in sync with the women I work with – I feel passionate about giving women a voice and helping them work on their boundaries and what they want to allow in their lives. As women, we have secrets: miscarriages, mothering through difficulties, termination. Society tells us to feel ashamed, but it's part of who we are.

Lisa in front of music posters of memorable gigs in Camden, north London

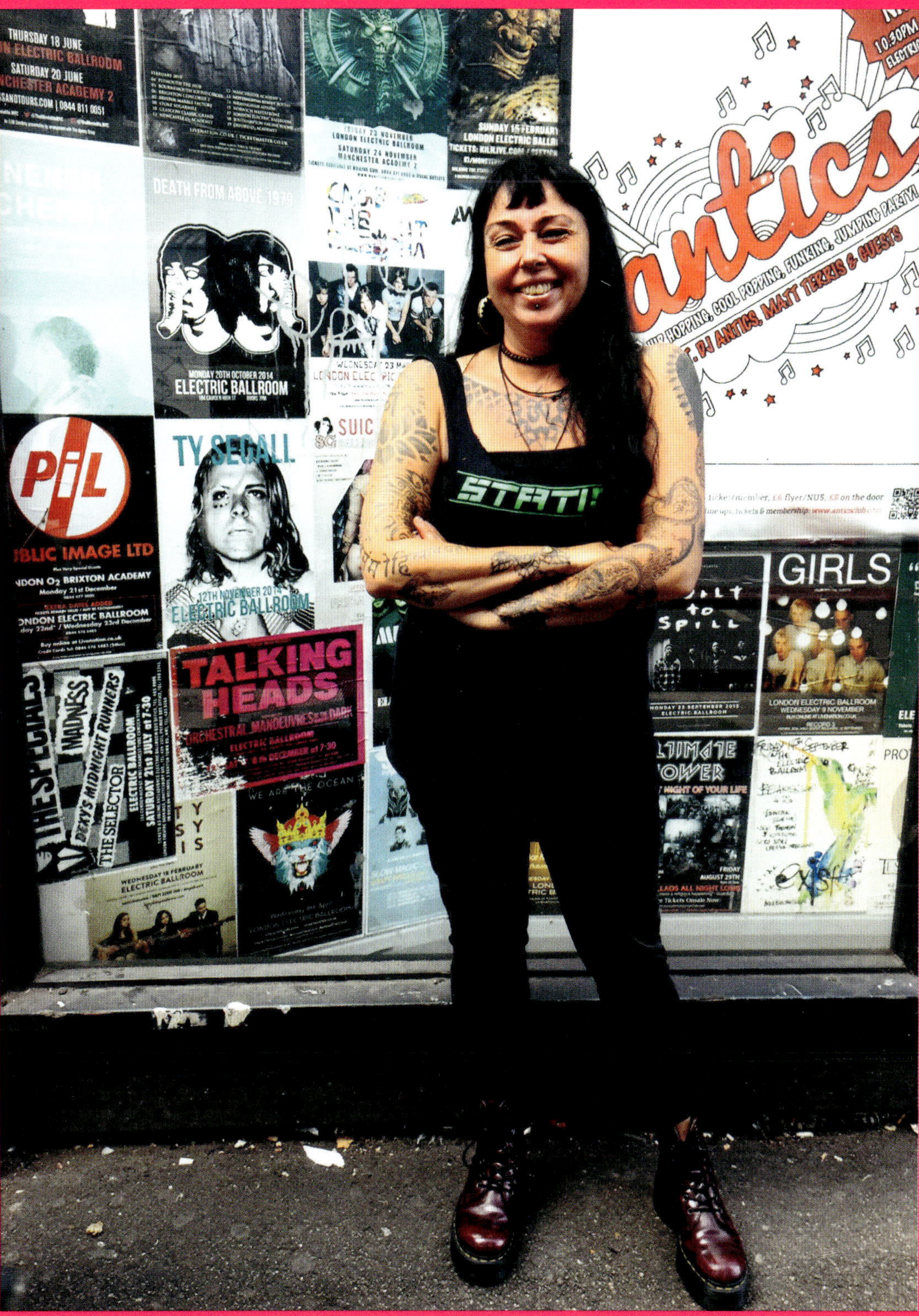

Lisa stands under the railway bridge between Kentish Town and Camden

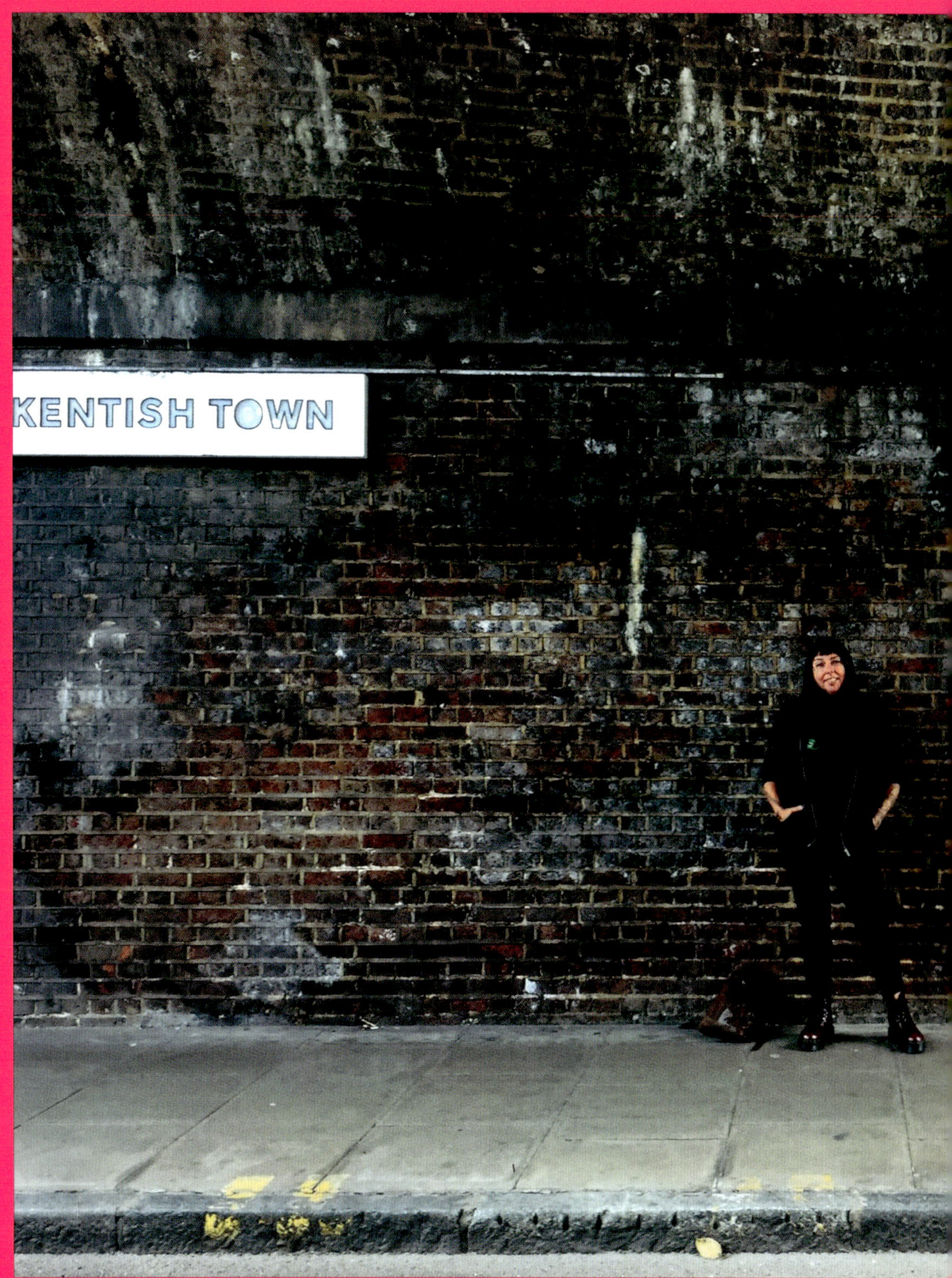

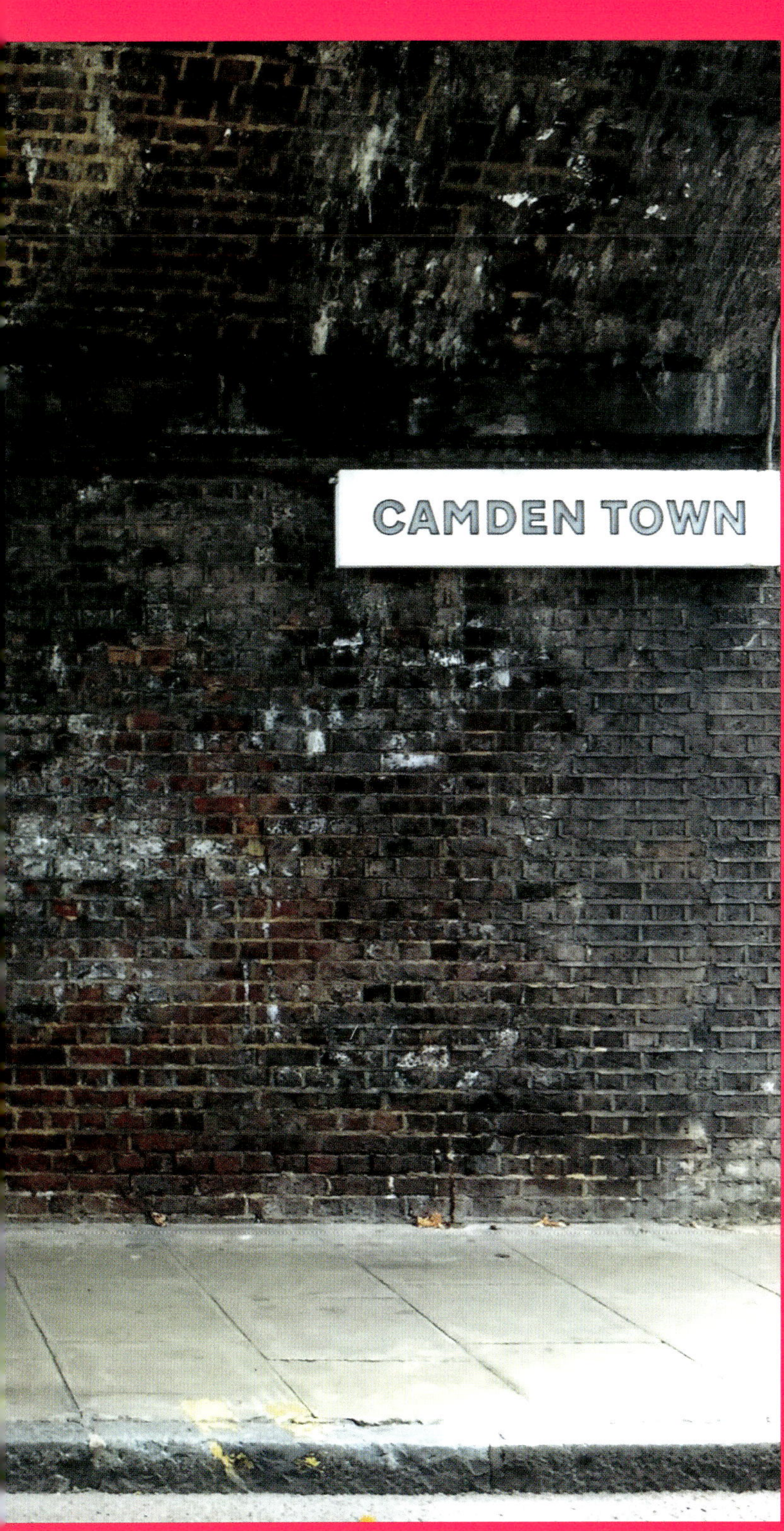
CAMDEN TOWN

CAROLINE

She / Her

Clapton, London
Age 49
Learning support

Feel more or less the same (so far). Able to blame anything and everything on my age! Finding out it's not the end after all. Rock on, sisters!

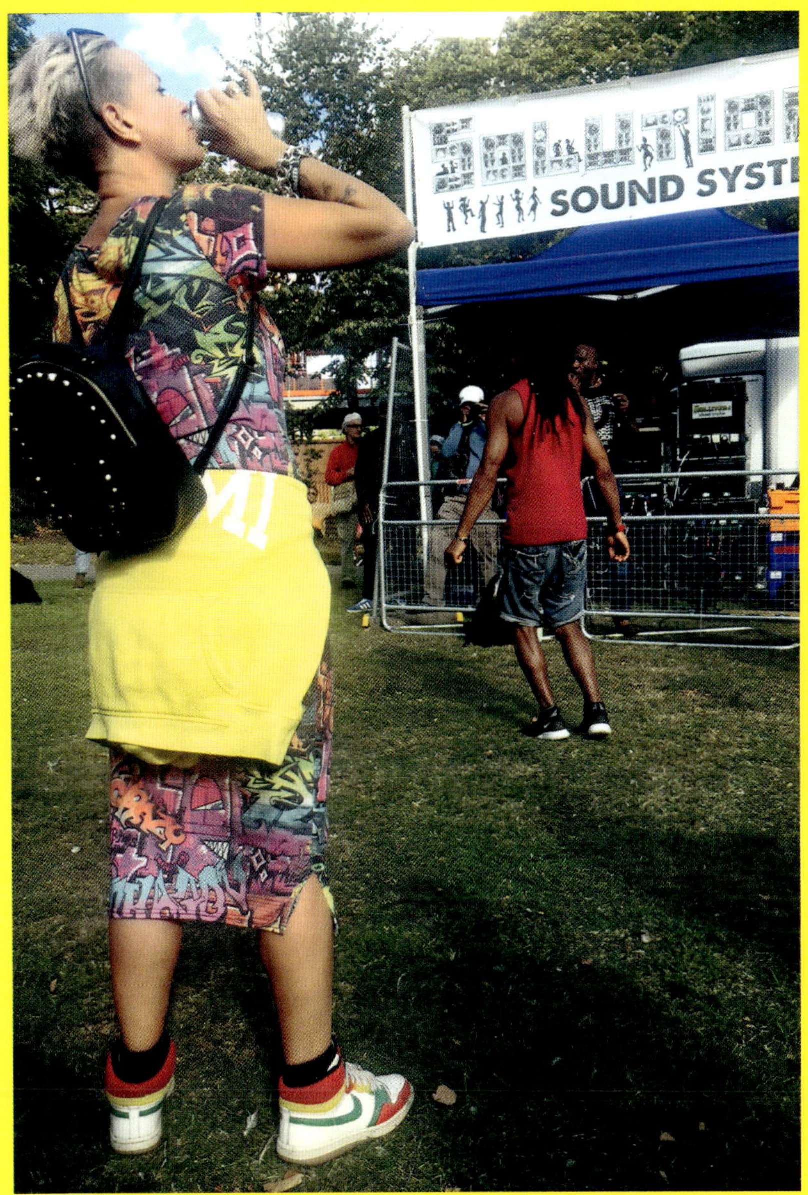

Caroline at Hackney Carnival

ABLE TO
ANYTHI
EVERYT
MY

BLAME
NG AND
HING ON
AGE!

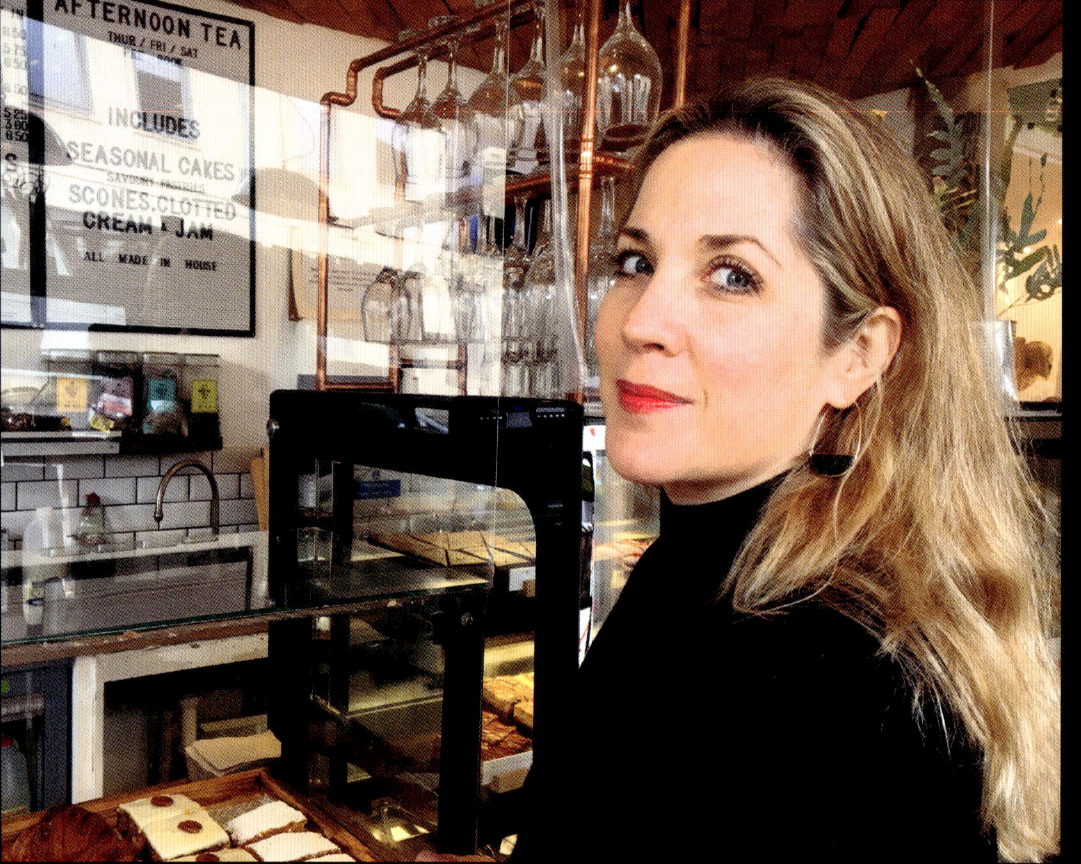

Emma likes to grab a coffee in Queen Square, Bath

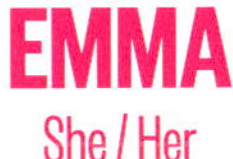

She / Her

Bath, Somerset
Age 50
Theatre stage door
supervisor and student
psychotherapist

The massive paradox about menopause is losing but equally gaining confidence. Shedding constraining stuff, like body image. Having my photo taken, that's difficult, I don't like looking at myself. Growing up, appearance was spoken about and evaluated in the family, and I took that on. In early adulthood I felt I presented well – got good jobs, had partners and, weirdly, thought that was about how I looked, to the detriment of developing myself.

Having children, partners, failed relationships, an abusive marriage, which was horrendous, make you question your identity: where you've got to and how. Then menopause hits, like a seismic shift. Demystifying it is important, so that it's real. Women sharing their experiences is imperative. Hopefully, it will shift and challenge the misogynistic medical profession – women coming out of doctor's surgeries with antidepressants; I had mental health issues around my pregnancies, and hormones where never thought about.

Multiple panic attacks hit really badly within six weeks of me having my daughter (she's now 19), and then a couple of years ago I had another one. When that happened, it was devastating. I panicked, thinking "I can't go back there", and started reading about perimenopause. I was fortunate to go to a specialist who had accreditation up to the hilt, an absolute expert. I said, "I'm anxious, gaining weight and lost libido." I had barely any examination and she said, "Right, you're going on gel," because it's that basic. Every woman should get access to the same level of expertise, but a lot don't get to that point.

GEORGINA

She / Her

Ticehurst, East Sussex
Age 67
Retired lawyer,
mother and volunteer

I started my periods aged ten. We knew who was on their period because we weren't allowed to go to swimming lessons. My mother was always very matter of fact about it. She said, "You know what's happening, don't you?"

We were the first generation that, as unmarried women, the pill was available to. Social, economic and career issues were important. If you were pregnant, you had to resign in some professions, even if you got married. You were being a bad mother if you worked. Unless you could afford a nanny, your economic status dipped. There were these unspoken assumptions; the world was a different place then.

I've supported friends who adopted children and I've parented two children, through sperm donation, with a former same-sex partner. The option was put on the table for me to get pregnant with the second, but I didn't want to. The idea of it didn't appeal to me.

Getting older has it's own challenges apart from the physical one. You become slightly "invisible", and if you try to become more senior at work, you're not considered. Friends have stopped putting their date of birth on their CV. Menopause should be acknowledged as something that's supported and managed, rather than a weakness. People get maternity, paternity and adoption leave, for example. It would just be a reasonable adjustment for people who struggle, because hopefully it would pass. My menopause passed without any really significant effect on me, but that is just the luck of the draw.

There's a kind of freedom. Women are generally living longer. I've already lived longer than my mother. Realising that life will continue for another 30 to 40 years is liberating. So, menopause isn't the defining moment for the rest of your life. You should use it to your advantage.

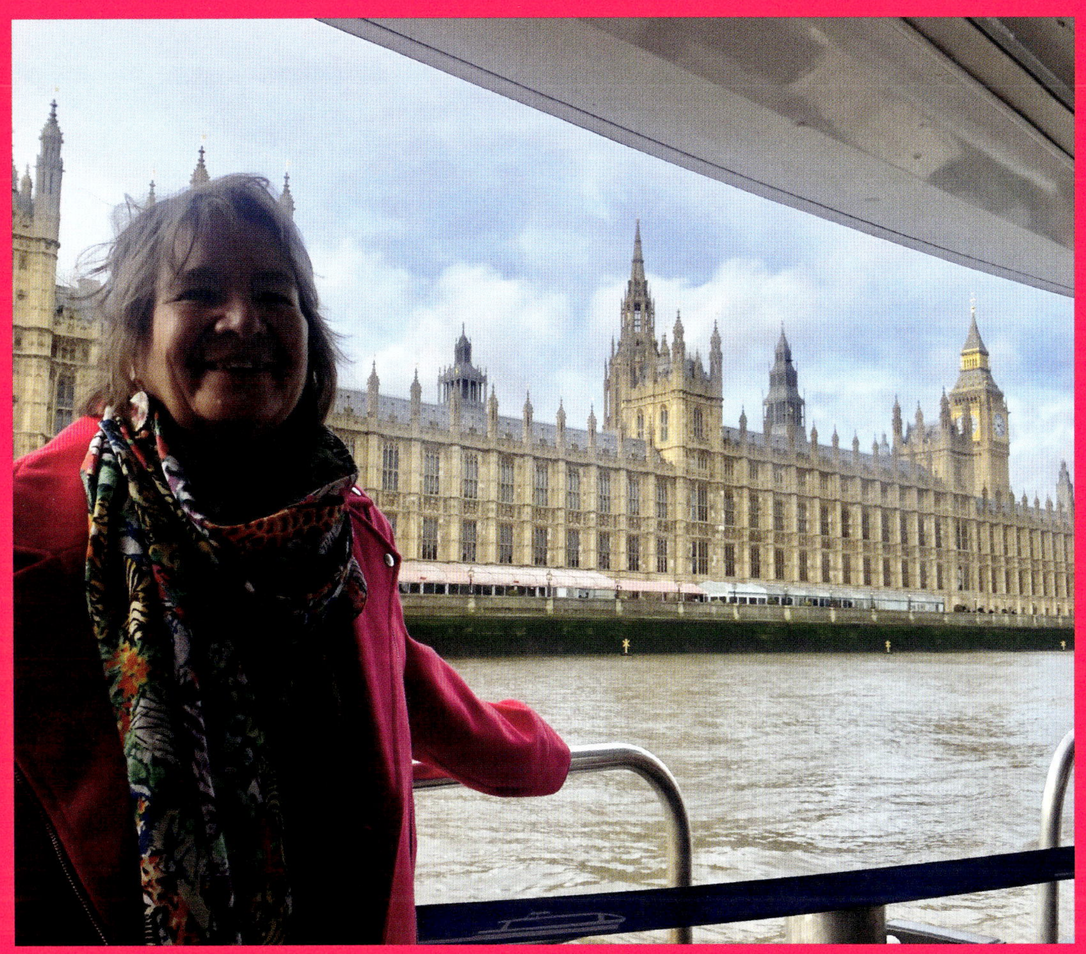

Georgina passes the Houses of Parliament on a river boat on the Thames

ACKNOWLEDGEMENTS

I'd like to thank all the people who shared their stories and allowed me to photograph them. Without you, this book would not exist.

My entire family – mum, brother, sister-in-law, nephew, niece, as well as my cousins, second cousins, grandparents, aunts, uncles, all of you. Thanks for always lifting me up and, most of all, believing in me and my work.

Paul, who I miss every day.

All my friends, for being there when I needed you most.

My partner-in-crime, Tindara Sidoti-McNary, for asking if you could make a film by the tidal pool in Margate, and for being a brilliant and generous collaborator and friend.

Lara Clifton, for helping me write, and rewrite, the Arts Council bid for this project.

The Arts Council, for funding the book and all the other projects of mine you have supported.

My tutors at Central St Martins College of Art and Design, for showing me I could be an artist.

My circus friends and all my ex-raver friends in Leeds.

Diane Danzebrink, for sharing your story and enabling me to find the right treatment for my menopausal symptoms.

Jessica Voorsanger, for introducing me to Black Dog Press.

Serena Bobowski, for curating my first photography exhibition and for encouraging me to keep going.

Ludo, Richard and Anton at Black Dog Press, for making this book.

Margo in Margate, for being so cool and for writing the foreword.

My beautiful and wonderful female friends who didn't make the menopause – Emma Insley and Carrie Franklin. You both inspire me every day to live life to the full.

All the artists who came before me whom I admire and whose art keeps me wanting to make more work.

Layla Stevens, for being such an extraordinary PA, without whose help I certainly would not have been able to make this book.

My dad. I wish you could have held this book in your hand. I know you would have loved it.

Mabel, my dog, for being my constant companion and a funny and loving soul.

Summer, for coming into my life.

© 2025 SJH Group, the artist and authors.

This book is published by Black Dog Press Limited, a company registered in England and Wales with company number 11182108. Black Dog Press is an imprint within the SJH Group. Copyright is owned by the SJH Group Limited. All rights reserved.

Black Dog Press
The Maple Building
39–51 Highgate Road
London NW5 1RT
United Kingdom

+44 (0)20 8371 4047
office@blackdogonline.com
www.blackdogonline.com

Design by Richard Seymour
Printed in Lithuania by Kopa

ISBN 978-1-912165-61-2

British Library Cataloguing in Publication data. A CIP record for this book is available from the British Library.

Neither this publication nor any part of it may be reproduced, stored in a retrieval system or transmitted in any form or by any means, electronic, mechanical, photocopying, recording or otherwise, without the prior permission of the SJH Group or the appropriately accredited copyright holder.

All information in this publication is verified to the best of the author's and publisher's ability. However, Black Dog Press and the SJH Group do not accept responsibility for any loss arising from reliance on it. Where opinion is expressed, it is that of the author and does not necessarily coincide with the editorial views of the publisher. The publishers have made all reasonable efforts to trace the copyright owners of the images reproduced herein and to provide an appropriate acknowledgement in the book.

black dog press